D0507349

MANAGING
TRAINING
IN THE
ORGANIZATION

— BOOK II —

THE NUTS 'N BOLTS OF PERSONAL, PEOPLE AND RESOURCE MANAGEMENT

Third Edition

Compiled by *DAVE ZIELINSKI*
from articles that have been published in

TRAINING
The Magazine Covering the Human Side of Business

and
Training Directors' Forum Newsletter

❧ Lakewood Publications

The Complete New Training Library:

Book 1 *Basic Training: The Language of Corporate Education*
Book 2 *Adult Learning in Your Classroom*
Book 3 *The Best of Creative Training Techniques Newsletter*
Book 4 *Designing Training for Results*
Book 5 *The Training Mix: Choosing and Using Media and Methods*
Book 6 *Managing Training in the Organization, Book I*
Book 7 *Managing Training in the Organization, Book II*
Book 8 *Delivering Training: Mastery in the Classroom*
Book 9 *Evaluating Training's Impact*
Book 10 *Using Technology-Delivered Learning*
Book 11 *The Effective Performance Consultant*
Book 12 *Making Training Pay Off on the Job*

Bulk reprints of individual articles may be quoted and purchased through:

Reprint Services
315 Fifth Avenue N.W.
St. Paul, MN 55112
(800) 707-7798 or (612) 633-0578

LAKEWOOD BOOKS
50 South Ninth Street
Minneapolis, MN 55402
(800) 707-7769 or (612) 333-0471
Fax: (612) 333-6526
Web Page Address: http://www.lakewoodpub.com

Editorial Director: Linda Klemstein
Editor: Dave Zielinski
Production Editor: Julie Tilka
Production Manager: Pat Grawert
Cover Design: Julie Tilka
Copy Editors: Audrey Kupers and Dave Zielinski

Lakewood Publications Inc. is a subsidiary of VNU/USA. Lakewood Publications Inc. publishes *TRAINING Magazine, Presentations* magazine, *Training Directors' Forum Newsletter, Creative Training Techniques Newsletter, The Lakewood Report On Technology for Learning Newsletter, Potentials In Marketing* magazine, and other business periodicals, books, research, and conducts conferences.

ISBN GET ISBN 0-943210-55-0

10 9 8 7 6 5 4 3 2 1

THE NEW TRAINING LIBRARY

Contemporary training and performance improvement ideas, strategies
and techniques for managers and HRD professionals

Welcome to *The New Training Library*. Before you read on, there are a few things you should know about this series of books and how it came into existence.

Each book in *The New Training Library* contains articles originally published in *TRAINING Magazine, The Training Directors' Forum Newsletter, Creative Training Techniques Newsletter,* or *The Lakewood Report On Technology for Learning Newsletter,* all Lakewood publications that explore contemporary human resources development issues, trends and ideas from different angles and perspectives. While there is some overlap among the books in the series, each of them stands on its own.

Our editors selected articles to illuminate a particular theme or subject area — from the dynamics of adult occupational learning, to managing and running a corporate training function, to designing cost-effective training programs, to powerful performance consulting. And more.

The pervasive style of the selected articles is that of magazine and newsletter journalism, opinion and commentary. In this accessible, nonacademic style, the authors address the real and immediate challenges you face as practicing HRD professionals or as managers and motivators of people.

The edited articles are contained between the covers of the books in *The New Training Library.* Not, to repeat, as the definitive texts or final words on any one subject area, but as books that serve a different and (depending upon who you are) maybe even more useful purpose.

As the training profession evolves, it demands a solid understanding of the original ideas, theories and systems that shaped its development. Today's training professionals also must be prepared to absorb, assimilate and put into perspective an astonishing amount of new information. Like doctors, lawyers, bankers or other professionals, HRD professionals can never stop learning. Not if they want to be effective. Certainly not if they want to get ahead.

The publications that form the core of *The New Training Library* have become among the most widely read and influential in the field because their editors have never forgotten that fundamental need. In addition to featuring the best writers, theorists and practitioners in HRD, each publication also meets the HRD professional's need to understand the newest techniques, strategies and approaches to tough workplace challenges within the context of the established body of HRD knowledge.

Thus, each publication I've discussed here is carefully balanced to appeal to relative novices in HRD as well as to seasoned professionals. And so are the books in *The New Training Library,* which represents a comprehensive and systematic collection of current ideas and practical responses to meeting workplace challenges (in many cases, articulated by those who first formulated them) within the context of HRD's most enduring, time-tested fundamentals. In other words, these books manage to be both timeless and relevant to the challenges you now face in the rapidly evolving American workplace.

Plus, the books in *The New Training Library* are designed so you can find useful information fast. And with that information, you probably can meet a challenge, solve a problem or defuse a crisis right away. It's a fact that HRD changes constantly, especially today. But I think you'll find, due to the care with which the contents of these books were selected and to the editorial strengths of the publications in which this material first appeared, *The New Training Library* series will be as useful many years from now as it is today.

Philip Jones
Editorial Director
Lakewood Publications

TABLE OF CONTENTS

CHAPTER 1

SKILLS AND TOOLS OF THE EFFECTIVE TRAINING MANAGER

Sometimes Training Skills Are a Second Priority 3
  By Brian McDermott
  • 10 Tips Help Training Execs Avoid 'Spineless Marsupial'
    Syndrome / *Randall Johnson*

10 Management Musts for HRD Directors 7
  By Geoffrey M. Bellman

Training on the Cheap 9
  By Bob Filipczak

Ducking the Ax 15
  By Brian McDermott

Home Alone: The One-Person Training Department .17
  By Bob Filipczak

Yes...You Can Weigh Training's Value 21
  By Jac Fitz-Enz
  • The Fallacy of the Burden of Proof

Simplifying ROI 25
  By James Hassett
  • E-Mail Evaluation: 2 Inexpensive Techniques Yield
    Multiple Benefits / *Dave Zielinski*

To Meet Just-In-Time Training Demands, Trainers Turn to 'Short Bite' Training 31
  By Sarah Fister
  • Outsourcing Short-Bite Training Works for Bayer Corp.

How to Get the Most Out of 360˚ Feedback 35
  By Gary Yukl and Richard Lepsinger

Evaluating Your Management Performance 39
  By Brian McDermott
  • Think You're a Good Training Leader?
    Your Staff's Review Will Tell / *Dave Zielinski*

What Trainers Can Learn from the Sales Force 43
  By Virginia Sweet Lincoln

Training Directors as Change Agents 47
  By Brian McDermott

Training, MIS Functions Struggle to Define a New Relationship 49
    By Dave Zielinski

The Myth of Soft Skills Training 53
    By James C. Georges
    • How to Make a Level 3 Evaluation of Soft Skills Training
      Pay Dividends / *Dave Zielinski*

Making Competencies Pay Off 57
    By Timm J. Esque and Thomas F. Gilbert
    • Competencies vs. Accomplishments
    • Give Leader Competencies Some Bite — Tie Them
      to Near-Term Goals / *Dave Zielinski*

Deciding Who to Train 63
    By Brian McDermott

The Care and Breeding of Global Managers 65
    By Beverly Geber
    • AT&T Grooms Middle Managers with New-Look
      Leadership Program / *Dave Zielinski*

Avoiding Copyright Traps: It Pays to Know the Rules 71
    By Dave Zielinski

Dos and Don'ts of Questionnaire Design 73
    By Dean Spitzer
    • Save Time By Asking Trainees to Do Own Needs Analysis
      with Database Tool / *Dave Zielinski*

Constructing Tests that Work 77
    By Marc J. Rosenberg and William Smitley
    • Using 'Dailies' to Keep Training on Target

CHAPTER 2

STAFF ISSUES

The New Trainer 83
    By Marc Hequet
    • Up Close and Personal at Arm's Length

How One Training Leader Is Turning His Staff into 21st-Century Trainers 89
    By Dave Zielinski
    • Community Colleges Offer High-Tech Resources for Training Your Trainers

How to Hire the Right Trainer 93
    By Chris Lee
    • How to Find the Right Training Job

The Care and Feeding of Trainers 99
    By Beverly Geber

Just Passing Through 103
    By Bob Filipczak

Using Subject-Matter Experts in Training **107**
    By Tom Goad

How to Select Good Technical Instructors **109**
    By Ruth C. Clark and Phyllis Kyker

A Three-Part Plan for Making Your Training Staff More Effective **113**
    By Dave Zielinski

HRD Degrees: Who Needs Them? **115**
    By Margaret Kaeter
      • Which Comes First: The Professionals or the Profession?
      • Engineering a Degree Program
      • Resources for Degree Programs

Toning Down Young Trainers — Without Turning Them Off **121**
    By Frank T. Wydra and Kathleen Whiteside

Instructive Moments: Every Trainer Has One of Those Days **123**
    By Marc Hequet
      • Maybe It's Not *You* They Hate
      • The Lawyer and the Cockroach

Performance Reviews: Practicing What We Preach **127**
    By Stephen P. Becker

The Power of Positive Feedback **129**
    By Donald V. Schuster

Zeroing In On Your Staff's Performance **133**
    By Dave Zielinski

Taking Care of Troubles **137**
    By Brian McDermott
      • How to Decide When to Fire a Problem Staffer

Building Trust **139**
    By Stephen P. Becker

CHAPTER 3

USING OUTSIDE RESOURCES:
Vendors, Consultants and Contractors

Calamitous Consulting — A Cautionary Tale of Using Outside Help **143**
By Beverly Geber
      • Tips for Working with Consultants

The Who, When & Why of Hiring Consultants **147**
    By Brian McDermott

Use of Contract Trainers, Designers Now Strategic Tool for Training Leaders **149**
    By Dave Zielinski

Inventive Outsourcing Helps Trainers Thrive Even As Staff Sizes Dwindle **151**
    By Dave Zielinski

More See Community Colleges as Attractive Outsourcing Option **159**
  By Chris Busse
  • Guidelines Help in Creating Partnerships
    with Community Colleges

Can You Outsource Your Brain? **161**
  By Marc Hequet

Choosing the Right Training Solution **165**
  By Thomas D. Conkright

How to Choose a Feedback Instrument **167**
  By Ellen Van Velsor and Stephen J. Wall

How to Choose a Video Producer **171**
  By Roy B. Cohn
  • It's (Almost) All in the Script

Out of the Can: How to Customize Off-the-Shelf Training **175**
  By Bob Filipczak
  • Massaging the Media

CHAPTER 1

SKILLS AND TOOLS OF THE EFFECTIVE TRAINING MANAGER

Sometimes Training Skills Are a Second Priority

Business knowledge is essential to the success of training.

BY BRIAN MCDERMOTT

Management skill, not training expertise, is the most important factor in determining how successful a training executive can be in improving the status of a training function in an organization. Participants in the Training Directors' Forum White Paper Project agree that training skills are obviously essential, but find that acting as a business person first and trainer second is what contributes most to increasing training's strategic importance to an organization.

In broad terms, management skill at this level translates as the ability to plan, communicate, politick, and respond in order to help address a corporation's or public agency's most pressing concerns and fulfill its business goals and objectives.

How does that translate into day-to-day activities? The application for the Training Directors' Forum Training/HRD Executive of the Year asked a similar question: "In what ways have you employed your management skills, personal training expertise, knowledge of your company's business, creativity, and interpersonal skills to make yourself and your training function integral parts of your company?" Excerpts from several responses follow.

Jo Moyer: *Director of corporate training and development, Freddie Mac.*

The three years prior to joining the training department at Freddie Mac, Moyer says, were characterized by abortive attempts to establish a coherent internal training system. With limited offerings and a suspect performance record, training was perceived as non-responsive and out of the mainstream of corporate life, she adds.

At the same time, Moyer says, the organization's training needs were increasing rapidly because deregulation in the industry demanded more flexibility, better customer service and the ability to be proactive. For the first time, the need for strategic planning and change-management skills came to the forefront. "Doing more with less, streamlining operations, and increasing corporate creativity were imperatives." Armed with that knowledge of the business, Moyer believed training could play a major role in helping the corporation achieve long-term success, so she set about changing training's image and services.

First, she met with every vice president "to hear firsthand their perceptions of corporate training needs; a second agenda was to establish a rapport with each. The interviews allowed us to establish a corporate training advisory council. I asked each executive vice president to appoint two influential individuals from each department. To help ensure the council's success, we made sure members received written feedback concerning our response to their input; we copied their bosses on each set of meeting minutes. We reinforced that they were chosen because they are perceived as movers and shakers, and most importantly, we changed in response to their direction."

To become more customer focused, Moyer says, the department was reorganized and policies modified to make it easier to say yes to clients. "We created a service-based department mission statement, developed standards for responding to customers, and tracked our performance."

Moyer's group also created a communication plan to promote their services and successes. They developed a database to use in reporting to management about program usage, cost-benefit analyses and program evaluations. They also used internal publications in a year-long campaign to position the department as being a "responsive and corporately responsible part of the organization."

To further establish training as an integral part of the corporation, Moyer's group developed an integrated curricula for supervisors and managers. The curricula covered key skills needed by each management group now and in the future, and offered expanded education about their industry. The number of courses was increased and more broadly distributed to regional locations. "Timeliness and professionalism helped us be acknowledged as business partners with line operations. To ensure timely courses, we identified a cadre of consultant/designers who could get to know our organization, and upon whose skills we could depend. We relied primarily on in-house staff to present courses to increase our credibility with clients."

Ann Atkinson: *Formerly vice president of training and management and organization development for Days Inns of America (and now consulting).*

"When I started at Days Inns there was no training function. The new owners had decided their strategic plan was to begin aggressively franchising. They realized that part of the sales strategy was to offer franchisees sound training. When I came to the company, I conducted listening sessions with senior management to consolidate their expectations into a strategy upon which I could base the training function. Then I went into the field and conducted listening sessions with 150 general managers. At the same time I worked every job in the hotel so I would have firsthand knowledge and empathy for the jobs, responsibilities, and concerns of the employees. I then visited training centers of other hotel chains to examine format, delivery, strategy, and focus...and to determine where we could make a difference. The answer seemed to be to develop classes in an intimate atmosphere, and to hire exceptional trainers, credible in their deliveries and styles.

"To sell this idea to senior management, I had to focus on the results they expected: satisfying the franchisee. So the training mission became that of selling franchise...and, oh, by the way, we do it through training. The president and chief financial officer attend every corporate training class and make a presentation."

One training goal, Atkinson says, is to meet every request for services within five days. "If this department can't fulfill the need, we take the responsibility of finding someone who can. Because of this credibility, our budgets are approved without delay, and the department is seen as a major player in the company's continued success."

Walt Thurn: *Manager of employee development, Florida Power Corp.*

In 1980, Florida Power was suffering from high turnover, a poor safety record, and decreased productivity as a result of a decade of rapid growth — from 1,600 employees and 500,000 customers to 4,000 employees and 900,000 customers.

Thurn says senior management asked the training department for a plan to help solve those problems. Our final recommendation was to implement a performance-based training system. Management was briefed that the program would require 10 years to implement.

"That was eight years ago. Today, performance-based training is an integral part of the organization and has helped produce the following results: "Promotion time (from entry level to journeyman) has been reduced from 7.2 to 4.1 years. Florida Power won a national award for its safety. Turnover in one major department was reduced from 48.5 percent to 9.2 percent (influenced by a pre-employment program designed by the training department). Productivity of our linemen is among the highest for an electric utility our size. Supervisor decisions for employee promotions are partially based on measuring competency using the training system. The training budget and staffing requirements have stayed level for two years [reflecting Thurn's philosophy that training departments should look for ways to reduce client training demands, not increase them, by eliminating performance problems]. And productivity improvements have helped flatten employee growth."

Those successes, Thurn says, depend on the involvement of line managers in the design and implementation of training, the delegation of authority and creativity to the training staff, and his own knowledge of the company's business and his willingness to work with clients.

Chuck Wolfe: *Director of management development, The Hartford Insurance Group.*

Wolfe introduced his staff to a process for managing change, which was used to create a future vision for training and to outline the stages needed to make the transition to becoming a business partner within the company. "The idea was to contribute in strategic and operational planning, and to improvements in the quality of work life."

The first step, Wolfe says, was to design and implement a comprehensive, cost-effective, and practical curriculum — presupervisory to executive levels. Initially, he says, the key to

---

10 TIPS HELP TRAINING EXECS AVOID 'SPINELESS MARSUPIAL' SYNDROME

BY RANDALL JOHNSON

Keeping the training department in the organizational decision-making loop is a constant challenge in virtually every organization, say Roger Cole, vice president of operations and planning, and Tom Roney, director of corporate training at The Circle K Corp. in Phoenix, AZ. But some careful "strategizing, prioritizing and positioning," they say, ensures training executives will have top management's attention when it counts.

The two offered these 10 tips for "making training make a difference" at a recent Training Directors' Forum Conference in Tempe, AZ:

• **Don't be a spineless marsupial.** People who come to senior management's table with ideas that are well thought out, clearly articulated, and backed with plenty of punch in the form of demonstrable support will get attention at the top.

Top managers expect bold, take-charge thinking from those it endorses. Don't come to top execs looking for support. Come to them with support in tow, with everything as close to "go" as you can reasonably get it without their approval.

• **Make friends in low places.** In the end, nobody knows as much about a company as the people on the front lines. Don't rely on paper or phone surveys of the hourly wage-earners for your information. Go out and talk to people. By building trust through ongoing relationships, you'll be able to glean information not available through any other channel. Says Cole: "If a crisis hits the organization, it's likely you'll be the only person sitting at the conference table who knows what's really going on and why."

• **Learn to move fast.** Training needs are often immediate. If you take six months to fill a curriculum request, chances are you'll miss the window of opportunity. As people become aware of what a time-intensive proposition new training is, they'll ask for less and less of it. The end result is a poorly trained organization that sees training as a nonentity. And when major strategic initiatives come along, the training department won't be a primary player.

A prototype for most programs can be designed in two weeks. "Try to get a test model built and tested within a week," Cole says. "If you've got ingenious people, which you probably have, they will do it."

If you can have it 90% ready in a month, that's better than waiting three months or longer to be 100% done.

Don't spend weeks "thinking." Make your first discussion a curriculum design session.

• **Don't be the patron saint of lost causes.** "Don't be the person who always says, 'The people in accounting are upset again,' " Cole says. "Of course they're upset. They've always been upset. It's their job to be upset." If you make these kind of negatives a part of every message you deliver to top managers, you'll be written off as

success was how the program was sold internally by his supervisor, his staff, and himself. "It was critical to establish a quick series of successful programs. I brought in Zenger-Miller's Supervision program, ODI's Managing for Productivity program, the Atlanta Consulting Group's Managing Relationships at Work for executives, and a negotiations program.

"Managing for Productivity proved most successful when regional managers took the program as a team and dealt with real issues rather than the ODI case studies. Managing Relationships at Work produced the best results with executives who had structural conflict built into their roles. The program can produce strong bonding, and when we have conducted it with field and home-office executives, it has often significantly improved working relationships." The negotiations training, Wolfe says, is credited with helping bring in $20 million in sales and cutting expenses by $3 million.

The second step of the program is to complete a development system that can improve productivity and service with reduced staff sizes, fewer management levels, and more competition. "It is critical that every executive, manager, and supervisor develop and train employees to improve bottom-line performance by helping them become more effective in their jobs." Training's job, he says, has been to develop a system and to work with line managers to make it work.

The most effective method for implementation, Wolfe says, has been to start with executives and work down. For instance, working with one senior vice president and his staff has led to development plans for the first time for directors, officers, and vice presidents in the department.

Edie Hutton: *Vice president and director of training and development, Landmark Bancshares Corp.*

"The training and development department acts as a business within a business. Our mission is tied to the company's mission. Our goal is to meet the training needs of the company as defined in the bank's long- and short-range goals. We meet regularly with clients to assess the bank's performance plans and to identify the programs and services that will be provided to help the company meet its goals."

The best strategy in securing scarce resources, Hutton says, is to provide results-oriented management of the department, and deliver high-quality programs, job aids, and tools that aid performance.

"The training department is expected to participate in senior management planning sessions, task forces, and ad hoc committees. Our department is called on by the bank's line managers to help identify performance problems and their solutions. More often than not, training is not required, and managers implement the alternate management actions we recommend."

Hutton says the training department is also respected for its nontraditional approach to problem solving, management, and design and implementation of programs and services. "That was very risky at first, but now we are asked more frequently, 'What

---

the pessimist you are. Choose your battles carefully, and then fight to win.

• **Learn the business.** Increasingly, training executives are crossing industry lines. If you've just come to healthcare from the petrochemical field, don't assume your years of wisdom are still valid.

One mark of the ineffective training department is a growing stock of generic programs, those of the "Teamwork 101" sort. Teams have various skill needs in different organizations. Ask your friends how your generalized programs can be tailored to meet their most immediate, specific needs.

• **Practice the 80/20 rule.** The bromide says 80% of the results come from 20% of the effort. "The training team that tries to be all things, to do all things, will end up succeeding only by chance," Cole says.

Says Roney: "Many of us conduct a six-month needs analysis when we could have found out 80% of the same information with only two or three phone calls to the right people — to our friends in low places."

The hardest part is learning to say no. If someone has a request for training and you see it as part of the less-useful 80% of the effort, you need to tell them.

• **Speak the language.** Every business has one, and if you aren't fluent in it, you're going to fall somewhere between misunderstood and ignored. Also remember to leave your "trainer-ese" in the training center. Neither top managers nor other training customers want to talk about performance objectives; they simply want to know what you're going to do to make their problem go away.

"When trainers begin to speak in organizational development jargon, odds are they will be discounted immediately," Cole says. "If you haven't learned your subject well enough to talk about it in English, go back and learn it again."

• **Learn the critical success factors of the business.** Look for those training possibilities that have the highest probability of influencing the bottom line in a major way — and always focus on those first, not the "nice to haves."

• **Be opportunistic — even when no opportunities for success are evident.** Sometimes training is not so much about education as about strategic management. If a manager comes to you with a report of poor performance in his department and a demand for training, you can benefit from helping him even if you know training isn't his real need.

Says Cole: "Call your friends in low places to get five keys to assembly, put together a one-page reading with questions on the back. Then put a nice cover letter on it from the manager, saying how concerned he is and how he wants everyone to take this 'course' within 24 hours."

What have you accomplished? First, you've got the manager off your back. Second, you're dealing with what you suspect are the real problems — low expectations and low follow-through on management's part.

• **Match training budget to pressing needs.** To make a difference in the organization, you need to figure out how much of your budget is going against what issues. Determine whether dollar allocations are proportional to the strategic importance of issues addressed by your training, and then redirect spending to match top corporate strategies.

do you think?' Many managers with a long history of 'tradition' in banking are changing, modeling the behaviors of our department as they relate to the management of their own resources."

Another guideline, Hutton says: "We will not and do not deliver training programs or services that are not based on need, or are not of good quality. As a result, we can convince clients that what they need is what they want."

Gary Schulze: *Corporate director of human resources development, McGraw-Hill Inc.*

Schulze's first challenge was to fulfill the promise made to the Board of Directors by the company's CEO, to provide a development program for senior executives in less than four months.

"Despite the commitment to the board, made before I was hired, nothing had been done about the program. The project required a great deal of diplomacy and tact; the work had to be done through a hoard of trustees, which included my boss, the senior vice president for personnel, and the senior vice president of administration. As administrator of the program, I made sure to keep both men posted on every step of the project, and gave them an opportunity to take full credit for the eventual success of the program."

Schulze launched the program with help from the Harvard Business School and has been building on its success ever since. The attendees of the first program, he says, were 23 of the company's most senior executives, many of whom became operating company presidents and corporate executive vice presidents. "The opportunity gave me a tremendous advantage since it gave me credibility with this group. It made it easier to establish programs at lower levels later. It also gave me a chance to sell myself with the CEO."

The establishment of a corporate training curriculum required buy-in from all of McGraw-Hill's operating companies, Schulze says. "To accomplish that I established and chaired a corporate management development committee made up of executives from each operating company, all of whom reported directly to their company presidents. This helped greatly in getting line support for my activities and provided a sounding board for testing new ideas and programs.

"Once we knew the kinds of programs we needed at each management level, I hired American Management Association consultants to help design and implement supervisory and management programs customized to our environment. Our CEO also agreed that if we were to have a truly effective and viable management development program, corporate human resources development had to have a budget protected from arbitrary cutbacks at the operating company level. *To this day we have a budget that can only be cut by the CEO.* When it does get cut, my department determines what can be given up with the least amount of damage to the corporation's business strategies and overall training effort."

Notes:

10 Management Musts for HRD Directors

Which is the best-managed department in your organization? It should be yours, thanks to the special opportunities and responsibilities that HRD directors have.

BY GEOFFREY M. BELLMAN

Managers of HRD (human resources development) functions have many of the same problems that all other managers face. And they also have a special opportunity as custodians of human resources development within their organizations. Because of their special responsibilities, they usually have more formal knowledge of how to develop human resources and, more specifically, of the techniques of management.

The following 10 suggestions come from my own experience as an HRD manager and as a consultant to HRD managers in other organizations. They contain obvious biases, but these biases have been useful to me and may well stimulate your thoughts in related areas.

1 First and foremost, manage. When you are consulting with a client, you are not managing. When you are training supervisors, you are not managing. You may consult or train well, but when you do, you aren't managing.

Management may not be a full-time responsibility for you because of the size of your department or your organization. But there are times when you must put on your managers hat and concentrate all your energies on deciding where this function is going to go and how you are going to take it there.

2 Delegate. If you spend more time managing, someone else is going to have to do much of the training and consulting you normally do. You say they don't have the skills to do that

work? Or they don't have the time? Or you don't have confidence in them? Have you ever heard those same complaints from line managers who won't let go of their technical work to do their managerial jobs?

Learn about how difficult it is to delegate by delegating yourself. Learn about the problems line managers face as they move from being individual contributors to being managers.

3 Establish ideals. What do you want your HRD department to be in the long term? What are your hopes for it? What are the HRD ideals that you want to serve? Consider these questions with your staff, and together write a statement of ideals that your department will constantly work toward. Further, measure your department against these ideals on a project-by-project, objective-by-objective basis, always asking, "Does this project or objective serve the ideals we're reaching for?" You will find that much of the work you undertake doesn't move you toward your ideals, but don't punish yourself for this. If, however, you feel that few projects are moving you in the direction of your ideals, then stop to reconsider what your purposes are and whether you, individually or as a department, can get what you want through continuing to work in this organization. It's also a good idea to reconsider your ideals to see if they are the same guides you want to continue to follow.

4 Be a model for your clients. If you train people in performance appraisal, use performance appraisal within your HRD group. If you work with others on meeting skills, use

meeting techniques in your own group meetings. If you encourage line managers to be more open regarding organization information, risk being open with information in your own group. If you teach MBO (management by objectives) in workshops, use MBO in planning in your group. If you believe managers should build teams, then build a team within HRD.

In HRD, we too often ask for changes from others in areas that we don't want to change ourselves. As a general rule, don't ask clients to try new supervisory or interpersonal skills or systems that you haven't tried first in your own organization. As you try these new skills or systems, pay attention to your own comforts and discomforts and use these feelings to adjust your approach to your line clients. When clients see that you believe enough in what you say in your workshop and consultation to use certain techniques, they will be more likely to use them as well. In the process, you will learn how to manage better and more realistically.

5 Risk managing innovatively. What new management process or technique have you tried in the last three months? What have you tried within the last year that didn't work?

In HRD, we have access to much knowledge on alternative ways of managing. We should be trying out these alternatives, just as we expect our clients to be open to new ways of managing. Even an occasional failure lets us know that we are testing management limits rather than operating too conservatively within management boundaries. When a new approach to managing doesn't work, discuss it in the group and move on to something that you hope will be more successful.

6 Manage in ways respected within your organization. Innovation is fine, but most of your management practices should be along established lines within your organization. "Established" not in the sense of what is done, but in the sense of what people say should be done in a particular organization. When you show a healthy respect for the "establishment," other managers will realize that you know how to do well on their terms. Your success at managing according to the "mores" of an individual organization will make it easier for clients to trust you.

7 Don't rely on promoting from within. For many HRD functions (especially in larger and more technical organizations), the day is past when you can promote well-intentioned and motivated people who do what makes sense. There is a rapidly expanding body of knowledge and skills in human resources development. Many of those skills should be practiced by your staff, especially if yours is a corporate-level staff. If you don't hire talent from outside to supplement your well-intentioned and motivated internal people, your staff may rely entirely on its own past experience. It also takes you much longer to develop the skills you need in a staff inexperienced in HRD than it does to hire someone with HRD experience from without. In addition to hiring people with HRD talents (full-time or part-time), encourage reading, attendance at workshops, the practice of skills within your group and the use of outside experts.

8 Multiply yourself. Long before HRD departments came into formal existence, training and consulting were done between line and staff departments. In fact, most training and consulting are still done without your involvement, and that's how it should be. Seek out the line personnel who are operating as HRD consultants and trainers as a part of their regular responsibilities as managers. Help them build their human resources skills, so they can do the work they're already doing more effectively. This approach allows you to multiply yourself and to demonstrate the importance of human resources development across the line organization.

9 Insist on a line review. Too many of us spend too much time avoiding contact with management. Our fear of them stems from the possibility that they won't like what we're doing or that they won't understand the importance of what we're doing or that they might take some drastic, irreversible action.

Although it's difficult to operate with people outside our control and of greater organizational power, that's exactly what we must do. We shy away from being measured, but if management doesn't see fit to measure us, how important are we? Remember, management keeps a close eye on anything it considers important to the organization. So if we expect management to think of us as important, we should expect them to hold us accountable. Insist, or at least work toward, being reviewed regularly by the line management of your organization. Use that review time to report on what's happened in the past and what you plan to do in the near future. Use that time to get management's commitment.

10 Don't worry about working yourself out of a job. Many HRD managers are working hard toward the day when they no longer will be needed. In fact, many of us use that as a kind of slogan for ourselves as we talk to the people around us. But I think "working ourselves out of a job" is an unfortunate expression.

The HRD function is a legitimate and continuing one, as real and important as the law, accounting or personnel. Ideally, there is no way for you to work yourself out of a job; your function will always be needed. True, your own or your organization's performance can result in the HRD department being trimmed down or eliminated, but the need for human resources development will continue.

The notion of "working ourselves out of a job" is based on a problem-centered image of HRD; that is, once we solve these few problems, we'll no longer be needed. But that's not the way the world of work really is. Problems are not the exception waiting to be resolved so we can return to a more idyllic workplace. Instead, what we call problems are the rule, the very essence of our work and work life. The HRD function exists because of the natural day-in and day-out occurrence of situations between people who are trying to complete a task together. As you use your own and your department's resources more effectively within your organization, more work will come to you as organization managers begin to understand how HRD can help them be even more successful.

Notes:

Training on the Cheap

If you're not constantly looking for ways to save money and still train effectively, you should be. Here's some help for that next meeting with the accounting department.

BY BOB FILIPCZAK

It might be a blinding flash of the obvious, but training is an expensive proposition. Much as we might wish otherwise, training still shows up on the "cost" side of most accounting ledgers. That means the training department is often on the defensive, justifying the money spent to improve the skills of employees and, ultimately, to increase the performance of the organization. If meetings with your corporate bean counters are as much fun as a root canal, it might pay to add some cost-cutting techniques to your training toolbox.

Of course, the arguments in favor of training are many and diverse and often quite convincing. At the core of the training-cost debate is a variation on the popular adage: If you think education is expensive, try ignorance. Substitute the words "training" and "poor performance," and you can get even the most recalcitrant number cruncher's attention.

Cheap training isn't really cheap if it's not effective. Even the phrase "cheap training" raises the hackles of most training professionals; the human resources development (HRD) community seems to be full of people who understand that there is no easy or inexpensive way to improve performance. Cheap training seems too good to be true — and it often is. Consequently, the money-saving ideas we're passing on here have already passed through the "effectiveness" filter. We'll be describing training ideas that are both good and cheap.

It's also important to remember the training costs that don't usually show up on budget reports. Time away from the job is a cost that has received more attention recently (see "No Time to Train," *TRAINING*, November 1995), and it's one that many trainers are trying to minimize.

TRAINING Magazine's Industry Report (October 1995) found that $52.2 billion was budgeted for formal training in 1995. But that figure does not factor in the salaries of all the trainees taken away from their jobs and put in classrooms. According to Joe Harless, president of the Harless Performance Guild in Newnan, GA, and a member

---

The ultimate money-saving idea: Avoid training altogether.

---

of the HRD Hall of Fame, adding trainee salaries to the pot would raise the true cost of training to more than $100 billion. When he started talking about the additional cost of the productivity lost while trainees are in class instead of out on the factory floor, we got so scared we almost hung up on him.

His point is well-taken. For the purposes of this discussion, time is money.

Harless described several principles of training cost reduction, among them this ultimate money-saving idea: Avoid training altogether. This isn't a suggestion to abandon all training, but to make sure that training is the solution to the problem you're trying to solve. Often, it isn't.

It's long been dogma in the performance-technology wing of the training profession that training is useful only if employees are short the skills or knowledge they need to do their jobs effectively. If the performance problem isn't related to skill level or information, says Harless, training isn't going to help. Nevertheless, he points out, training tends to be the universally suggested solution when a performance problem crops up. His research over the years shows that, in fact, performance problems are rarely a matter of skill or knowledge gaps.

Figuring out whether you need to train means doing some up-front work — usually a time-consuming needs assessment. But it's time well spent. Anything you can do to minimize the amount of time productive employees spend in a classroom is going to save the company money in the long run, says Harless.

Companies often overtrain employees, contends Saul Carliner, executive vice president of Fredrickson Communications, a training consulting firm in Minneapolis. Typically, he says, companies train employees to use new computer software by putting them in a classroom for four or five days and teaching them every facet of the program. "They will learn every in and out of that application whether they need it tomorrow or not," says Carliner.

His advice: Give employees just enough training to get them up and running on the software, and then teach them how to find out about the more advanced features when they need them. After they've learned the basics, you can teach them more of the software's features in a few weeks, when their confidence is high, says Carliner. Applying this bare-essentials philosophy, he recently trimmed what was supposed to be a four-day course down to one hour after quizzing his client about the real training needs.

It's also OK, says Carliner, to let employees stumble through tasks they seldom need to do. If a person uses the conference-calling function on her telephone once a year, let her figure out how to use it on her own. "That's OK," says Carliner, "because to fumble through something for 10 minutes is a lot less expensive to the company than having someone spend an hour on it in training class and never use it."

Challenging one of the training world's most sacred notions, Carliner questions whether we even need to teach employees how to write. Maybe we should just admit that some people can't write, he suggests, stop trying to train them, and figure out how to automate that task so they can do it with the least amount of hassle. For example, Microsoft's latest version of Word, its popular word processing software, includes a bunch of form letters that employees can personalize with just a few words here and there.

If a needs analysis shows you really do need to do some training, Harless' second principle of cost reduction comes into play: Make sure only the people who really need the training get it. He decries sheep-dip training — in which all employees are run through a course whether they need it or not. "[It] is the most expensive thing that I can think of," Harless says.

His third principle is related to the first in that it seeks to keep people out of the classroom as much as possible: Use job aids instead of training. Job aids are written instructions employees take to job sites and use as references when they have questions about something. Harless sees job aids as simple, alternative information-storage mechanisms that save trainees from trying to store everything in their fallible memories. If you use job aids well, says Harless, you can cut your instructional-development time by a factor of two or three, and cut your training-delivery time in half. He once reduced two weeks of classroom training to two hours just through creative use of job aids, he says.

Jeff Nelson, president of Expert OJT a training company in Newport News, VA, helps companies develop their own job aids. He teaches a team of subject matter experts (SMEs) how to write either electronically or paper-delivered job aids and eventually lets them take over the process. When he works with companies, he says, he tries to push the control of the training down to the front line, where people are actually doing the work. In many businesses, says Nelson, "the training department owns the process. Our whole approach is that the people who own the processes for real ought to own the training process."

Nelson says he and 12 front-line workers designed machine-operator training for an entire manufacturing company in two weeks by writing extensive job aids. His approach is to create job-aid templates so people who don't know a lot about training can plug information into the appropriate areas and write effective instructions. "They've got the information in their heads," says Nelson. "They just don't quite know how to express it in a way that others can follow."

Creating effective job aids means finding the "why" of the instruction, the point at which an employee might get stuck and turn to a job aid for help. The job aid should also include a list of the tools needed, all the steps in the right order, a description of the outcome, and something that tells the employee if he performed the task correctly. At the end of the process, for example, he has repaired a diesel

---

Job aids save trainees from trying to store everything in their fallible memories.

---

engine and knows he did it correctly because it starts.

Nelson uses decision tables in job aids, a series of "if-then" statements that lead people through the task. In a job aid for routing mail, for example, the decision table reads: "If the mail is marked priority and the day is Monday, then place it in File A." He says he prefers them to flowcharts because they are more intuitive; almost anyone can pick up a decision table, without any training, and use it right away.

There are also ergonomic issues with job aids — which is business-speak for, "Where are you going to put the damn thing?" Nelson says some workers fasten job aids to the sides of their machinery so they can grab them quickly and store them easily. In one case, computer users lacked room on their screens for on-line documentation, so Nelson modified a three-ring binder into a kind of mini-flip chart by turning it inside out and putting it on the desk next to the computer. "It wasn't high-tech, but it worked great," says Nelson.

One warning about job aids: Never tell people that job aids will make their jobs simpler. "It's just psychological," says Nelson. "People have been working at their jobs for many years, and you tell them, 'Hey, I can take your entire job, and I can put it on two pages.'" Not a great way to make friends.

It's the oldest trick in the training book, but of late, there has been talk about making on-the-job training (OJT) a more useful, more structured experience than it has been in the past. Traditionally OJT meant one person learned the job by watching an experienced worker and asking questions, a variation on the apprenticeship model that predates even Malcolm Knowles.

The trouble with OJT, as Harless points out, is that you may lose two employees' productivity, and the bad habits of the experienced worker get passed on to the new one. If, for example, old Stan knows a shortcut that bypasses some of the safety requirements, he'll probably teach it to Joe as they work together.

Michael Jones, an adjunct professor of human resources management at Ohio University in Chillicothe and co-author of *Structured On-The-Job Training*, recommends a disciplined approach that minimizes the problems of traditional OJT.

Jones suggests being very selective about who provides structured OJT. These trainers can be peers or supervisors, but the primary requisite is that they have a good work ethic and can correctly model the behavior that the new employee will be encouraged to emulate. OJT trainers should go through a train-the-trainer course, says Jones, so they understand good training technique and how to facilitate learning. They also analyze needs, design the training, deliver the training, and evaluate the training. In Jones' model, OJT instructors perform all of these tasks right at the work site.

Structured OJT requires an up-front investment in time spent developing trainers and instruction, but the approach can be cost-effective in terms of skill mastery. Employees' learning curves are very steep, says Jones. His research shows that structured OJT can get workers up to speed on their jobs in half the time it usually takes.

Careful selection of on-the-job trainers is key, he says, because new employees will often turn to these people in the future for information and help. These trainers become de facto mentors for a lot of employees — an important point to keep in mind when you say, "Go sit by Nellie" or "Go follow Joe." In OJT, says Jones, "other things are going on that many managers aren't aware of. But by carefully selecting and training that [OJT trainer], we can control those factors."

Both Jones and Nelson concede that training on the job doesn't always provide the ideal learning environment — the press of regular work frequently interrupts the training. There are ways to minimize interference, though most blur the boundaries between OJT and "formal" training. One of Nelson's clients scheduled a training shift, an extra shift in the plant's schedule during which time and equipment would be available for uninterrupted instruction. Jones also suggests scheduling structured OJT during downtime. If that's not possible, he says, set aside an area on the floor for training and make sure everyone knows which days training will be conducted. Jones says most employees are very considerate about making sure training doesn't get interrupted if they know it's going on.

Regardless of *how* you deliver training, it will pay to keep in mind Harless' fourth principle of training cost containment: Make sure that training is performance-based rather than knowledge-based. That means employees get time to practice their new skills and are able to do something different — not just think differently — when they get back to the job. The most expensive training is the kind that doesn't transfer, says Harless.

A close relative of structured OJT is peer training; non-trainers are given some background in effective adult learning and then let loose to teach their co-workers either on the job or in a classroom (see "Frick Teaches Frack," *TRAINING*, June 1993). Many small companies use peer training because most don't have any formal training department at all. In fact, most small businesses have no trainers or significant training budgets. If anyone has to wrestle with training employees with a minimum of resources, it's owners of small businesses.

One of the peer-training strategies small companies use to stretch their shoestring budgets is what we will call, for lack of a better term, boomerang training. That means sending one employee out for training, usually to an external supplier, and having her bring back what she learned to the organization. She then trains her co-workers.

That's one of the strategies Brenda Schissler, president of Staffmasters, a small temporary agency in Louisville, KY, uses to train her 10 permanent employees. Most of her employees are well-versed in training techniques

because they go out and train customers in things like customer service and telephone skills in addition to supplying temps. Each employee specializes in a particular topic, like office safety, and briefs the rest of the staff during meetings.

Nevertheless, boomerang training isn't always reliable, acknowledges Schissler. Individuals get different things from training they attend, and that subjectivity affects what they teach co-workers. Steve Braccini, president and CEO of Profastener, a San Jose, CA, distributor of components to the electronics industry, has found a

---

"I think these people learned as much from their colleagues as they ever did from the book."

---

way around the possibly skewed perceptions of boomerang trainers. He always sends two employees so they can do a reality check on their perceptions of the training before they bring it back to Profastener's 165 employees.

One key to most boomerang training, and many other dollar-stretching ploys, is an effective train-the-trainer program. Employees without a training background need to acquire at least the fundamentals of good instructional technique. Braccini makes sure all boomerang trainers have a train-the-trainer course under their belts before they attend any program. In fact, he won't send an employee to training strictly for personal development anymore; he always sends someone who can bring the training back and deliver it effectively to other employees.

Be careful when you try to turn employees into trainers, cautions Bob Pike, president of Creative Training Techniques, a consulting firm in Minneapolis.

Pike says he's seen some pretty frightening examples of train-the-trainer courses. One was a public seminar taught by someone without a training background who told the audience that lectures are the most effective way to train, that using visuals just distracts the trainees, and that games aren't an appropriate learning

medium for serious subjects. "Here are 45 people that, in my estimation, are getting misinformation," says Pike.

As vice president of the federation programs and services division of the U.S. Chamber of Commerce in Washington, DC, Roger Jask's charter is to provide low-cost training for small businesses as part of the recently developed Small Business Institute. The Small Business Administration used to give money to universities to develop courses specifically for small businesses. The funding for that, however, has been cut.

At the same time, small businesses that don't have training departments or functions have become more interested in training their employees, says Jask. He suspects that many businesses today are started by middle managers who have been axed by large corporations. These new entrepreneurs are convinced, from their experiences with HRD in mega-companies, that training offers them a strategic advantage. Consequently, says Jask, they pursue cost-effective ways to get their employees trained.

To help answer that need, Jask's division developed 35 self-study courses for small businesses. The training focuses on seven areas his research identified as the core competencies that keep small businesses alive: marketing and sales; budgeting and finance; legal issues; human relations and communications; productivity improvement; quality and customer service; and supervision, management and leadership.

Jask picked five books in each area from Crisp Publishing, a publisher of training books in Menlo Park, CA. Jask's division changed the book covers to feature the Chamber of Commerce logo, and added a test at the end of each book. Small businesses can buy the books for less than $20 apiece. Employees read them, do the exercises that follow each chapter, complete the test, and send it to the Small Business Institute. Jask's division grades the test on a pass-fail basis. If the employee passes, she gets a certificate of completion and earns between three-tenths and six-tenths of a continuing education unit.

While a small business may buy the books, it's up to the employee to read them. "Most small businesses are hoping that training will be a two-way street," explains Jask.

Staffmaster's Schissler uses the Small Business Institute's self-study courses and says they fit her needs pretty well. She likes the fact that the books aren't too long and employees can read them at their desks.

That brings up an important concern among small businesses that want to train employees: How long will they be away from the job? In some cases, cost plays second fiddle to the time investment. A small business, struggling with either survival or growth, can't afford to lose a couple of employees for a day of training.

It's difficult to get small businesses to let go of their employees for training at local community colleges, says Elaine Gaertner, director of economic development for California Community College's Economic Development Network (ED>Net). "I think we could, in many cases, almost offer it to them free, and we might have a hard time getting the critical mass to put together a class," says Gaertner. One community college she was helping called 300 small businesses before it could fill one class on how to turn your company into a high-performance workplace.

One of the more interesting shoe-string-training ideas that seems to be gaining momentum is a book club within the organization. Profastener's Braccini started a book club about three years ago that concentrated on the work of quality guru Philip Crosby. The employees in his group would read a chapter and then get together to discuss the ideas. Braccini would often prepare some questions ahead of time to keep the discussion going. He says the book discussions were important as the company moved toward total quality management and ISO 9000 certification because everyone shared a common language and philosophy. The book club was discontinued when it evolved into a more formal training system, but he's starting another club to study *Moments of Magic* by Shep Hyken.

Another book club, started at a not-so-small company, has also been successful. Susan Keen, manager of corporate education at Sunquest Information Systems, a 600-employee computer-information company in Tucson, AZ, discovered that the future of computing was something called object-oriented programming. OOP allows average computer users to assemble their own programs by linking icons that represent programming routines.

Keen met with Sunquest's SMEs to ask them what employees needed to know about oop. Because it was new stuff, however, she didn't have much of a budget for formal training on the subject. When a couple of outside suppliers estimated a cost of $250,000 to acquaint about half the company's employees with OOP, Keen and her experts hit upon a solution drawn from their college days: study groups.

The gist of the plan was to buy a textbook by Grady Booch, one of the gurus of OOP, and have the SMEs facilitate study groups for one hour each week to discuss the concept. When Keen announced the formation of the groups, the first 60 participant slots were filled immediately. She

---

Training isn't just a competitive advantage to organizations; it also helps individual employees stay employable.

---

purchased the textbooks from a college bookstore, and coached five SMEs in facilitation skills.

After the first group completed the program, it was clear that the textbook the experts had picked out was way over the heads of most participants. Because Keen bought the books from a college bookstore, however, she could sell the used books back to the college and use the credit to buy a more accessible text.

Most of the studying and reading was done on the employees' own time, reducing "time away from the job" costs. But the key to the success of this venture, according to Keen, was a mandatory orientation class. Three weeks before the first meeting, materials were distributed, facilitators were introduced, questions were answered, and expectations were clearly defined. Since this was a rapidly changing field of knowledge, a few ground rules were set. For example, the SME/facilitator would be the final arbiter of any disputes. Moreover, participants agreed that the textbook was the definitive source if any arguments over vocabulary occurred.

Keen's final cost analysis indicates that her study-group approach was a

bargain. It cost the company $4,800 for books and $3,200 for other materials. Add in incidentals, and Keen estimates the cost of the training at about $17,000, or about $56 per person, not including employees' time.

The ripple effects from these study groups are also worth noting. People talk about the importance of interactivity in training — what could be more interactive than a discussion group? "I think these people learned as much from their colleagues as they ever did from the book," says Keen. More important, since the groups were a mix of people from different departments, employees who rarely encountered each other suddenly discovered they could discuss important concepts together. "Marketing is actually talking to the developers now," says Keen. That could set a dangerous precedent.

We've still got two of Harless' principles of cost-effective training to go. Number six is: Use traditional instructional design rules. Most training, he contends, uses an inductive instructional methodology, in which trainees are prompted to "discover" the general principles by adding up the particular facts. This extends delivery time — making it more expensive — and is not proven to be any more effective than deductive instruction, which Harless recommends. Deductive training doesn't sneak up on the participant; it clearly states the general concepts, cites examples that support them, and leaves it up to the trainee whether to believe them.

Principle number seven on Harless' hit list is: Minimize travel and lodging of trainees. That simply means that instead of taking the mountain of trainees to Mohammed, you would be wise to take the trainer to sites where trainees live and work.

This is hardly a complete list of cost-effective training ideas. Trainers save time and money in a variety of other ways. Brown-bag sessions, for example, bring employees together for short training meetings during their lunch hours and minimize time off the job. Such sessions have been popular in the past and are even more prevalent in today's "do more with less" environment. Another simple idea: Create an informal training cooperative. Schissler's company bought training videos with a few other small companies to create a shared video library.

Trade organizations are another

potential source of subsidized training for both large and small companies. Jay Long, director of employee development for Ruppert Landscape Co. Inc. in Ashton, MD, sends employees to training offered by a couple of trade organizations. Small companies that supply larger organizations may also find their customers willing to provide training. A large company committed to TQM or ISO 9000 certification may invest in training a supplier's employees to ensure it receives the highest-quality materials for the products it manufactures.

Another idea is a training consortium, a concept that's been around for a while but one that speaks directly to training on a shoestring. Training consortia are groups of companies that band together and agree to share some of their more generic training programs. If United Glop has empty chairs available in its time management program, it contacts Amalgamated Gramis and invites it to send some employees over (see "Training Consortia: How They Work, How They Don't," *TRAINING*, August 1994). The primary problem with training consortia is keeping them together and tracking who did what to whom.

Western Learning Systems in Santa Clara, CA, offers a variation on the training consortium idea. Your organization buys a membership to the organization (like a health club), and you can send employees to a variety of training courses for $189 a head.

Community colleges also can be a resource for companies trying to stretch a tight training budget. These colleges have become more savvy about providing training for companies, large and small (see "Community Colleges Go Corporate," *TRAINING*, December 1995).

There's been a significant increase in interest in training among small businesses, says Jack Zenger, president of the Times Mirror Training Group, a collection of training companies that includes Zenger-Miller Inc., the San Jose, CA, firm he founded. Zenger-Miller has begun contracting with community colleges to offer programs aimed at small businesses. For Zenger, partnering with community colleges has been a marriage made in heaven. In the past, he says, his company had no way to reach out to small businesses; now, community college instructors can be certified in Zenger-Miller's programs, enabling the schools to offer training, classrooms, and economies of scale to smaller companies.

One last idea: Ask employees if they have any ideas about getting the training they need. Training isn't just a competitive advantage for organizations; it also helps individual employees stay employable. That new fact of life can provide employees with a strong incentive to get training by hook or by crook. Consultant Carliner says many informal employee networks provide a place where information is exchanged and skills are enhanced. "Employees themselves are quite ingenious in finding ways to get trained," says Carliner. They just might come up with new ways to get trained that will fit your budget.

Notes:

Ducking the Ax

Protecting a training budget when finances are tight requires timing, sales skills and corporate perspective.

BY BRIAN MCDERMOTT

Top management swinging the budget ax in your organization? If so, it's probably too late to prevent deep cuts in your department's spending unless you've already invested a large percentage of your time selling the importance of training.

Robert Schull, chief of operational air crew training at Scott Air Force Base, led a group discussion, "How to Keep Training the #1 Priority," at a recent *TRAINING* Conference. The main idea the group agreed upon, Schull says, is that training managers must keep alive the perception that vital organizations must continually nurture their people. Therefore, training must be unencumbered and the last entity to be cut when trimming budgets.

"The group had a variety of experiences. Basically, what we came up with is that to make training a top priority, chief trainers need to keep the impetus alive at staff meetings through memos to CEOs, and through reports on the numbers and needs of people to be trained. Every department director in an organization has a view of what the department cannot afford to lose. But the only common thread throughout any organization has to be the training program. You must have commitment."

Schull presents a variety of data in statistical formats to make his case for the training he provides to all military airlift aircraft personnel: The percent of personnel totally qualified for particular jobs; lists of people who are not fully trained; projections about how many people must be trained in each of the next five years, based on attrition and promotions.

"If a training officer sits back and says nothing, training will be pushed aside. You have to understand how people get into power positions in organizations; it's the top sales people or the top production people who move up. And those people don't always have the management skills or the knowledge of what it takes to make the whole corporation work. Either a top manager has a brainchild of his own and will support a training program, or you have to put him through the program up front to get the support. You have to get the support from the top down.

"If training is going to succeed, we need to be vibrant, aggressive and action oriented. We've got to make people understand why these things are important and why anything less than the ideal might not have the desired impacts." Schull spends about 33 percent of his time selling the importance of training. "It's all the time I have. The majority of it is involved in protecting my budget."

An Alternative View

Often, Schull says, training directors say no to new concepts suggested for training due to a lack of funds. He suggests, however, that reevaluating how training dollars are spent can lead to restructuring that might satisfy the need for the new concept while retaining the integrity of existing training.

"The hardest thing for a training chief is to see what could be deleted, if necessary, to add something new. Often times it becomes a matter of restructuring a training system in order to increase the learning and retention and so it can be delivered less frequently. It might mean making a program self-paced or creating training from which people can test out.

"There are so many different kinds of training programs that I can't say there is any one way to make decisions. But I have to look and see where the pitfalls of my own programs are. That's difficult for most of us because we like to protect our programs, but not to dissect them. It's like learning to walk. You have to look at the basics and question if the old concept is still valid. Just because we have done something one way for 50 years does not make it right."

Schull warns: "I got the feeling from some people in New York that they feel their management is totally supportive of training. That's fantastic. But you can easily get complacent and that's when you are most susceptible — the time when a budget cut is going to come down and you are not going to be prepared."

Management changes. Profit and loss statements change. As a result, Schull says, it's likely there will always be budget cuts to contend with. It's up to training directors to anticipate and control how those cuts will be handled in their departments.

"There's no 10-page booklet for prescribing how to sell management on training, but it is the number-one priority for my job. All the trainers out there have to have this in the back of their minds; will they have problems in a year or two even if they're not now. We've got to be ready to defend what we have."

Learning to Sell

One of the best things a training executive can do to promote his or her department is to take a sales training course, according to Lou-Ellen Barkan. Barkan, formerly a senior vice president for training and development at Shearson Lehman Bros., is a vice president and senior compensation consultant at Citibank in New York.

"The best training model is the best sales person you know because selling is the essence of getting commitment. The same skills used to sell a product can be adapted by a staff person selling a service to clients. You have to learn to handle objections. You have to learn how to present the benefits, to understand and articulate the needs and to create awareness."

It is critical, Barkan says, to learn the business and the concepts of your organization. "What do people do all day? You've got to read the proper journals; understand the company; articulate your projects in the language of your clients. If you are talking to sales people, deal with them in sales terms. You have to know how the people in your organization talk to each other, the jargon, the feeling. Don't come in talking like an academic or you'll probably find that people don't want to talk to you."

The first step in making any sale, Barkan says, is gathering the information. "Some people call it a needs analysis. I call it talking to people about the pragmatic realities of what they need. You have to make sure that what you propose as a solution meets the parameters of the client's work world.

"Next," she says, "come up with a number of possible solutions. List the benefits and risks. Sort out the possibilities and then let the line management people decide what they want to do. I don't defend the things I do. People have very real business needs. It's my job to be very clear about what the missed opportunities might mean; it's somewhat like a spreadsheet analysis. If clients are not aware of the down side of a project, I feel the person proposing the program is in error." And how that information is received by clients, Barkan says, again depends on sales skills.

The best way to win respect and cooperation for training efforts is to do something right, Barkan says.

"Make something work. Some people think you can only establish credibility by doing something big. I think you can gain credibility by doing small things quickly. People are interested in doing things that way. You are providing value added. And it leads the desire to go on working with you."

To overcome resistance to new training techniques or programs, Barkan says, give people service that is as close to what they want as possible. She says, however, the reality is that senior management must be sold on training efforts in order for them to succeed. "If they are not sold on the importance of training, you might as well stay at home and bake cookies."

Notes:

Home Alone: The One-Person Training Department

Trials, triumphs and tricks of the trade from the lone wolves of corporate education.

BY BOB FILIPCZAK

It's enough to make any sane person scream. Outside your office door, belligerent supervisors complain about taking their people off the job to attend some harebrained training program. The executive committee, concerned with keeping its collective butt out of a courtroom, demands that workshops begin at once on sexual harassment, performance appraisals and interviewing skills. Needs assessment questionnaires are piled waist deep in the corner next to a stack of OSHA regulations that you'll have to translate from Swahili. And here comes the CEO with some diseased song and dance about the pressing need for customer service training that will make your company globally competitive.

Welcome to the world of the one-person training department.

Take Mike Williams. Besides holding down a full-time job as a bond broker for J.B. Hanauer in Livingston, NJ, Williams is head of Hanauer's training department. He's also the entire staff of the training department. Though his income still depends on commissions earned from the bonds he sells, Williams took on the training job because he has a background in education and seemed the logical candidate when the company recognized a need for ongoing training.

Consultant Carolyn Balling works part time as the sole in-house trainer for Collagen Corp., a manufacturer of skin-care products in Palo Alto, CA. That makes her a half-person training department. She trains the company's 300 employees in management skills, total quality, sexual harassment, compensation issues, performance appraisals, interviewing and selection. If she falls idle, there's always new-employee orientation. "I don't have time to sit around and do the vision thing," she confesses.

That broad range of topics is not particularly unusual for a one-person shop. Many staffless training directors juggle lists of projects and cours-

---

As various programs, got the ax, it was surprising how often nobody seemed to notice.

---

es ranging from half-day time management workshops to multileveled diversity programs to three-year customer service curriculums. Though these courses generally lack the glamour of an executive vision-building retreat in Kuala Lumpur, they represent the kind of meat-and-potatoes training that keeps a company going day in and day out.

Starting from Scratch

One-person training departments often share a common origin: The person in charge is the individual who started the department in the first place. Sometimes the birth spark comes in the form of a mandate from above. Sometimes the department evolves as a natural outgrowth of duties the person has gradually taken on.

Andoni Lizardy, a San Diego-based human resources consultant, sees these people as "pioneers" in a very real sense of the word. Instead of braving tornadoes, deserts and mountain passes, they often face resistant managers, hostile employees and an unnerving lack of empathy from others in their companies.

One of the first challenges they face is course scheduling. The problem is a chorus sung by managers to the tune of "I Won't Let My People Go." Supervisors who aren't used to having a training department around tend to resent efforts to drag their subordinates away from work. The trainer will argue, of course, that this seminar will be good for the employees and will provide a significant return on investment in the long run. The manager's response, however, may run along the lines of: "We've done fine for 20 years without a training department, so why do we need one now?"

Scheduling has always been the most common snag for Judy Berry, director of staff development for the city of Edmond, OK, who started her one-person training operation two years ago. With the timetables of 500 employees to juggle — everyone from the city attorney to the street sweepers — Berry finds that getting people into the classroom is a major hassle. To help reduce scheduling problems, she has set up a training library, a place where employees and managers can check out books, manuals and videos. A person who wants some training can take material home. Managers who can't find time to release employees for classroom training can at least check out a video from the library and show it to their work groups when convenient.

Show and Tell

Perhaps the best way to overcome resistance to a fledgling training department, especially among top executives and watchers of the bottom line, is to demonstrate that the department can save the organization some money. Before Berry set up shop, for instance, the city of Edmond sent all employees who requested training to outside suppliers. Now, only technical training that Berry can't handle is provided by outside suppliers. All other requests are filled by the training department, saving the city substantial sums. That's an effective way to achieve instant popularity.

Another way to overcome resistance to a newly launched training department is to develop a high profile within the organization. This is primarily a matter of internal public relations and finding ways to build relationships. Berry organized a program that sends city employees into public school classrooms to explain to the next generation what their jobs involve. This has gone over well with the employees, the students and especially the taxpaying parents of the students.

Charles Evans, now a senior associate with Barnes & Conti, a human resources consulting company in Berkeley, CA, formerly ran a one-person training department for Office Club, a Concord, CA-based retailer of office products that recently was acquired by another company. In 1991, while working for Office Club, Evans won an award from the *Training Directors' Forum Newsletter* for "holding down costs while maintaining quality service." He says the first thing he did upon launching the new department was to walk around the company and talk to everyone who would spare him a minute. That accomplished two things: It gave him a good idea what the organization's priorities were, and it gave him instant visibility as the training manager.

Lizardy also extols the advantages of establishing relationships, at all levels, before any training begins. That way, he says, "When people come in the [classroom] door, they'll have a positive view of who the trainer is rather than seeing him as some stranger that the company shoved down their throats."

Chris Smith, director of import training and development for Expeditors International of Washington, a Seattle-based broker and freight forwarder, says that about half the training she develops revolves around manuals. Most of the manuals help employees fill out forms, follow regulations and adhere strictly to procedures so customs officials don't delay the company's freight. She could cloister herself in her office writing manuals and instructor guides eight hours a day, five days a week, and still not get caught up. But she believes it's more important to keep in touch with the 1,000 managers and employees at her company's various sites around the West Coast and Midwest. Because managers and supervisors are responsible for delivering most of the training she develops to front-line employees, Smith considers it vital to build

personal relationships with them. She must be more to these manager-trainers than some faceless manual machine back at headquarters who churns out program after program.

Smith feels so strongly about internal public relations that she writes a daily newsletter for all Expeditors International employees and customers, sending it via fax and e-mail to the company's 22 sites. Realizing that her constituents have to keep afloat in a sea of information, from trade magazines to changes in customs regulations, Smith scans various

---

If you want to overcome resistance to training, carry a big stick. And there's no bigger stick than the backing of top management.

---

publications and notifications, and includes in each daily edition a one-page list of briefs that summarizes the points most important to the company's business. She says this takes about an hour every morning. Needless to say, her briefings generate much good will by saving people the trouble of wading through some publications on their own.

The Big Stick

If you want to overcome resistance to something — and persuasion alone won't get the job done — it helps to carry a big stick. In the training world, there is no stick bigger than the serious support of top management. Evans discovered this early when he encountered some problems scheduling training classes. People were just too busy, it seemed. When Office Club's executives made it known that employees would be wise to find the time to attend courses, openings in busy work schedules miraculously began to appear. In Evans case, it was the CEO who insisted that the training department be established in the first place and who announced that training henceforth was going to be an integral part of the way the business was run.

None of the staffless training managers to whom we spoke expressed any complaints about top-manage-

ment support. All said they had as much access as they needed to the CEO. That might seem curious, considering the training field's tearstained history in this area — the decades of wailing about top management's woeful lack of interest in employee development. But the fact is, many one-person departments are born at the express command of a CEO. Then too, most single-trainer operations are in small companies, where practically everyone is likely to have access to the top banana.

Not all one-person training departments start from scratch, however. Sometimes larger departments shrink into solo operations as the result of downsizings. Lisa Schuermann, training manager for Purina Mills, a St. Louis-based manufacturer of products for the agriculture industry (not related in any way to Ralston Purina, also in St. Louis), watched her department dwindle from five people to a solo act over the last nine years. She delivers product knowledge, sales and management training only for the field managers located at 56 branch offices. Purina Mills set up a training center at headquarters after the cutbacks, so she doesn't have to travel to all the different sites. She has forged an alliance with the research and development department — particularly with the vice president of R&D — that gives her access to many subject-matter experts who conduct some of the training for her.

Schuermann is unsentimental about the cuts to her staff and to the company's training offerings. "Things we'd always been doing because we'd always been doing them no longer got done," she shrugs. In fact, the shrinking of the company's training function provided a harsh lesson in employee perceptions. As various programs got the ax, she says, it was surprising how often nobody seemed to notice.

Since Schuermann has only the time and resources to concentrate on truly important training issues, she focuses on those that are important not to her, but to her constituents. "If I don't have customers [who want a course]," she says, "I don't have training."

Kim Vogt, personnel manager for Workbench, a New York furniture retailer, also was left doing a solo act after a cutback, though in her case the training department was cut only from two people down to one. She admits that the economy can't really support another person to help her. Her survival strategy is to make sure her offerings match the needs of supervisors and to build a trusting relationship with upper managers so they will support her efforts.

Peer Training: It's Not Just a Good Idea

People who run solo training operations are not shy about asking for help. That usually translates into finding managers or employees who have some interest in and aptitude for training, and helping them develop classroom skills. In some cases, these peer trainers are already in place on a more or less informal basis when a new training department opens for business. In other cases, they have to be recruited.

In the first situation, the task is to get the existing peer instructors into some train-the-trainer workshops. When Expeditors International's Smith started her one-person department, managers and supervisors had been delivering all the company's training for some time. They were delighted when she began to supply them with written materials and train-the-trainer workshops, she says.

At Office Club, Evans also had a clan of store managers — one from each store — who delivered training to the front lines. In hindsight, he wishes that top management had built in more incentives for these people. While training duties were written into their job descriptions and some extra money was kicked into their salaries, Evans believes a more formal incentive system would have overcome some of the resistance he got from managers who didn't really need the extra work. If, for instance, managers had received special recognition for the training they did or if conducting training became a privilege reserved for fast-trackers, it might have seemed less like a chore. Any idea would be worth a try, Evans says, to make training "seem like an opportunity and not just one more thing to put on a plate that's already full."

Suppose the training manager can't find recruits with any real aptitude for teaching? What do you do if you're a one-person shop and you know your peer trainers can be competent, but never great, when they get up in front of their next class? Lizardy has a suggestion: Become an expert at producing slides, overhead transparencies, videos and any other visu-

al medium you can master. If you can't give people a good trainer, he argues, you can at least give them good handouts, well-designed job aids, clear visuals and logically organized information. That way, when they leave the classroom — even if they've been cataleptically bored a good deal of the time — they'll have learned something. And good handouts can be studied later.

This raises another question. Regardless of who delivers the instruction, who should develop the actual course? The pros and cons of building

---

Always agree on a budget — in writing — before you take on a job as a one-person training shop.

---

one's own training vs. buying it from a supplier apply to the one-person department as much as to larger training shops. Off-the-shelf programs obviously can make life a whole lot easier for a solo trainer, but only if the budget is there to buy them. One complaint is that off-the-shelf courses are very expensive, and that only big corporations get price breaks. Balling asks the age-old question: "Why am I paying this much for something if I only like half of it?" Other lone wolves buy off-the-shelf courseware whenever they can. Sure enough, they say, it makes life a lot easier.

Where's My Budget?

Whether they work in large training departments or solo shops, trainers are often accused of financial naïveté. Lizardy claims it is not unusual for an individual with a background in training to agree to start up a one-person department without ever asking the people in charge what the budget is.

His advice: Always agree on a budget, in writing, before you take the job. And demand that the budget include money for your own personal development as a training manager. You'll hesitate to demand this, fearing that it implies to management that you don't know all there is to know about training. Nonsense. Your argument should be that only a skilled, up-to-date pro-

fessional will be able to deliver effective training and squeeze all the value out of the programs on which management spends its money.

Evans admits that failing to get the budget up front and out in the open was one of his biggest oversights when he started his training department. Since the company didn't budget enough, he was forced to get creative about finding and leveraging funds. When he dealt with suppliers, he negotiated price breaks by promising a long-term relationship with a growing company. In one case, a training supplier who showed some mercy in pricing got a three-year contract with Evans' company.

Another creative financing package Evans obtained came in the form of a grant from the state of California. The Employment Training Panel, part of California's unemployment insurance system, gives companies grants for employee education. Evans secured half a million dollars and expanded his training department from one person to four. After the grant, his department was able to conduct sales training, personal development seminars and some workshops on managing change for front-line employees.

Other financing tactics used by small training departments include memberships in video libraries and training consortiums. Balling bought a membership for Collagen in a private consortium called Western Learning Systems in Santa Clara, CA. Once a member company pays the initial charge, it can send employees to the consortium's courses for a nominal fee.

The idea of expanding the one-person training department got mixed reviews from the trainers with whom we spoke. There was nearly unanimous agreement that the freedom that comes from calling all the shots is the greatest advantage of running a one-person department. This view was especially strong among those who had moved from big corporations with large training staffs.

Marshall Foo, for example, used to train aircraft maintenance personnel in the Navy before he became the training vice president for Mediline Service Corp. of Springfield, MO, a company that provides computer services to the medical industry. He likes the atmosphere of a smaller company. "All the decisions come from me," he says. "It makes things easier because you're not always having to pass it through a filter of several people."

Workbench's Vogt adds that the pleasure of staying in touch with the whole organization and having "your finger on the pulse of everything" is something a trainer in a larger department is unlikely to experience.

On the other hand, most people who run one-person departments can think of plenty of things they'd do if only they had the staff. The most common concern involves an inability to follow up on training, to see if it "took." Given a few staff people, most lone wolves would put them to work on follow-up and evaluation projects to document the return on investment of various training programs.

Parting Words

We asked several of these people for a few words of wisdom they might like to pass along to other one-person training departments. The central theme of most responses boiled down to this: Stay focused on key business needs and on building the skills that will keep your company alive. Anything else is superfluous. How do you distinguish a driving business need from a management fad or a random bee that has gotten into some vice president's bonnet? Talk to people — all kinds of people, at all levels of the company, all the time.

A few sources had more specific words of advice for trainers who are home alone. We'll close with those:

"See everything, overlook a great deal and correct a little."
— *Carolyn Balling,*
quoting Pope John the XXIII

"It helps if you can type 120 words a minute."
— *Chris Smith*

"Know the price of your commitment."
— *Mike Williams*

Notes:

Yes...You Can Weigh Training's Value

Even soft, interpersonal-skills training can be evaluated in dollars-and-cents terms. But you have to begin at the beginning.

BY JAC FITZ-ENZ

The enduring belief that you can't quantify the benefits of a corporate training program has been punctured many times over the years. Yet the myth persists. We still hear incessantly that the effects of training interventions — especially "soft-skills" training — cannot be traced objectively and quantitatively to an organization's bottom line.

Once again, the myth has exploded. And this time, the evidence doesn't come merely in the form of a single evaluation project that documented the dollar value of a training program in a single organization.

In the fall of 1992, 26 companies joined forces to search for a universal method of training evaluation. After more than a year of model development, refinement and field testing, a standardized training valuation system (TVS) emerged. It is built around a relatively simple set of analytic tools and has been tested across a range of training interventions.

The system employs a four-step process, starting with an in-depth situation analysis (similar to a needs assessment) and concluding with the dollar value added to an operation by training or other causal factors. The methodology can be used to identify specific, current and potential values before training is conducted. It also measures value obtained after training. And if the training fails to produce the anticipated results, the method helps us determine why.

On the surface the process is deceptively simple. There is little in it that will sound new or surprising to anyone familiar with the literature of human-resources development or with the work of HRD Hall of Fame members Bob Mager, Thomas Gilbert or Joe Harless. But the most elegant solutions are the simplest. And the key to this approach is the relationship that develops between the trainer and the customer — usually a line manager — as a result of the situation analysis. The strengthening of that relationship is also a key benefit, one that may be as important as the evaluation itself.

Throughout the process the underlying question is: "What difference would that make?"

The idea for what came to be called the Training Evaluation Project (TEP) arose from conversations in the summer of 1992 with training professionals at Miles USA, MCI, and Du Pont Merck Pharmaceuticals. For the umpteenth time we discussed the barriers to objective and quantitative evaluation of work-related training. We agreed that in its most basic terms the age-old evaluation demon in training has been the perceived inability to connect training outcomes to changes in organizational quality, productivity, sales or service. The question has always been: When people gain a new skill or enhance an existing one through a training program, how do we trace that change to one or more of the organization's key performance indicators?

That fall, 23 other companies joined the discussion. The method subsequently developed and tested in this project followed the classic outline: Analyze the performance problem — the gap between the results we're getting and the results we want; if training appears likely to solve the problem, develop and deliver the training; find out whether behavior has changed, back on the job, as a result of the training; and finally, determine the value of that behavior change to the organization. What made this initiative successful where others have foundered is the relationship that was forged with the customers (line managers and top executives) and the way the problem-analysis questions were structured. Both factors were critical; one without the other would not have been sufficient.

Objections

The ancient bugaboo preventing the sort of evaluation we wanted to do is the issue of proof: With so many variables affecting a company's overall performance, how do you prove that some particular gain resulted entirely from a training program and nothing else? We began by agreeing that this so-called obstacle is largely a straw man (see box on p. 22).

The question is not, "How can we prove beyond the shadow of a doubt that a given training program produced a given result?" but rather, "What will we accept as persuasive evidence that the program produced the result?"

The answer is: We will accept the informed judgment of the line manager. Only the manager knows the vagaries of the work environment. If we assume that the manager is competent and honest, then that person's testimony must be acceptable.

The catch is that "informed judgment" requires the line manager to be intimately involved in the training initiative from the beginning. And the trainer needs to know how to help the manager dig out and specify the value that the training is intended to add to the manager's operation. Here we meet with three objections.

Objection A claims that most managers cannot be persuaded to take part in a needs assessment — what we call the "situation analysis" of the performance problem. This is really only an admission of the trainer's inability to strike a working partnership with the customer. None of the 26 companies in our project considered this a roadblock. Indeed, in many cases it was the customers who provided the evidence of success or failure of the trial programs these companies conducted and evaluated.

Objection B states that the manager naturally will want to justify his decision to invest in training. Therefore, the argument goes, he will be a willing co-conspirator in the trainer's attempt to prove that the course was worthwhile. Frankly, this is more often a specious excuse than a reasonable argument. But even if it were a fair criticism, it would be simple enough to bring in a third-party auditor to check the results.

Objection C asserts that even if the manager is willing and reliable, she will only be estimating the bottom-line value of the training program. The fact is that almost all line managers and professionals have a wealth of operating data sitting about un-used. When asked in the right way, they are able to find data related to the process and outcomes in question. The operative phrase is, "in the right way."

These objections do not do the training profession justice. Managers and executives make value judgments every day, with far less analysis, about everything from paying for performance (How much is Judy's performance worth compared to Joe's?) to whether a quarterly sales increase is "caused" by the new marketing plan or merely a seasonal fluke. One can only conclude that the objections are obfuscations put forth by people who don't have the energy, imagination or courage to evaluate their training.

Having agreed that these barriers are self-imposed, the participants in our group set out to experiment with the TVS model. Over the next eight months, only 11 companies committed themselves to a full and fair trial, but all 11 were successful. That is, they found the model did what they hoped it would: It gave them a way to measure and evaluate the quantitative value added — or not added — by their training interventions.

For Instance...

You can't really evaluate the success of "soft-skills" training? Don't tell that to Vicki Brown, Joan Shaughnessy and Priscilla Smith. Brown and Shaughnessy are training specialists and Smith is vice president of human resources at Prudential Insurance and Financial Co. in South Plainfield, NJ. They chose as their pilot project a course that taught "coaching skills" to middle managers.

They began with some in-depth questioning of higher-level Prudential managers — the bosses of the intended trainees. "What skills do you see as being essential in good coaches?" the trainers asked. The managers responded in general terms, talking about motivational skills, analytic skills, communication and listening. The trainers dutifully listed these things. But then they pressed on, addressing each skill individually, probing for the tangible value of applying the skill and the tangible

THE FALLACY OF THE BURDEN OF PROOF

BY JAC FITZ-ENZ

One of the self-imposed barriers to seeking the concrete value of training programs is the mistaken notion that the trainer must present proof, with a capital "P," that training had a specific effect on the organization's bottom line. So many factors affect the human and financial performance of a company, it is said, that isolating the pure contribution of a training program is impossible.

In laboratory terms, this is true. In real-world terms, it's utter nonsense. Demonstrating causality of that type is impossible for everyone in business, not just for trainers. Practically speaking, in business there are almost no opportunities to prove causal relationships between given activities and specific effects. Proving causality demands control of all variables. In the real world there is no such phenomenon as control.

But many line functions have established "unspoken agreements" in which they assume some correlation between certain actions and subsequent results. This has been going on for so long that people speak of these connections as if they were provable. The most obvious example is sales. If a salesperson meets the quota, the assumption is that the person is a competent seller of the product. There is no proof of that. Buyers buy for many reasons that have absolutely nothing to do with the salesperson. Salespeople do not control customers.

Likewise, manufacturing managers do not control suppliers of material and equipment or even their own employees. The chief financial officer does not control the cost of capital. Control is a concept, not a reality.

All of us struggle to influence our environment, but none of us control anything. Only in the laboratory can control be demonstrated, and then only within a very small field of investigation.

"Statistical proof" is a misconception. Statistics only try to show that the null hypothesis was probable, not that the stated hypothesis was proven.

So before trainers hang their heads in futility they should understand the fact that when we talk about business, the word proof has no place.

The objective of a valid and reliable evaluation effort that assigns a specific value to the outcome of a training program is simply this: To demonstrate that there is a probable correlation between the training event and a subsequent change in quality, productivity, sales or service. The methodology should imply the following:

"Given the conditions as stated, and assuming other things being equal, the observed effect quite probably is the result of the training."

Before you jump all over that as a disclaimer, please note that the principle of ceteris paribus (other things being equal) is the foundation for all attempts at proof. And it is precisely the assumption that underlies all business planning and subsequent evaluation. As business managers we prepare budgets for the coming year making exactly the same assumption. After the budget year has passed we will know what the results are, but we often won't know and seldom can "prove" what caused us to be over or under our projections.

The old argument has it that trainers shouldn't try to determine the dollar value of their programs to a company because they can't prove that training — and nothing but training — produced a particular business result. That argument is a hollow sham.

consequences of failing to apply it. For instance, managers agreed that "poor listening" might result in rework or missed assignments. The trainers pressed further, asking for specific examples of rework and missed assignments: How often do these things happen? What's the cost when they do happen? From there, hourly pay rates could be used to arrive at a plausible estimate of the dollar value of "good coaching."

Then, by tracking rework, missed assignments and so on after the training course, managers themselves could collect the data that would confirm or contradict the initial estimates of the coaching program's value.

This approach relied on planned, specific questions and a structured questioning technique (more about that in a moment). The questions focused initially on the work process, not on training. As the conversation evolved from the general to the detailed, tight connections were established between processes and outcomes. This eventually led to descriptions of expected value. When the program was actually conducted and results obtained, the customer-managers would see for themselves the effects of training.

The critical difference between this and typical questioning methods occurs at two levels. First is the connection drawn between specific acts and specific outcomes. All too often when trainers question managers in the course of a needs assessment, they settle for vague, undemonstrable connections between certain behaviors and certain business results. When this happens, any hope of assigning a concrete value to a performance problem — or to the training course that solves it — is lost.

Second is the projection and later verification of the tangible, dollar value that comes from those specific results. Throughout the process the underlying question is: "What difference would that make?" If a supervisor were a better listener — so what? If production workers were better team players — so what? The manager's answers are continuously probed until some visible, tangible outcome is revealed — an outcome having to do with quality, productivity, sales or service. Once this outcome is uncovered, it is usually easy to put a dollar value on its effects.

It is as important to identify the reason for failures as it is to evaluate successes, and a reliable evaluation methodology ought to do both. This was, in fact, the case with Prudential's effort. The initial study concluded that if trainees acquired the coaching skills taught in the workshop and demonstrated these skills on the job, the value added would be three times the worth of the investment. Post-training assessments determined that the workshop wasn't meeting expectations. Only 55 percent of the members of the pilot group were found to

---

All too often trainers' questions during needs assessments are hopelessly vague.

---

be using the new skills successfully on the job, while 45 percent were not. Working with the unit manager, the trainers reviewed the data (which was clear, specific and plentiful, thanks to the preparatory work) and were able to identify the problem. They are now moving to correct it.

If behaviors taught in a course aren't transferring to the job, that's good to know. The key point there, however, is not that the coaching course failed to hit its target. It's that this soft-skills program had a target, one expressed in monetary terms: It would repay the company's investment three times over in traceable dollars.

A process that can assign a value to training can also be used to discover the cost of not training. As part of a downsizing and cost-cutting program, Alberta General Telephone Ltd. (AGT) of Edmonton, Alberta, Canada, decided to save training expenses by shortening the entry-level training program for customer service reps from two weeks to one week. Rudy Nieuwendyk, manager of HR education and development, decided to track the effect of that decision.

By using performance measures already in place, and tracking the variables other than training that have an impact on performance, he found that reps who completed two weeks of training were able to complete a call in an average of 11.4 minutes, whereas those completing only one week of

training took 14.5 minutes.

The bottom line of this analysis was that the extra time required to complete calls cost the company more than $50,000 in lost productivity in the first six weeks. In addition, the cost of lost quality due to increased errors, increased collectibles, and service-order error rates exceeded the amount lost due to decreased productivity. So the cost to AGT of cutting back on training amounted to more than $100,000. Management decided to restore the two-week training program. The company is thinking about expanding it even more.

Nieuwendyk's next goal is to apply the TVs approach to the company's quality-training efforts. "We delivered a lot of quality training over a four-year period," he says. "It would have been heresy to question the value of quality training. [But] after the training was done, we came to understand that we hadn't clearly identified what it was that the training was to affect. We had no reliable method to determine who needed training in what to affect what behavior to obtain what measurable result. What we are beginning to do now is to determine the what, who, why and how before we invest the training dollars."

The Model

The TVS approach breaks down into four basic steps.

Step 1: Situation.

The "situation" is the business problem or opportunity with which we're concerned; that is, it's the pre-training status of somebody's (or some group's) performance. We analyze the situation by asking managers a series of questions that uncover and clarify the source of value within the function and the key processes for obtaining that value. In other words, what do these people do that is important to the organization, and how do they do it? Once we know that, we can settle upon definitions of acceptable and current levels of performance. Finally, we establish the value of the gain we would achieve if the current level of performance were brought up to an acceptable level.

The situation analysis shows what the issue looks like strategically, how it works tactically, how it affects the organization, and what it costs. This is the most important step in the process. It requires considerable detail and precision. It begins and ends with a focus on value. When done properly, the potential measurable value of training (or some other intervention) becomes clear.

Step 2: Intervention.

This step has two components: problem diagnosis and training description. In diagnosing the problem, we study the performance shortfall to find its source and a likely solution. The solution may or may not be training. A checklist, based on the seminal work of Bob Mager on analyzing performance problems, points to the true source of the problem.

Following Mager's lead, we ask a series of branching questions: Is there a performance discrepancy? If yes, is it important? If so, could the person do the job if her life depended on it? If not, is it because she lacks certain skills? If so, can training help? If it isn't a skill issue, what is it? And so on.

Based on the outcome of this diagnosis, we decide whether to attack the problem with training or to seek a different solution. If we decide to train, we naturally want to develop a course that builds the specific skills people will need in order to close the gap between the current level of performance and the acceptable level.

Step 3: Impact.

Suppose we've decided that training is the remedy. We have designed and delivered the training. Now the question becomes, what difference do we observe in the trainees' behavior and performance after they have completed the course? An impact statement describes:

- The variables that might have caused the difference in performance.
- The relative effect of each of the variables.
- How employee behavior, as a result of the training, changed and

affected performance (as in the AGT example).

- Why training did or did not affect performance (as in the Prudential case).

Step 4: Value.

Value is the monetary worth of the effects of changed performance. It is a measure of differences in quality, productivity, service or sales, all of which can be expressed in terms of dollars.

This approach can help forge a stronger partnership between trainer and client.

Sometimes the dollar value is immediately evident, as with increases in market share or margin on sales. Other desirable outcomes, such as a reduction in time to market or an increase in customer satisfaction, can be converted to dollars.

One company in our group, a pharmacy chain, developed a 240-hour, state-approved course to certify pharmacy technicians to expand their role to include counting and pouring prescriptions. A change in state regulations, which previously had reserved these tasks for registered pharmacists, made this expanded role for technicians possible. Since technicians are paid less than pharmacists, the company saves money every time a prescription is processed by a technician. With some uncomplicated math, the company determined that the value added by the certification program — its payback after expenses — amounts to $318,422 per year.

Typically, the "impact" and "val-

ue" steps are the missing links in attempts to determine the concrete worth of training programs. This is where the disclaimers crop up and everyone starts backpedaling from definitive statements of value added. But when the link is strongly forged right at the start, in the situation phase, the impact and value become relatively easy to determine. Sometimes they're quite obvious.

Partners

Training veterans may say they don't see anything new in this process. All it does, after all, is identify a business problem, suggest a solution, and estimate the value of the result. But I would argue that two factors make this approach noteworthy.

The first is methodological. Right from the beginning, in the situation phase, the trainer employs a focused analytic method with a set of directed questions. These help managers dig answers out of their operating results — answers to questions about what good performance looks like and why skills matter.

Second, the approach forges a strong partnership between the trainer/performance analyst and the client/manager. And since a very tight focus on value is maintained throughout the process, the partnership is based on the manager's core concern: performance. Tangible values are identified for each skill to be taught. There is no vagueness or backing off from visible, quantitative evidence. The result can be a powerful bonding of trainer and customer — a bond that exists all too rarely in organizations today.

It is clear, at least to everyone involved in this project, that the door is open to objective training evaluation. All we have to do is walk through it.

Notes:

Simplifying ROI

Elaborate studies of return on training investments
are terrific if you've got the time and money.
Here's an alternative if you don't.

BY JAMES HASSETT

Everyone can always use more training. Every single person in your organization could probably benefit from learning new job skills. On the other hand, everyone could also use a week off, another $10,000 in the bank and fresh mints on their pillows each night.

On any given day, managers would rather see their employees working on the job rather than in a classroom or training center learning how to become more efficient. The costs of training are always easier to see than the costs of not training. Therefore, the question of whether employees need more training inevitably comes down to time and money. Will the time and money you invest today in training be repaid — with interest — in the next week, month, year or decade?

How do you measure a particular training program's contribution to the bottom line? Several state-of-the-art cost studies prescribe exacting methods for tracking return on training investments. These methods are certainly worth considering. However, a more modest four-step procedure called training investment analysis can be an attractive alternative. This procedure can help you obtain a simple, straightforward estimate of the impact of any training program on your organization's bottom line.

ROI Research

There's a long, rich history of research on the effects of training — both economic and noneconomic. From anthologies such as Lakewood Publications' *Evaluating Training's Impact* to Donald Kirkpatrick's classic

1975 article "Evaluating Training Programs" in *Training & Development* magazine, innumerable researchers and practitioners have offered models and words of wisdom on evaluating training.

Kirkpatrick delineated four levels of training evaluation: *reaction* ("How did you like the training?"), *learning*

**If you look at everything
that happens after
a training program
as the result of
the training program,
you are falling
into a classic fallacy.**

("What do you know now that you didn't know before?"), *behavior* ("What do you do differently?"), and *results* ("How did the training affect your organization?"). Each succeeding level of evaluation is a bit more difficult to perform and less frequently done than the one before it.

Measuring results does not necessarily mean measuring a monetary return. For example, our company has worked on a series of training programs regarding new computer systems used by flight standards inspectors in the Federal Aviation Administration. The primary mission of the FAA is to increase aviation safety. In this context, a results study would focus on using the computer systems or on the effectiveness of inspection programs for aircraft and personnel, not on profit and loss.

Even profit-making institutions have training programs that are not designed to increase profits. In the banking industry, for example, employees are trained to comply with government regulations.

However, in any organization that seeks to make a profit, one of the most compelling demonstrations of a training program's effectiveness will be its effect on the bottom line, or what is often called return on investment (ROI).

In 1990, *Training and Development* published "Return on Investment: Accounting for Training," a special report by Anthony P. Carnevale and Eric R. Schulz that summarized the American Society for Training and Development's research on this issue. In that survey, two out of three training managers reported they felt increasing pressure to show that programs affect the bottom line. However, only 20 percent of these same organizations did ROI studies, in part because they felt this type of evaluation "takes too much time or is too costly."

Another review (published in *TRAINING*, August 1991) cited a Federal Express analysis as a good example of the state of the art in measuring ROI. The study focused on 20 employees who went through the company's two-week training program soon after being hired to drive FedEx vans. Their performance was compared with a control group of 20 other new hires whose managers were told to do no more (nor less) on-the-job training than normal.

Performance was tracked for the two groups for 90 days in categories such as accidents, injuries, time-card errors and domestic air-bill errors. The 10 performance categories had dollar values assigned by experts from engineering, finance and other groups. The cost of each accident, for example, was placed at $1,600.

The basic math for computing the ROI was straightforward. The annual cost of errors for untrained couriers was estimated at $4,833, vs. $2,492 for trained couriers. That works out to a training-produced difference of $2,341 per person per year. This is $451 more than the cost of the $1,890 training course (a price tag that includes instructors' and trainees' salaries, as well as the costs of hotel, meals, airfare and covering couriers' duties during training). When this savings of $451 for one courier is multiplied by the 1,097 new employees who went through the program in a recent year, the ROI for that year was $494,747. This represents a very healthy 23.9 percent return on investment. The study itself cost about $10,000 and took five months.

This kind of rigorous evaluation doesn't make sense for every training program, however. Would you spend $10,000 to evaluate a $5,000 program? Even if you can afford the cost, can you afford the time? The ASTD report cites the case of a $40,000 study conducted by New England Telephone to measure the effectiveness of a technician training program. Trouble was, by the time the report was completed, "everyone familiar with the evaluation had left the department that financed it." The need for a more modest approach, at least in some cases, is obvious.

Meanwhile, Back in the Real World

Many people seem to believe that corporate bottom lines provide an objective measure that can be used as the basis for a harsh brand of frontier justice: A manager makes a decision, it increases profits or it doesn't, and the manager gets a raise or is fired as a result. In the real world, managers and accountants know that nothing is ever that cut-and-dried.

Anyone who has ever written and enacted a business plan knows that financial predictions often fail to match reality. It would be nice to have a simple, inexpensive and unambiguous system for deciding what actually caused a business venture to succeed or fail. But in practice, this is somewhere between prohibitively expensive and impossible. This leads directly to a key fact underlying the rationale for training investment analysis:

Fact 1: *Many interrelated factors affect profit and loss; training is just one.*

This seems painfully obvious. Training, by itself, almost never determines the bottom line. But it is easy to lose sight of this fact when you are doing a study that focuses on training's ROI.

Intuitively we know that, under some conditions, training does increase efficiency and profits. If you want people to sell a complex product, they must know what it is. If clerks are to enter orders on a form, they must be trained to fill out forms accurately. For those who distrust such intuitions, the Federal Express

study is just one in a long series of studies that supports this conclusion.

However, it also follows that, under other conditions, even the best training will not increase profits.

Suppose an eccentric entrepreneur believes that 8-inch floppy disks are going to make a comeback due to a ground swell of support for used computers. He believes that training his sales force is crucial, and he hires the best trainers in the business. But his prediction is wrong: Nobody buys the used computers or the disks.

Does that mean that the training was at fault? Of course not.

Or suppose that a full-service brokerage firm is concerned about losing clients to discount brokers. It decides

---

Whenever possible, judgment calls that quantify the effects of training should be made by decision makers or management.

---

that training its employees in customer support will reverse this trend. The firm invests in a customer service training program for all of its brokers and support personnel.

Unfortunately, the company also decides to continue charging an 8 percent front-end load to cover sales commissions and 4 percent per year for marketing expenses. The week that the training is completed, the cover of Money magazine gives the firm an award for the all-time-worst buy in mutual funds. Again, in profit-and-loss terms, the training likely will have no impact. But the reasons customers go to the competition have nothing to do with the training.

External factors (such as the state of the economy and the world) are difficult to analyze and nearly impossible to control. If you look at everything that happens after a training program as the result of the training, you are falling into a classic fallacy. Logicians even have a special name for this error in thinking: "post hoc ergo propter hoc," which means "after this, therefore because of this," which is not logically correct.

Thus, a definitive analysis of a training program's ROI is impossible

until enough time — months or years — passes and the impact becomes clear. Even then, the results are never entirely unambiguous because it is so difficult to unravel the effects of training from other variables.

All of this leads, indirectly, to a second fact underlying training investment analysis:

Fact 2: *The most important analysis of training's return on investment occurs before a training program is offered — not after it is over.*

A year after the training, your company will move on to new challenges. If the training worked, it may be no longer relevant. And if the training failed, it may no longer matter.

According to an old Chinese proverb: To prophesize is very difficult — especially with respect to the future. Yet that is precisely what we do with each new business decision and each new training program. It follows that training investment analyses that are performed after the fact are mostly for the record book. They have a place in long-term corporate policy, but the most important training to evaluate is not last year's, it is next year's. That's the program you will go ahead with or cancel. And that's the program that will affect the bottom lines you care about most: this year's and next year's.

ROI Focus

Before you begin a training investment analysis, ask: Will (or did) this training program give employees knowledge or skills needed to meet organizational objectives that are not directly measured by short-term profit and loss? If the answer is "Yes," then a single-minded focus on the bottom line is misplaced. Instead, you should consider analyzing noneconomic results of the program, such as improved compliance with regulations or safety procedures.

If the training is aimed at increasing profits, assess how profit is measured in your organization and whether it is necessary to show how profit is linked to training. Seek out the views of key decision makers, and talk to them first about their expectations and needs.

For example, in a December 1991 article about Federal Express in *Training & Development*, founder and chairman Frederick W. Smith says: "You could never cost justify the cost of our FXTV network or our interactive video training system. But if you ask me, those would be among the top 10 highest payoff projects we've ever done at Federal Express. Maybe even in the top three."

As the article explains, Smith believes it's important for the company's leadership to support things like quality and learning "that cut across the organization and don't have a clear ROI." This strong corporate belief would make a study of training investment analysis at best redundant, and at worst subversive.

The KISS Rule

It is hard to go wrong following the KISS rule — Keep It Simple, Stupid.

Training investment analysis explicitly recognizes that in many situations, the best available information is an informed estimate. That being the case, the accompanying work sheet is designed to simplify the process so that these informed estimates can be reached as efficiently as possible and then put into action.

Note that training investment analysis represents a small retreat from more formal evaluations with control groups, before and after tests, and complex methodology. But also note that an easier analysis procedure makes it more practical for you to focus on the bottom line when it mat-

ters most: as you plan your training.

Here are the four steps to a training investment analysis:

1 Determine the information your organization needs. A training investment analysis should always use the same financial procedures and terminology that other departments in your company use when they evaluate a potential investment in equipment or software. If another department has produced a report, get a copy. You may find that others avoid the term return on investment, and use an alternative accounting concept such as the payback approach or the

---

E-MAIL EVALUATION: 2 INEXPENSIVE TECHNIQUES YIELD MULTIPLE BENEFITS

BY DAVE ZIELINSKI

More training managers are reporting multiple benefits from delivering course evaluation forms via electronic means. Not only do their response rates typically rise, but the act of receiving, completing, and then returning the survey via e-mail attachments gives students additional computer skills practice.

Dave Ferguson, senior project manager of training and performance support at GE Information Services in Rockville, MD, is among those expanding his use of e-mail to deliver evaluations. His group recently created and sent an Excel evaluation worksheet, formatted to look like a paper-based evaluation form, to employees who had completed a five-day training course. The forms were sent four to five weeks after graduation.

The course involved training employees of a GE client company how to use computer hardware and a variety of software tools. Particular focus was given to a new sales automation software package.

At the class conclusion, a level one "smile sheet" evaluation was done, but Ferguson wanted more detailed data on training transfer. Because using spreadsheets was part of the course, he created an evaluation in spreadsheet format that was sent to trainees as an attachment to an e-mail message. "Since participants had all learned to use e-mail — including using attached files — we thought this was also a good test of their new skills," he says.

The survey asked trainees to rate their skill levels in 50 specific skill areas taught in class, using a scale of one to four (from "can't do at all" to "can do easily"). Skills rated included things like creating memos within the e-mail package, entering formulas or text in spreadsheets, building a list of planned customer visits in Excel, and transmitting sales data electronically to headquarters. "We also added 10 questions about the frequency of use, or how often trainees said they were having to use these skills," Ferguson says. "We wanted data on how important some skills were to performing well day to day."

Survey Received 50% Response

Some 1,150 of 2,200 students who were sent surveys responded — a 50% plus response rate that thrilled the training function. Perhaps most impressive was that given three different ways of returning surveys — print out and mail, print out and fax, or return via attached e-mail file — over 80% of these previously computer-averse students chose the latter method. "We believed this was the most difficult of the three vehicles, so the respondents surprised us with this testimony to the skill they acquired," Ferguson says.

Returned forms are tallied in a large Excel database that allows Ferguson to run detailed breakdowns of data based on a number of indicators and create graphs and charts that trainees' managers have found valuable.

Sprint Asks Managers to Rate Training Services Via E-mail

At Sprint's University of Excellence, the telecommunication company's training, assessment, and OD arm, Karen Mailliard, director, decided to change her approach to evaluation.

Instead of sending director-level clients a lengthy paper-based survey to rate the UE's services at year-end 1995, she decided to send them just one question via e-mail. She asked them, "How would you rate the contribution UE made to your unit's success in 1995 on a scale of one to seven?"

"Before 1995 we had sent these directors a 20-question year-end survey that asked them to rate all of our many services," she says. "This really simplifies it."

The one-question survey supplements other evaluation done throughout the year at lower levels in the company by the UE, including quarterly report cards from internal customers.

Respondents sent many unsolicited comments along with their numerical feedback, Mailliard says. "Some of it was 'we still need help in this area,' so we got more work out of the surveys. Everyone who responded received a follow up phone call from us."

TABLE 1
TRAINING INVESTMENT ANALYSIS WORK SHEET

Objective: _____

_____

Audience: _____

Returns measured over: _____ One year _____ Other _____

PART 1: CALCULATING THE REVENUE PRODUCED BY TRAINING

OPTION A — ITEMIZED ANALYSIS

Increased sales:
- _____ Additional sales per employee
- x _____ Revenues (or margin) per sale
- x _____ Number of employees
- = _____ Revenue Produced by Training

Higher productivity:
- _____ Percent increase in productivity
- x _____ Cost per employee (salary plus benefits plus overhead)
- x _____ Number of employees
- = _____ Revenue Produced by Training

Reduced errors:
- _____ Average cost per error
- x _____ Number of errors avoided per employee
- x _____ Number of employees
- = _____ Revenue Produced by Training

Client retention:
- _____ Average revenue per client
- x _____ Number of clients retained
- = _____ Revenue Produced by Training

Employee retention:
- _____ Average cost of a new employee (training plus lost productivity)
- x _____ Number of employees retained
- = _____ Revenue Produced by Training

Other: _____ _____

TOTAL Revenue Produced by Training: $ _____

OPTION B — SUMMARY ANALYSIS

_____ − _____ = _____

| Revenue After Training | Revenue Without Training | Revenue Produced by Training |

PART 2: CALCULATING THE RETURN

_____ − _____ = _____

| Revenue Produced by Training | Cost of Training | Total Return on Training Investment |

© 1992 Brattle Systems, Inc.

---

net present value approach or the rate of return approach. If so, you should do the same. Learn to speak the same language as your financial people, and calculate costs the same way they do.

If your organization requires a sophisticated analysis, you may be able to apply models developed in previous studies of training ROI, such as:

• Ives and Forman's multilevel ROI model, including cash in-flow benefits and depreciated costs (*CBT Directions*, June 1991).

• Spencer's step-by-step model for calculating the costs and benefits of an HRD program (*TRAINING*, July 1984).

• Godkewitch's examples of financial utility equations (*TRAINING*, May 1987).

• Schneider, Monetta and Wright's innovative use of a management inventory to measure the ROI of a supervisory course (*Performance and Instruction*, March 1992).

However, if your organization does not demand this level of analysis, these methods may be overkill. This leads to the second step in training investment analysis.

2 Use the simplest and least-expensive method possible for finding the information you need.

In many settings, the Training Investment Analysis Work Sheet will provide all the structure that you need to calculate the returns from your training program. You can use it to predict the effects of a new training program or to study the effects of an old one. It also can be used to generate the best guess or a range of possible effects — from the lowest return to the highest possible return.

At the top of the work sheet, record the overall objective of the training program, its audience and the time period in which you expect the training to produce significant economic results. For most organizations, one year is a good place to start.

If your company is known for its fiscal patience and its emphasis on long-term results, you may want to look at effects over two or three years, since longer periods will generally show greater effects. At the other extreme, if your company's stockholders prefer instant gratification, and anything beyond the next quarter or two is considered the distant future, you may be forced to analyze the return over three to six months, even if this underestimates the total value of the training.

Part 1 of the work sheet calculates the revenue produced by training. Two options are provided. Option A, itemized analysis, provides a list of ways in which training may increase revenue: increased sales, higher productivity, reduced errors (for example, in manufacturing or billing), client retention, employee retention, and other. For example, let's say a sales training program for computer networks results in five additional sales per person per year. If each sale produces a marginal profit of $10,000, and there are 20 salespeople in the department, the total revenue produced by training is five times $10,000 times 20 or $1 million.

Some of the figures requested here are unambiguous, such as the number of employees and revenues per sale. However, in each category, at least one of the figures requires an informed estimate of training's effects, such as the additional sales per employee, the percent increase in productivity or the number of errors per employee avoided as a result of training.

This leads to one of the most important elements of training investment analysis: Whenever possible, judgment calls that quantify the effects of training should be made by decision makers or management. Admittedly, these figures will be informed estimates rather than unassailable truths. However, if decision-makers are responsible for making the estimates, they will be far more likely to accept your final conclusions. Their participation in your estimating process is likely to increase their support of training investment analysis. At the least, this process will make it clear that the training department is sensitive to bottom-line issues and is doing as much as possible to tailor its training programs to increase profits.

After all of these judgments have been made and the calculations have been performed, the total revenue produced by training is the sum of the estimates from all categories.

In complex situations in which it's difficult to assign the effects of training to distinct categories, the only practical way to calculate training's effects will be to use Option B, the summary analysis. Very simply, this calculates the difference in revenues with and without training. Suppose, for example, the current sales forecast for next year is $4 million in profit. But key decision makers believe that with the added boost of a sales training program, this figure can be increased to $5 million. The revenue produced by training is then $5 million minus $4 million, or $1 million.

Once Part 1 is completed, Part 2 calculates the return by subtracting the cost of training from the revenue it produced. In the case of our mythical sales department, if it spent $200,000 on a custom-designed training program, the return would be $1 million minus $200,000, or $800,000.

3 Perform the analysis as quickly as possible. There is always a trade-off between the rigor of a study and the time it takes to perform. Clearly, training investment analysis sacrifices rigor for simplicity and immediacy.

There are many times when a rigorous study of ROI is justified and possible. But remember the New England Telephone study, which was out-of-date by the time it was completed. The training investment analysis approach is designed for situations in which time and money are severely limited. The work sheet focuses attention on the elements of a training program most likely to have an impact on the bottom line and then makes an educated guess. This can improve the accountability of the training department in a way that is visible throughout your organization.

4 Publish and circulate the results. Ideally, summary of the results should be a desktop publication with the quality one would expect of any important corporate document. It should reinforce the idea that training is an investment and could include information on training expenses in other companies.

If you find that a particular training program will cost more than it will produce, publish and circulate the results just as quickly as you would with a positive study. It will increase your credibility as someone who is willing to face harsh bottom-line realities and adjust to them.

With any luck, your study will provide irrefutable evidence of what trainers have known all along: Many training programs pay for themselves by increasing profits and/or reducing costs.

Notes:

To Meet Just-In-Time Training Demands, Trainers Turn to 'Short Bite' Courses

How to trim the fat without losing the meat.

BY SARAH FISTER

Multiple-day training courses are becoming less common as shrinking workforces and dwindling budgets call for shorter, more efficient training options. Everyone, it seems, is starved for time, and in an effort to accommodate employees' busier schedules trainers are finding they need to deliver information-packed courses in half the time they used to.

While few trainers are happy with the situation, many have come up with creative ways to trim away the fat without losing the meat of a course. Typically, this means reducing a course to only the information employees need to meet immediate performance goals.

But what's the cost of this trend? Les Courtney, training coordinator at Chevron Research, fears short-bite training courses aren't adequately preparing Chevron's employees for the future.

"Just-in-time now drives everybody's motivation for attending our classes," he says. "But I'm afraid we'll get five years down the road and realize we haven't addressed any of our long-range development needs."

On the up side, says Courtney, the limited amount of time employees now have available for training has made them — and trainers — more accountable for their training choices. Employees can no longer sign up for every course offered as an opportunity to get out of work for a few days, because taking time off for extended classes means facing piles of work upon their return. Employees must have a good business reason for taking time out to train, says Courtney.

At the same time, trainers can no longer get away with tossing out four-day seminars on the history of change in the workplace. Employees have only enough time get the information they need, when they need it. Practice must be done on their own and when time permits, says Courtney.

Cutting to the Core

Courtney first encountered a demand for shorter courses in 1992 when Chevron went through a major restructuring. The size of work teams was dramatically reduced, but workloads stayed the same. The full-time training staff was also slashed from six people to two.

"We were given a mandated time frame of one day for courses and we had to make a case each time we added four more hours to the training," he says. Considering many of Courtney's courses lasted three or four days, this dilemma called for more than just cutting the fluff. He had to substantially trim back course content without diminishing the quality of the product.

• Courtney started by setting a target duration for each class and working back from that. Then he took a hard look at the overall content to decide if all of it was necessary. "If you can cut nonessential parts of the content there is a greater opportunity to reduce the course," he says.

• Next, he dissected each course, isolating its core tools and concepts in lists. Using that information, Courtney built in short practice and experiential exercises, but cut away most of the interactive exercises, practice time, and case studies. "The only way to reduce course time, but keep the high-level content, was to give trainees

responsibility for reading material and practicing on their own time," he says.

• The easiest courses to cut were the computer classes and softer, "psychology of achievement" courses, says Courtney. He had more trouble cutting soft skill courses with high levels of technical content, like writing classes. "Trainees need more time to practice to fully understand the meaning and concepts behind the information," he says.

• He also developed a new program of "learning bites" where a professor or subject-matter expert gives a one- or two-hour presentation — sometimes delivered over lunch — on a specific subject like financial planning. Courtney is always looking for speakers who can offer employees short-bite seminars that will directly apply to their job performance.

There are, of course, some courses that could not be shortened — like heavy technical courses and safety courses — but Courtney didn't have any trouble getting management to understand that. "Some of these courses have very heavy technical content and are very expensive. But they're of high value to the organization and we fill the classes constantly."

Courtney doesn't necessarily like the short-bite trend. "It's a compromise but it seems to be working," he says. Employees however are pleased with the new shorter courses and Courtney encourages their input on design. For example, when he pilots a new course, he offers it in a one-day time slot and asks early participants if it should be shorter or longer.

The Value of Chunking

Judy Martins, vice president of training at Chicago-based Equis Co., uses the theory of "chunking" to design courses that fit shorter training slots. She designs courses so they can be broken into small chunks of information that cover one skill or part of a skill. That way she can offer it as a longer course that includes a series of chunks built on top of each other, or as one- or two-hour mini courses on individual chunks.

"That way you don't have to eliminate as much information — you just break it up into smaller pieces," she says.

It's easier to do this with some courses than others, she says, especially those that involve a series of unrelated skills like time manage-

OUTSOURCING SHORT-BITE TRAINING WORKS FOR BAYER CORP.

Jay Duffy, training manager at Philadelphia-based Bayer Corp.. turned all of his short-bite training over to Business Link Training (BLT), a private consulting firm that is customizing a program to fit Duffy's changing training goals. BLT works with companies to shrink or redesign courses into shorter modules. It's worked with Westinghouse-Armco Corp., Joy Technologies, and the North Allegheny School Systems in Pittsburgh.

Duffy and BLT's president, Peter Steiner, worked together to reorganize Duffy's training program and created the BLT (Steiner's name for the shortened courses). The courses are two-hour modules focused on Bayer's 20 key corporate competencies, says Duffy, including topics like performance management, succession planning, and visions and values.

Duffy outlines material for either a new course or a course he wants to shrink, and Steiner does research and develops the material. Steiner also employs a staff of freelance trainers to teach the courses in classrooms at Bayer headquarters.

When Duffy decides to shrink a course, he and Steiner analyze the material and break it into a series of skills. They decide which of the skills would have the most impact on students and build a module around it. For example, they shrunk a two-day "Giving Good Feedback" course into two hours by focusing on being specific, because "if you can be specific with feedback the rest is relatively easy," says Steiner.

Unlike other short-bite courses that rely on lecture and encourage participants to practice on their own time, Steiner's BLT's are dominated by interaction and role playing, says Duffy.

Participants are assigned prework assignments before the course, so they can immediately focus on the topic when they come into the classroom. There are no introductions or long explanations. Students are given one generic example, then they immediately start applying it to specific practice situations. For prework in the feedback course, students summarize an episode in which they gave feedback. In class, they briefly share their work, then immediately begin working on written exercises, identifying specific and general feedback, writing their own feedback and comparing notes with other students.

"My philosophy is for trainees to do the cognitive learning on their own. The classroom is for practice," says Duffy. If participants come unprepared to a course they are asked to leave.

Employees have embraced the new format. The courses are offered every other Friday twice in the morning and once in the afternoon, and each course is offered throughout the year so employees have a greater opportunity to attend.

"Before, people were waiting eight months to attend courses," says Duffy. "The BLT's shortened that considerably. Now we can create a course in five weeks."

The shortened courses allow Duffy to deliver all of the training on site, eliminating the costs of renting hotel lecture halls and travel. The cost of outsourcing is less than if it was designed in house, says Duffy. Steiner's courses cost from $4,000 to $8,000 depending on the subject. This includes everything from the initial research and prework to the final course materials and training manuals.

In another effort to save employees time, Steiner and Duffy developed *The Flash*, a USA Today-styled newsletter that contains BLT information in self-learning formats, says Duffy.

Employees read the newsletter and pick out courses they need. They can use the information for their own knowledge or use it to be certified in the course.

For certification, a BLT trainer calls the employee within a few weeks of getting the material and asks the employee a series of questions about *The Flash* course. If they answer the questions correctly and then have a manager verify the information has been used on the job, they are certified in the course.

The Flash, along with videos and audiocassettes of BLTs, are available in the lobbies of many buildings at Bayer Corp. so employees take them home or use them during free time at work.

Duffy still offers traditional longer courses because it's what people are used to, but says he is trying to "evolve away" from them. Steiner has redesigned over half of the training curriculum at Bayer.

— S.F.

---

ment classes. Sales and computer classes, for example, are difficult to offer in chunks because they require a series of prerequisite skills linked together to reach a goal.

The most important thing is to closely analyze the objective and desired outcomes of courses, Martins says. Find out what skills or information trainees absolutely need to take away from a course, and force yourself to stay focused on those.

Guy Vollendorf, training director for Network USA, Pensacola, FL, has also broken many of his courses into smaller learning segments. He finds this works especially well with computer training. The beginner course gives employees just enough information to perform the basics of their jobs, he says. A month later he offers the next level of information.

Vollendorf prefers to do this training in-house to maintain flexibility in his scheduling. "Outsourcing training of this type means losing people for the whole day," he says, "and they end up getting more information than they can retain — which means they won't use it. Bits and pieces are a lot more effective."

Getting Line Managers Involved

Vollendorf found that cutting course times alone will not guarantee better attendance. Just as essential is being flexible in his scheduling to work around employees' and managers' time constraints.

"I study the major departments to find out when their most intense hours are and I don't schedule anything during those times." He also offers the same class at numerous times during the week so everyone who needs to can attend. Sometimes a class may have a very poor showing and others are packed, he says, but it makes it easier for managers to keep the day-to-day business going.

The most crucial part of designing courses and course schedules is working directly with managers, he says. When he involves managers in planning courses, he finds they are more willing to let their people take time off to attend training seminars.

"Anytime you are getting ready to do training you need to approach the managers and get them more involved. I think trainers forget to do that. It took me awhile to realize I can't do anything unless I get the managers' support. Get them involved with the scheduling and let them decide who goes when. In return, they make the commitment that those people will show up."

Because of a limited training staff, Vollendorf had to recruit subject-matter experts to deliver some of the newly created short-bite training courses. New SMEs go through a three-month train-the-trainer course that meets twice a week to cover facilitation skills, presentation, and speaking. When they complete the course, they become company-certified trainers, says Vollendorf.

"It's a way for them to give their expertise back to the company so everyone benefits from it," he says, and it allows him to offer courses far more often at small expense to the organization.

Enabling Just-In-Time Training

The tide toward short-bite courses is enabling a lot more just-in-time training, says Martins of Equis Co. When a manager comes to her and says, "We need this skill now," she can easily pull a chunk of information from a larger course and schedule a mini-course for the next day.

"They may not be getting the depth I would like, but at least they can get some information as they need it."

The downside of just-in-time training like this, she says, is it's hard to evaluate how well employees develop skills because there is little or no in-class practice or follow-up.

Martins has offered classes in as small as 15-minute chunks delivered during a management meeting, but she prefers not to work in that small a time frame. She always includes handouts or job aids with more detail, and resources for finding more information.

Courtney of Chevron believes all training is just-in-time. "There is not a lot of call for courses in long-range development needs," he says, but adds that much of his just-in-time training provides employees with skills used over the long haul, like computer knowledge or risk analysis.

Computer-based-training (CBT) is also being used to accommodate just-in-time learning needs and busy work schedules. Chevron built a local area network to link 2,000 on-site computers for training on using an automated financial system. It allows users to log on when they have free time to take a self-paced training course.

"Attention spans are better in these shorter courses. They are designed to get quickly to the core information," says Courtney, "but that's all people want. They just don't have the time for anything else."

Notes:

How to Get the Most Out of 360° Feedback

Managers who find out how others see them:
(a) become willing to change
(b) become defensive and vindictive
(c) go back to business as usual

BY GARY YUKL AND
RICHARD LEPSINGER

Feedback from multiple sources, alias "360-degree feedback," is currently something of a rage among training professionals. Consultants and practitioners alike tout it as the optimal tool for enhancing leadership and management capabilities, particularly when a company is trying to develop a more open, communicative culture.

More than many developmental tools, 360-degree feedback can prompt real, measurable changes in managers' behavior. The reason is simple: When people receive honest, specific feedback from their bosses, colleagues and subordinates, they often come to understand how their behaviors affect others — and the need for change in some of those behaviors.

Yet like other "magic bullets," multi-rater feedback often fails to bring about the advertised effects. Too often, 360-degree feedback is a one-time event that is forgotten as soon as managers return to the hectic world of work. When this occurs, the problem usually lies with the type of feedback that's being asked for, and how it is gathered, displayed, interpreted and acted upon.

Generally, the process works like this: Questionnaires are used to gather information about managers' behavior from those in a position to witness it on a daily basis: direct reports, colleagues, bosses, and sometimes suppliers and customers. Managers then receive feedback reports that summarize the responses given on these questionnaires. In most cases, participating managers also get the chance to discuss the feedback they've received during workshops conducted by a facilitator.

Many stumbling blocks can blunt the effectiveness of this process. Most fall into two categories: the design and administration of the questionnaire, and the design and facilitation of the follow-up activities. You can increase the likelihood that real behavior change will result from your 360-degree feedback intervention if you follow these recommendations.

The Questionnaire

In selecting a feedback questionnaire, look for the following qualities:

• **Well-researched:** Empirical research should show how each behav-

---

Action planning encourages managers to take control of their lives and decide for themselves how to become more effective.

---

ior itemized on the questionnaire is related to managerial effectiveness. Solid evidence that the behaviors are relevant for success increases managers' interest in getting and using the feedback. Providing feedback on behaviors that are not actually linked to effectiveness is a waste of time and money.

• **Behavioral:** The items on the questionnaire should describe specific, observable behaviors. People have difficulty giving accurate feedback when the descriptions of behavior are vague and general (such as "structures the work roles of direct reports"). The items should describe concrete behaviors: "Explains what results are expected when a task is assigned," or "Tells you when a task you are doing needs to be completed." Specific items like these provide the basis for feedback that is easier for managers to interpret and use for improvement.

• **Positive:** Behaviors should be described in positive rather than negative terms. Avoid questionnaires with items like, "Yells at you for making a mistake." Better wording would be, "Helps you understand the reasons for a mistake and how to avoid making similar mistakes in the future." Some direct reports will be leery about reporting that their boss does something that is ineffective (even if he does so only occasionally); they are more likely to say he does not use an effective behavior frequently. Moreover, a questionnaire full of negative items tends to make managers feel defensive and less likely to participate voluntarily in the feedback process. Finally, feedback about ineffective behavior does not tell people what they should be doing — only what not to do.

• **Personal:** Whenever feasible, behaviors should be described in terms related to the individual answering the questionnaire. It is better, for example, to ask for a response to "This manager praises me when I carry out a task effectively" than to "This manager praises direct reports who carry out a task effectively." Respondents shouldn't be expected to hazard guesses about a manager's behavior with others. This kind of wording also gives a more accurate picture when the manager behaves differently toward different people. Of course, such wording is not appropriate for behaviors that involve more than one person ("Holds a special celebration after the group successfully accomplishes a project") or for behaviors the manager performs alone ("Reviews performance reports for the organizational unit").

• **Multidirectional:** Managers tend to behave differently with people depending on their organizational relationship with them. For example, our research indicates that managers use different patterns of influence behavior when they are dealing with direct reports, with colleagues and with bosses. That's why feedback from different perspectives provides a more complete picture of a manager's behavior. But don't solicit 360-degree feedback about behaviors that are used exclusively in one type of relationship. Delegating, for example, is something managers do with direct reports. Colleagues and bosses generally will not have firsthand knowledge of a manager's delegating behaviors. Thus, you may need different versions of the questionnaire for respondents with different relationships to the manager. Each version should include only the behaviors that are relevant in that kind of relationship.

Administering the Questionnaire

A successful feedback system depends on enlisting the cooperation of a sufficient number of respondents who have knowledge about the manager's behavior. Managers need guidelines for how to identify appropriate respondents and gain their cooperation.

Some useful guidelines:

• **Select respondents carefully.** In most cases, the participating managers select respondents to fill out the questionnaires. This gives managers a greater sense of control over the process and increases the likelihood that they will accept the feedback. Some trainers worry that managers will distribute questionnaires only to their friends, but even friends will usually provide honest responses if they know their feedback will be held in confidence.

Still, advise managers to select a representative sample of people who are most critical to their effectiveness on the job. Also encourage them to identify people who are in a position to provide accurate feedback — ideally, those who have interacted with them on a regular basis for a year or more. Respondents should have had the opportunity to observe a manager's behavior for at least four months.

• **Ensure an adequate number of respondents.** The number of respondents should be large enough to ensure adequate sampling and to protect the confidentiality of the sources. You'll need at least three completed, usable questionnaires from subordinates, for example. Because some people invariably fail to return the questionnaire, the initial sample should be larger than the responses needed.

People asked to complete questionnaires also need guidance to help them provide accurate feedback:

• **Explain how the data will be used and ensure confidentiality.** People who are afraid of adverse consequences will be reluctant to fill out a behavior questionnaire, and, if they do complete it, they probably won't provide honest answers. This problem is especially acute when direct reports are asked to describe the behavior of a boss who is defensive or abusive.

To gain cooperation from potential respondents, explain the purpose of the survey, how the results will be used, and how confidentiality will be ensured. You might want to explain

---

Gather information about managers' behavior from those in a position to witness it on a daily basis: direct reports, colleagues, bosses and sometimes suppliers and customers.

---

in a cover letter that the questionnaire results will be used to provide feedback, and emphasize that individual respondents' answers will remain anonymous. (One way to protect confidentiality is to ask respondents to mail their completed questionnaires directly to an external consultant who will analyze the results and prepare the feedback report.) Feedback should not be reported if there are too few respondents to protect individual confidentiality.

The boss's feedback presents special problems if it is displayed separately from other feedback. Obviously, the boss's feedback won't be anonymous. Although the power relationship reduces the risk of adverse consequences, the boss may decline to participate in the process out of a desire to avoid embarrassment or to avoid the perception that this is some kind of formal performance appraisal. It should be easy to get the boss to cooperate when the purpose of the feedback is purely developmental; the boss is able to provide relevant and unique information about the participant's

behavior.

• **Help respondents avoid common problems in rating.** It's difficult to remember how much or how often a manager used a given type of behavior over the past several months. Instead, raters may base their responses on their general feeling about the manager. Thus, you may get a "halo effect" — that is, a manager who is well-liked may be given high ratings on all scales, regardless of her use of particular behaviors. Conversely, a manager who is strongly disliked may be rated negatively even on those behaviors that he performs often.

Another common bias ("attribution error") occurs when a manager who is known to be effective is rated highly on any scales the rater believes are relevant to effectiveness, regardless of the manager's actual behavior. For example, a manager may work well with individuals, but do little to build team spirit.

When raters fall victim to these biases, their feedback becomes less useful. Even managers who are very effective in general can benefit from identifying areas for improvement, but you'll have a tough time pinpointing their weaknesses if the feedback is biased.

You can alert raters to these biases, and urge them to rate each type of behavior independently. An even better solution is a short training session that teaches respondents to rate behavior more accurately. But rater training is costly and may not be feasible unless your organization plans to collect behavior ratings on a regular basis.

The Feedback Report

There are many different ways to summarize respondents' feedback, some of which are more useful than others. In general, however, the feedback report should:

• **Clearly identify feedback from different perspectives.** Behavior descriptions from different perspectives — direct reports, colleagues, bosses — should be presented separately. Aggregating feedback from different sources tends to make it more difficult to interpret. For example, if a manager tends to use consultation frequently with colleagues but seldom with direct reports, aggregate data will obscure that the manager treats people differently based on their relationship and position in the organization.

• **Compare feedback from others**

with the manager's own perceptions. Most feedback reports compare what others say about a manager's behavior to self-ratings by the manager on a parallel questionnaire. Just going through the process of rating themselves helps managers understand the behavior scales better. Comparing their own ratings to those of others also helps managers interpret the feedback. A high level of agreement among the various raters confirms that the manager's self-assessment is probably accurate; large discrepancies suggest that someone is not perceiving behavior accurately.

Managers often rate themselves higher than others rate them. For example, a manager may indicate that direct reports are frequently praised for their accomplishments, whereas the direct reports report that they receive little recognition from the manager. This is exactly the type of discrepancy that should get the manager's attention and probably indicates a weakness to be addressed.

However, it's important to explore the reason for a discrepancy rather than jump to conclusions about it. Self-ratings may be higher because the manager is biased, his behavior may not be visible to the other raters, or the other raters may have interpreted the items differently.

A discrepancy in the other direction may also occur, but this is less common. For example, a manager may rate himself lower than others do on inspiring subordinates to greater efforts, perhaps because the manager does not realize the extent of his positive influence as a leader.

• **Compare the manager's ratings to norms.** It is difficult for a manager to know whether her score on a specific behavior is high or low without some basis for comparison with other managers. For example, our research shows that managers, in general, use rational persuasion very frequently when they try to influence others. Yet a below-average score on this behavior will not be obvious without the use of norms. Ideally, norms show where a manager falls in the distribution of scores for a large sample of managers. One good way to do this is to use a percentile score that indicates how many managers in the database got lower scores.

• **Display feedback for items as well as scales.** Most behavior scales or categories consist of several items. The behavior scale of "mentoring,"

for example, may consist of items such as: "Offers helpful advice on how to advance your career"; "Provides you with opportunities to develop your skills and demonstrate what you can do"; "Encourages you to attend relevant training programs, workshops or night courses to develop greater skill and expertise"; and "Provides extra instruction or coaching to help you improve your job skills or learn new ones."

Some feedback reports provide feedback for the scales, but not for the separate items that comprise them. Both types of feedback are useful. Item feedback helps managers under-

---

Just going through the process of rating themselves helps managers understand the behavior scales better.

---

stand the behavior scales because the items provide specific examples for each category. Feedback on individual items also reduces problems caused by missing responses. Once the scale scores have been computed, the fact that different respondents skipped different items that make up the scale is camouflaged. Omitted responses may be counted as "never does" or not counted at all, but either way, blanks distort the overall scale score. Reporting results for individual items provides a more accurate picture of a manager's behavior and makes the feedback easier to interpret.

The best form of item feedback is a mean score for each item (the ratings from all respondents on the item are totaled and divided by the number of respondents). Some feedback reports also present the range of scores (highest and lowest), and even the distribution of answers from different respondents (how many people in each group selected each response). Again, the score distribution should not be shown unless there are enough respondents to protect the anonymity of individuals.

• **Provide feedback on recommendations.** Feedback questionnaires typically ask respondents to describe what the manager does, not what the respondent would like the

manager to do. We have found that asking respondents for recommendations provides a useful supplement to feedback about observed behavior. In particular, these recommendations should show how many respondents said the manager should use the behavior more frequently, the same amount or less. This information helps managers interpret their behavior feedback and identify their strengths and weaknesses.

For example, even though a manager has a moderately high score on a behavior such as delegating to direct reports, some people may prefer even more delegation. Without the recommendation it would be hard to discover this opportunity for improvement. Occasionally, respondents think the manager should use a behavior less, although this does not happen as often if the questionnaire describes only positive behaviors. Because of the extra time required to complete a questionnaire that includes a section on recommendations, these questions should focus on scales rather than individual items.

The Feedback Workshop

Sometimes managers receive only a written report on 360-degree feedback, but it's better to have a facilitator explain the feedback and help managers use it to the best advantage. A feedback workshop with 15 to 20 managers is an economical way to use a facilitator. A number of workshop activities can help participants understand the feedback, accept it, and use it to improve their effectiveness.

• **Explain the purpose and benefits of the feedback.** Both the managers themselves and the people completing the questionnaire are more likely to cooperate if they know the feedback is to be used only for developmental purposes and not for evaluation of current performance.

• **Explain the underlying model of leadership and management.** The behavior questionnaire should be based on a theory of effective leadership that identifies behaviors important for managerial effectiveness. This theory should be explained to managers early in the workshop so that they have a basis for interpreting the feedback and focusing on its most important aspects. A good theory also helps managers understand the need to modify their behavior, depending on the specific situation and their objectives and priorities. If developing subordinates is a high priority, for example, more delegation is appropriate. Obviously, managers should delegate assignments more frequently to someone who is competent and trustworthy than to a person who is inexperienced or irresponsible.

• **Involve managers in interpreting the feedback.** In some feedback systems, computer programs provide a narrative interpretation of the feedback and tell managers what they must do to improve. Managers who are responsible for making decisions about millions of dollars of company assets may understandably resent having a computer tell them to change their behavior. With some assistance from the workshop facilitator, most managers are quite capable of evaluating their feedback and determining its implications; they also know better than anyone else about special circumstances that have affected their results. Moreover, allowing managers some room to interpret their results increases the likelihood that they will accept the feedback.

• **Emphasize strengths as well as weaknesses.** Research shows that people are more likely to reject feedback if it is consistently negative. The workshop facilitator should help managers keep a balanced perspective by stressing positive as well as negative feedback. The facilitator should emphasize that the feedback is intended to give managers a sense of what behaviors they should continue, not just what they should be doing differently. The facilitator also should be prepared to provide advice, encouragement and support to managers who are concerned about correcting weaknesses.

• **Ask each manager to develop an improvement plan.** Feedback is more likely to result in behavior change if each manager develops a specific improvement plan. This action planning encourages managers to take control of their lives and decide for themselves how to become more effective. Moreover, in combination with a leadership theory to guide the process, the action planning will help managers learn how to analyze the specific needs of their leadership situation.

Follow-up Activities

The benefits of a feedback workshop are more likely to be realized if supporting activities follow it. Useful follow-up activities include training, coaching and assessment of the feedback's effects.

• **Provide opportunities for skill training.** Skill training allows managers to learn how to improve their behavior, not just what behaviors need to be improved. You can tell a manager he needs to use influencing and inspiring behavior, but if he's not good at influencing and inspiring people, he's highly unlikely to get better at it without training that teaches him those skills. Training will also increase a manager's confidence about using the behaviors back on the job.

The feedback workshop can be expanded to two days to include a day of skill-building, or training can be provided in separate sessions at a later time. Considerations of time, logistics, participant needs, and the type of behaviors involved will determine the best approach. A combined feedback and training workshop takes longer to conduct, but the cost of travel, facilities and trainers may be lower for a combined workshop than for two separate ones.

• **Provide support and coaching.** Individual support and coaching for managers will help them apply what they have learned. One approach is to hold a follow-up session four to six weeks after the feedback workshop to review progress, discuss any difficulties the manager may be having, and provide encouragement and coaching. An alternative approach is to have managers meet with their bosses or with a human resource manager to review progress on their improvement plans.

• **Assess the effects of the feedback workshop.** One way to assess behavior change is to hold review sessions to discuss how well the managers have implemented their improvement plans. Another approach is to conduct a follow-up survey among the people who responded to the questionnaire for a specific manager six months to a year after the feedback workshop to assess the amount of behavior change. This way, the company gets valuable information about the return on its investment in feedback workshops, the facilitators get information they can use to improve the workshops, and researchers get an opportunity to learn more about leadership and training.

With all these benefits, you'd think it would be common practice to conduct follow-up evaluations of feedback and training workshops. Unfortunately, systematic evaluation is the exception rather than the rule. This situation may improve, however, as companies become more interested in measuring the return on their investments in training and development.

Over the years, we have learned a lot about using feedback effectively, but we still have much more to learn. Thousands of feedback workshops are conducted every year, but few studies evaluate them. We need more research to discover what works well and what doesn't.

Companies that conduct feedback workshops have an unprecedented opportunity to evaluate the effect of variations in how feedback is collected, presented and used. Many academics would welcome the chance to collaborate with practitioners in this area. It is time to begin exploiting the opportunities we have to advance our knowledge about this increasingly popular form of management development.

Evaluating Your Management Performance

Company goals should be a training manager's main focus

BY BRIAN MCDERMOTT

Where do I get off being so smug, telling myself I'm doing a good job managing my training department? That's something I ask myself a lot," says Constance Nohelty, manager of personnel, training and development for Nielsen Media Research. It's a variation on a question every training and human resources development executive faces: How do I know when I'm doing a good job?

Answers and evidence of success are as airy as "intuition" and as weighty as "bonus checks" and "oversubscribed courses." But the common denominator among executives interviewed by *Training Directors Forum Newsletter* is, as Christine Chriscoe, manager of training and development for Coca Cola USA, puts it, "Do I add value to the company? Am I helping the company meet its business goals?"

Categories of Concern

A second underlying factor upon which training executives seem to agree is that they prefer to be judged first and foremost as managers.

"There are only three things you can manage," Chriscoe says, "people, dollars, and things — so why should a training manager be judged differently than any other manager?" That means training managers are subject to the same criteria found in varying combinations on most managers' job descriptions and performance appraisal forms — judgment, decision making and problem solving, work relationships, oral and written communication, job knowledge, EEO and affirmative action compliance, and fiscal responsibility.

Alston Fergusson, training manager for Intel Corp., agrees. "I want to be measured as the manager of my group of 52 people. I am more than just a trainer. I hire people who are training experts. My role is to organize and manage these people just as if they were scientists or engineers. I've got to design [department activities] to match the tasks we are assigned, to understand the company's immediate goals, provide the needed resources, provide the training for my people. The job involves planning and getting resources approved, and then stewardship to make sure we get the maximum out of those people and resources.

"I need background in training to increase my credibility, but I want the focus less on that and more on the management skills, the people skills: motivating and rewarding, creating teamwork and a high morale and sense of mission. If you focus too much on the training technology, I think you will miss the boat as a manager."

Individual Focus

When focusing on the projects and progress specific to evaluating personal performance in training management, there are four broad categories (see "Performance Checklist" on p. 40). The four center on activities related to dealing with other managers, the training staff, the training courses, and personal skills, knowledge, and attitudes.

Fergusson looks for his success in an increased demand for services, early inclusion in important new projects, a general belief in training as a critical contributor to company growth, and respect for his compliance with Intel's high-tech-oriented corporate culture. He listens for how often line managers ask him for solutions to business problems, not just courses. He gauges his success with management by the extent to which training is financed, a clear indicator of whether the function is regarded as useful. And he listens for unsolicited customer feedback, usually an indication that something good has happened to motivate that individual's response.

Fergusson also judges the general mood of his department, the career growth of his staff, his ability to attract good people from within the company, and the staff turnover rate in evaluating his own performance.

Ron Korman, training director for Control Data Corp., says, "No news is good news. When I hear everything is cool out there, it tells me we are doing the job right. The most important way to know how I am doing, though, is to look at the impact I have on the company's strategic goals."

His group recently rolled out a successful management workshop on what the company expects in terms of commitment to quality, marketing, and people. And in this case, he says, training and corporate goals go together "like peanut butter and jelly."

Korman, too, believes much management success is tied up in how well staff members do and how they feel about their work. He meets at least twice a week with staff members, using an agenda that always leaves room for open discussion.

Nielsen's Nohelty also partially judges her success on the attitudes and development of her staff. "I make it clear that they are on their own track for advancement. I show them four job descriptions for the department and tell them they are on their own as to when they reach those goals. I'm not pitting them one against another. And I've tried to keep the department open to them because I believe my job is to make their jobs easier." That might not work at all times in all places, Nohelty says, but it is something she expects of herself right now.

High-Level Feedback

Thomas Tener, manager of management development for Southwest Bell Telephone, checks several sources to measure his performance. He solicits appraisals from a training steering committee. He writes annually to division presidents about what has occurred in training and asks for feedback on what worked well and

Performance Checklist for Training and Human Resources Development Executives

This checklist was compiled from interviews with six training and human resources executives. Each suggestion answers the question, "What specific things do you look at to determine if you are doing a good job running training?" There are 41 questions. "Yes" responses indicate positive performance skills.

	Yes	No
Management Related:		
Is top management committed to training (attending and teaching courses?)	☐	☐
Is your opinion asked by the "right" people?	☐	☐
Do you meet regularly with your superiors and potential customers?	☐	☐
Do you understand your company's business needs?	☐	☐
Do you help your company fulfill its strategic plan?	☐	☐
Are you involved early in roll-outs of new products and services?	☐	☐
Is there an increased demand for your services?	☐	☐
Is people development respected as critical to growth in your company?	☐	☐
Are managers asking you for solutions to their business problems?	☐	☐
Does management support your budget requests?	☐	☐
Can you influence parts of the organization where you don't really have the positional power to do so?	☐	☐
Do managers know what it takes to prepare and deliver effective training?	☐	☐
Staff Related:		
Does your staff willingly participate in daily department activities?	☐	☐
Do your people feel good about what they are doing? Are they enthusiastic?	☐	☐
Does your staff share responsibility for the success of the department?	☐	☐
Do you create an environment where people can develop?	☐	☐
Are job descriptions and development plans clearly defined so your staff knows what it takes to earn promotions or increases in responsibility?	☐	☐
Are your staff members earning promotions?	☐	☐
Do your staff members increase skills and knowledge from year to year?	☐	☐
Does demand for training warrant additions to your staff?	☐	☐
Do you motivate, develop and reward your staff so that people have high morale and a sense of mission?	☐	☐
Is your staff turnover rate stable and acceptable?	☐	☐
Do you attract good people to your staff from within the company?	☐	☐
Do you meet regularly with staff members?	☐	☐
Do you and your staff work together well as a team?	☐	☐
Course Related:		
Is there a market for what you produce?	☐	☐
Are people asking for more classes?	☐	☐
Are current courses fully or over-subscribed?	☐	☐
Do your courses compete favorably for time against other activities and job responsibilities that demand managers' and employees' attention?	☐	☐
Are courses developed and delivered at an acceptable quality level?	☐	☐
Do you follow-up on training?	☐	☐
Do coworkers see changes in your trainees back on the job?	☐	☐
Personal:		
Do you use business language rather than personnel jargon?	☐	☐
Do you know which training technologies and tools to use? Which to avoid?	☐	☐
Is your understanding of the training profession broad, current, and credible?	☐	☐
Do you make time for long-range planning and goal clarification?	☐	☐
Are you excited and enthusiastic about your work?	☐	☐
Are you creative?	☐	☐
Are you compassionate about your work and the people you work for?	☐	☐
Do you always have a few more ideas to explore?	☐	☐
Can you maintain a sense of humor even in the most trying times?	☐	☐

what could be done better.

"And the best barometer of all is the quarterly meeting I have with the people I work with when I have them tell me how I'm doing. We spend an afternoon trying to figure out what we have done well and what we could do better. I give them a questionnaire they can use to give me feedback, so they don't necessarily have to speak out. We discuss whether we work well as a team, if we are keeping focused on the future, the quality of our communication, and whether they are getting enough information to do their jobs. Sometimes I have to just sit up there and undress, so to speak, and ask what I did well or not so well."

Tener also keeps a log of telephone calls and judges by the content how he is doing. "If it is all problems or things that should have been handled lower in the organization, then I failed to get somebody to do something they should be doing. I also look at the kinds of things that are on my desk; should they be there? If not, what have I done that keeps them there?

"The biggest piece of my job," Tener continues, "is being an internal peddler. I'm nothing but a salesman. I have helpful ideas and concepts and processes for managers and supervisors. The second piece of my job is influencing the organization to do things that some people may not want but that have to be done. And the third area is coordination of all the management development in five states." When things go smoothly in each of those areas, he says, the desired quality and quantities of training are likely to be in place.

Marty Lewin, manager of group technical training for Allstate Insurance, says, "We have a reputation for being an effective training department — fulfilling commitments to present a certain number of classes of certain quality. But I think we are harder on ourselves than management. We are the professionals, and the way we evaluate training is more stringent. If we report that we've met our schedule, we are pretty much seen as being effective. But we have higher standards and we want to know that people are performing well. So I look not only at the process of putting something together, but also follow up on the results." Part of following up on a new customer service program, for instance, involved polling employees about changes in their managers who had attended the courses.

An important part of evaluating the process of managing training for Lewin, too, is in how well he develops his trainers. In addition to quarterly and annual reviews, he schedules regular classroom observations with each of his trainers. After each observation he meets for a coaching session to provide feedback and set goals for improvement. He also always has an ongoing career development plan for each employee, and makes a point to never miss a scheduled review. "They have to be done on time; that process has to be managed because it lets people know how they are doing, and it shows them that you care."

It's also important, Lewin says, "to have a feel for and understanding of all the elements of training. It surprises me sometimes that even people in training don't understand the time and work involved in doing training. Sometimes managers ask trainers to develop a two-week workshop that can be delivered next week...and some people say yes. You have to train management to know what effective training takes so you can get the proper support.

"Trainers are often out in their own little worlds; it's easy to forget that you work for the big company. But we can make a lot of contributions if we remember who we work for. That's part of managing relationships with the overall management team."

The other basics of judging his own performance, Lewin says, include looking at how he manages his own area, and the quality and success of the product, "which are not necessarily synonymous."

Coca Cola's Christine Chriscoe compares commendable management performance to being a most valuable player on a baseball team. "It's a combination of individual skills and the contributions you make to the team. I can build a wonderful training department, and have fantastic programs that any training pro would drool over. But if they don't contribute to the organization, they aren't worth much."

THINK YOU'RE A GOOD TRAINING LEADER? YOUR STAFF'S REVIEW WILL TELL

When was the last time you asked your training staff to rate your performance? If the answer is never, you're probably in the majority. It takes some guts — and an open mind — but letting your direct reports conduct an "upward review" can go a long way toward making you a better training manager.

That's why Melanie McCarthy, vice president of marketing for USA Net Inc., does it. It's a practice she started while managing the training function at the Home Shopping Network.

"I don't want to get complacent," she says, "and I want to make sure I don't miss anything important I could do to help my staff." When asking her staff for feedback, she gives them the option to do the appraisal anonymously or openly. She asks that they rate her performance using a 1 to 5 scale — "doing poorly" to "doing very well" — in areas such as these:

(1) How well do I state and clarify visions, goals, and objectives for the department?

(2) How well do I lead by example?

(3) How committed am I to employee involvement?

(4) Do I give helpful (and timely) feedback about your performance?

(5) How well do I encourage you to take risks?

(6) How well do I turn failed risks into learning opportunities?

(7) How well do I help you develop the skills you need to do your job effectively?

(8) How well do I provide support for your career development?

(9) How well do I coordinate work within the training department?

(10) How easy do I make it to criticize me?

— *Dave Zielinski*

What Trainers Can Learn from the Sales Force

Successful trainers analyze their audience, set objectives, plan content and make persuasive presentations. Here's how it's done, in plain language.

BY VIRGINIA SWEET LINCOLN

In your business, do you sell? I hope, you say "Yes." Even though you're a trainer, you're still a salesperson. You're always selling something: a product, a service, an idea, your programs — yourself! And outstanding salespeople share certain characteristics with outstanding trainers.

For one thing, you do certain things to ensure a successful seminar. You analyze your audience, set objectives, plan content, develop and deliver the training session. You then evaluate the results. Good salespeople also analyze their audience, set objectives, plan content, make the sales call and evaluate the results.

Both fields involve professionalism. The presenter must be knowledgeable and people-oriented. Salespeople and trainers need to value their clients and meet those clients' needs.

And both fields involve getting results. Some measurable difference occurs at the end of a sale that says you've been successful. That difference is called an order. You get immediate feedback about your degree of success. A measurable change similarly has to occur at the end of a training session, if you've been successful. The participants must be able to do something, or to do something differently, as a result of your work. As a trainer, you also get feedback.

How can trainers use sales strategies? Let's say you have an idea for a new training program. You may not have the authority needed to approve the budget and implement the program. You may need to sell your manager on the feasibility of your program. Here's where you can borrow from the work of top salespeople.

You'll want to do two things. First, analyze the benefits your company will get from adopting your new program. And second, analyze the benefits that your manager will get. Ask questions like: Will the program save the company money and time, improve safety, raise productivity, give us a competitive edge or reduce turnover? The more benefits the company gets, the greater are the chances for your program to be accepted, especially in today's tight economy.

Then look closely at your manager. What is important to him or her? Is it cost reduction? Is it increasing productivity and morale simultaneously? Is it recognition for outstanding cost containment? Is it being perceived as innovative and "on the cutting edge?" To get your manager's commitment, your program needs to have some strong benefits.

Once you've identified those benefits, you're ready to set up a meeting. For each phone call or meeting, you need to have an objective firmly in mind — and in writing. You must write behavioral objectives for your training programs so you can tell when you've reached the goal. (You'd also state a sales objective in measurable, behavioral terms.) Here's an example: "As a result of my meeting today with Tom, he will agree to a pilot test of my program in the accounting department to begin February 15."

It would be great if everyone were convinced on the first call that a training program is vital and should start immediately. But that's not reality. You may need to make several sales calls on a particular manager. You may have to revise your objective. Partway through your meeting, for example, you may find that the best you can hope to gain is another meeting with this manager after you've done further research. Training objectives (and sales objectives) are subject to revision. They may not be attainable at a given moment, so you need to create an enabling objective that you can reach.

Your original objective for the pilot program doesn't get tossed out, just delayed. It becomes your terminal objective. After additional research and further meetings, your enabling objectives can help you reach that terminal objective — the pilot test.

Whether or not you leave a meeting with your original objective met, always thank the person for spending time considering your proposal. And plan to follow up. Be sure to end the conversation with a reference to future contact: "I'll be back in touch with you..." and specify when.

Script Your Big Moments

If you're nervous about talking to top management, work out a brief script (see Example 1). Talk through your script much as an actor would read the lines of a play. Ask yourself: "What are the best and the worst things that can happen to me in this situation?" It will help you recognize that you are not in a life-or-death struggle when you set up a meeting about your training program.

Outline all the possible objections the manager may have to your idea for the training program. Gather convincing evidence to outweigh the objections. Suppose cost is a concern. Your first step is clarification: What cost is a problem? Start-up cost? Per-participant cost? Short- or long-range program costs? Salary involved? Downtime? Once you know what the specific objection is, you may be able to answer it with a cost/benefit analysis. You can compare the cost of sending a person through the program with the expected increase in productivity.

You may find that it's helpful to borrow certain critical attributes often seen in successful salespeople. Here are three big ones:

• **They are highly organized.** That is, they've worked out systems that help them track information and follow up (see Example 2).

• **They are persistent.** Initially they may get a "No" answer, but they recognize that a "No" often can be turned around. (Sales statistics show that 60% of all sales are made after the fifth call. Yet only 12% of all salespeople make more than five calls. If this statement were applied to training proposals, how would you measure up?)

• **They balance their empathy with their ego.** They can understand things from the customer's perspective and they listen well. But they also have enough ego involvement and self-confidence that they know they want to make the sale. They set up a win/win situation. Trainers can do the same thing as they work with top managers. Put yourself behind the manager's desk and look at things through a manager's eyes.

To find out more about the characteristics of successful salespeople, watch them in action. Read sales books. To further perfect your sales skills, attend a seminar.

It is important to qualify your manager, just as salespeople qualify customers: identify why he or she needs this program and whether he or she can afford it. And make sure you're talking to the person who can commit the dollars and give the go-ahead. You may want to develop some qualifying questions to determine whether your assessment matches the reality of your environment (see example 3).

Another successful sales strategy you can borrow is to call ahead for an appointment. Your managers will see you as a professional who values time — yours and theirs.

When you're on the phone, keep your voice low, quiet and calm. The telephone is designed to pick up certain frequencies. It is kindest to those voices at the lower end of the speaking range. (The phone company talks about the voice with a smile. Your manager can detect that smile even though most phones don't have television screens. How can you tell? Easy. When you smile, you relax your vocal cords and your voice sounds pleasant and relaxed. When you don't smile, the cords tighten up and you sound tense; your voice is pitched higher.)

Write out your objective before you pick up the phone. Set an objective for each management appointment you make. You might phrase your objective like this: "Set up meeting date and time with X. Purpose: to discuss the new pre-supervisory training program and schedule it for September startup. Possible meeting date 7/8 at 9:30 a.m. or 7/20 at 1:30 p.m."

The rationale for this is the same as for writing objectives for a training session. The objective tells you precisely what you want to accomplish with your call. And like your training-session objective, you can quickly tell whether you've met it or not.

When you make an appointment, offer the manager a choice of date and time: "Would you like to get together on Tuesday the 18th at 9:30, or would Thursday the 20th at 1:30 be better for you?" Ask for a set amount of time as well. After the manager chooses, repeat it. Then write the date and time on your calendar and tell the manager you'll phone on the appointed day to reconfirm. That's another demonstration of your professionalism.

Keep in mind that you are a walking advertisement for your program; your enthusiasm and confidence need to show. Remember the "100 factor," which Joe Girrard talks about in his book, *How to Sell Anything to Anybody.* He maintains that everyone you talk with knows at least 100 other people. They can influence 100 other people positively or negatively about you. That's why it's essential to value and respect everyone, and to show them courtesy and understanding even when they are difficult. Your attitude will give others a positive picture of you.

Prepare for your meeting by rehearsing what you want to say and how you'll say it. List the benefits you uncovered earlier. Consider the objections you believe will be made and how you plan to overcome them. Role play in front of a mirror and watch your body language. Again, you're borrowing a successful sales strategy.

Anticipate Questions

Think in terms of your manager. You may want to try a "Ben Duffy." He was a New York advertising man who learned that the American Tobacco Co. was about to switch agencies. After making an appointment to do a presentation, he checked into a hotel where, working undisturbed, he developed a set of 10 critical questions he would want an advertising agency to answer if he were the client.

When he arrived at the interview, the president of American Tobacco said, "It just so happens, Mr. Duffy, that I also made a list of question; let's exchange lists." They did. And Duffy landed the account — because 8 of the 10 questions appeared on both lists.

You can do the same thing for your manager.

During your meeting, mirror the manager's language when it's appropriate. Mirror body language as well. By doing this, you make the person comfortable with you. But if you get a negative reading in the body language and in the tone of voice, change your own body language to a more neutral stance. Try relaxing; it's contagious.

Ask your manager if you may take notes, then offer to give him or her a copy. Notes help you pick up on — and recall — key points of agreement and concern. You can use them to review the meeting. And if you have a second meeting, notes provide a discussion starter.

Listen Effectively

Ask questions. Clarify what the manager means: ask to have particu-

---

Example 3

Some Qualifying Questions

l. What would you like to see happen as a result of the pre-supervisory training program?

2. Assuming the program is successful, which departments would you like to see involved next?

3. How soon would you like those other departments involved?

4. Do you see any additional areas we should include in this program?

5. Are there particular presenters you'd like to see involved with this program'?

6. Would you give me your reactions to this "agreement for change" form that I've designed for the participants?

7. What do you like best about this new program?

8. What do you like least about it?

9. May I have your approval for the budget and the go-ahead for this pilot?

10. Who would you like to see in the first group of participants?

---

lar concerns explained in more detail so you have a complete picture. Combine asking questions with listening effectively. Few people are good listeners; you'll be more valued if you are.

Remember to agree with your manager at appropriate times. Let's say you just pointed out that your new program will save the company money by reducing accidents in the shipping room. Your manager leans forward and says that the program can also increase the morale of the people who work in that area.

It's time for you to agree strongly. The manager is buying into your program, and you need to give him or her recognition for being insightful.

Keep asking: "What are this manager's needs and concerns?" "How can I help her look good to her boss?" or "How can I help him meet his goals?" By finding answers to these questions, you are more likely to get support and approval of your program.

If you have set a call-back time, be prompt. You might even check in a day or two in advance. And if you've promised to get additional information to the manager, get it there as soon as possible. Whatever follow-through is needed, be sure it gets done. Again, always thank the manager for the time. As Peter Drucker said, "Good manners are the glue that hold organizations together."

After the meeting is over, evaluate it as you would your training programs. Identify what worked well and what didn't. Identify what you would do differently and why. Get moving on the action steps you need to take. You want to know what you do well in your talks with top managers, how you do it and why.

If you want to be as good in sales as you are in training, you'll need to practice. You need to get comfortable with your new image. You need to feel comfortable with the sales process. Try these ideas out for the next three or four weeks. Research shows that it takes about 2l to 28 days before a new skill becomes a habit.

Analyze your successes and repeat them. Pick up new ideas and information. Tune into your manager's interests; read; attend seminars and practice, practice, PRACTICE. That's how you became an outstanding trainer. And you can repeat that same success in the sales area as you sell your manager on your training programs.

Training Directors as Change Agents

If you have the nerve, you probably have the skills needed to facilitate cultural change in your organization.

BY BRIAN MCDERMOTT

The training department, because of its key charters, is the most logical agency to manage change in an organization, according to Malcolm Warren, director of training and organization development at CVS.

Warren reminded attendees at a Training Directors' Forum Conference that training directors carry the mandate to analyze performance and performance systems; they are responsible for design and delivery of interventions and planned actions that bring about predicted change, and are often mandated to have evaluation and feedback processes. These, Warren says, are the primary skills and tools needed to direct a department, a division, or an entire organization through cultural and structural changes. "To the extent that you or I are willing to undertake the perilous nature of leading in the introduction of change, we have the opportunity."

Determining Your Role

There are no pat answers about how, or even if, a training director should manage being a change agent in an organization, "There is no organization structure which is correct [for every organization], and no organization structure in existence is correct for long," Warren says. "There are many solutions to the problem of getting people to work together effectively."

Historically, however, the focus of most corporate education has been level four training — teaching individuals to do the correct thing continuously without cue. And that type of well-planned, well-executed intervention, Warren says, can be transferred to deal with an entire organization or a unit within an organization.

"If you want to determine if you should be into change agentry, use a basic strategy development technique. Assess what you want to be when you grow up. Do you want to be the training director five years from now? What do you want to be involved in? What kind of budget do you want?"

Specifically, Warren suggests:"
- **Technically examine your competencies.** How good are you really? — not how good do you tell management you are, or how good that management thinks you are.
- **Evaluate your markets.** Do a market-share analysis. List your primary clients, your secondary clients, and determine where you are dominant.
- **Identify your client system.** What are your clients' universes of acceptable solutions — what do they accept now and what are they likely to accept in the future? The biggest mistake you can make is to think you have the right answers. The only solutions that are right are those your clients accept.
- **Determine what your department is good at.** Who will buy what you offer? What can you market within your system in order to be chartered as the focus of change, the agent?
- **Evaluate your capabilities in terms of staff and energy.** Be certain you can serve the demands for what you offer. It is dangerous to move too quickly and then fall short of what you have promised or proposed.

Understanding Change

Perhaps the most important thing to consider about being a training director/change agent, Warren says, is that "you can't be the high priest of an idea for change." Unless an idea comes from and is supported by the client, it is unlikely to succeed.

"Our job is to articulate [the idea for change]. We are in the fortunate position — most of us — of being behaviorists. We can talk about conditions. We can talk about observed behaviors. We can talk about outcomes and results. We can define what it ought to look like. We can clarify and help an organization communicate an idea because we understand the communication media. We can help get the idea out to the right people at the right time. We can design the tests, provide the milestones and can also test something against what other companies are doing."

A change agent, Warren says, should be concerned with three main conditions in an organization: anthropology, psychology and politics.

"Anthropology is the basic tribal notion that every human system has values, notions of what is good and what is not good." Warren says that in business those notions revolve around items such as profit, growth, citizenship, appearance, discipline and structure. "Mostly they are unwritten and unspoken. The change agent helps identify the formal and informal norms, the correct values; points out the dissonances and dysfunctions. For instance, people may feel, 'Our organization values promptness,' but in reality everybody is always 10 minutes late for meetings."

Dealing with the psychology of change in organizations primarily means handling the fear of the new, Warren says. It is important to establish clear expectations and to work for small successes. "Most organizations assume that as soon as they identify a goal it has already been achieved. You must be very conservative about this, very specific about what happens when, and how long it will take. The change agent is in the position to help balance the stresses. The role of the change agent sometimes is to hold people back, not to be the implementer, the pusher, because once goals are articulated people really want to move. You have to be able to work within the universe of problems and help people find new ways to solve old problems."

The political aspect of change, Warren says, is to know who has the power to demand change and who has the power to "get in your way."

He suggests, "Capture power, if

only by association. Get drivers behind you. Catalog past relationships; who supports you and your department? You cannot delegate politics; a high title does not equal power."

Elements for Change

When working to change the way an organization behaves, Warren says, the critical data — what is perceived as being wrong and what might resolve that situation — should be gathered from within the organization. A change agent should employ techniques that allow clients to understand and define their needs, rather than imposing solutions that appear academic or foreign to the company's environment. Warren points out three criteria for achieving successful change:

• **Change must be driven by the client.** If there is an area where you want to be a change agent, you cannot go in and tell people what is wrong with them. The client must feel a need.

• **The unit you work with must have some autonomy to change.**

• **Successful change requires a driver,** a fanatic who desires change *so* much that he or she will commit time, energy and resources to make a plan work.

If these three pieces are in place, Warren says, you know you have a place to start to make changes. Next, begin work with the driver to define where that person wants to go and how.

Notes:

Training, MIS Functions Struggle to Define a New Relationship

These days it pays to get to know the folks in information services.

BY DAVE ZIELNISKI

As new computing technologies and software applications continue to play a larger role in the work lives of all employees — changing the way work is done and creating a new family of training needs — training functions face a dilemma. What kind of relationships should they forge with management information services (MIS) departments, which typically oversee the implementation and support of information technology? Should MIS workers conduct a greater share of technology-related training? Do training functions even house the requisite knowledge to orchestrate or influence more of this kind of training?

Some organizations, like the Home Shopping Network, are acknowledging the trend by reworking organizational charts, moving the training function out from under human resources (HR) and placing it under the control of the MIS department. Others, seeing once-insular MIS employees emerge to train and interact with more nontechnical workers throughout companies, are giving those employees new skills training to match new, "softer" responsibilities.

One thing's for sure: The growing dependence on computers and technology means training functions will probably need to form much more integrated and collaborative relationships with MIS departments to capitalize on growing opportunities for influence.

A Need for New Skills

The problem with many nontechnical trainers and their approach to technology, says Michael Woerner,

director of training and development for Wawa Inc., a 512-unit convenience store chain, is that many of them are what he calls "skills Nazis." Woerner refers to instructional and course designers, but the term could easily be applied to any trainer who looks at "creating procedural training for computers and software like they would procedural training for a forklift."

You know the drill, Woerner says: "Bring in a set piece of equipment, find a subject-matter expert, establish the procedures, design the appropriate training, deliver it by a frozen date." But information systems training today requires a much different approach, he says — one that means getting involved at the conception of projects involving new technology and developing an intimate understanding of user needs.

Taking a cookie-cutter approach to learning in environments where training needs are constantly shifting is "a recipe for frustration and ineffectiveness," Woerner says.

The change in skill sets required of information services professionals is also changing trainers' roles. Distributed client/server, object-oriented applications development, computer networking and data communications are all greatly complicating the learning needs of MIS professionals (see related story on p. 50). In the mainframe era, for example, training needs focused on basic programming technologies like JCL and COBOL. Through the "sheep dip" approach, a training unit could provide training for hundreds of people at once, and not have to worry that their skills would grow obsolete anytime soon.

Now MIS professionals need scores of specific courses — and fast.

A recent survey of MIS professionals by the Gartner Group, a high-tech research outfit, showed that 90% of respondents felt they had to be retrained to keep pace with growing job demands. Is your training function prepared to contribute to this training?

At USAir, Margaret Weiss, manager of training and professional development for an 800-person information systems division, says the window for assessing training needs has shrunk considerably. "You can't project needs a year or even six months in advance anymore," Weiss says. "The world is moving too fast."

Weiss now does a quarterly needs assessment, and finds even that is often not frequent enough. The rapid pace has meant a big change in the way her unit assesses training needs. Instead of focusing on what technologies MIS staffers need to master to be well-rounded professionals, the unit focuses on what they need to learn to complete the next project.

And the only way to do that is to involve MIS people in determining their own immediate needs, which Weiss does by having them answer six questions: What is involved in the project? What new or existing technologies might be used? What is the experience level of those who might be assigned to the project? What specific software applications or product training might be needed? How many people will need the training? And what support groups within information services (such as database, systems, or operations) might need tailored training for the upcoming projects?

Weiss says the learning needs of MIS workers are being redefined in other ways. Not long ago, few organizations thought much about the interpersonal communication and business skills of programmers, systems developers and other technology specialists, she says. Locked in an MIS world of their own, these specialists seldom "interfaced" with the rest of the organization.

But because of the way information systems reengineering is changing organizational charts, more groups need to work closely with technology specialists to define their own applications needs. At USAir that mean MIS specialists need training in leadership, time management, presentation skills, project management, meeting skills, and more.

Saying No to Training

The same forces expanding the training needs of MIS professionals outside technical areas are driving non-MIS professionals into technical areas. Many non-MIS professionals, suddenly immersed in information technology-based reengineering, must get savvy fast on a variety of technologies.

At many organizations that's leading to a new challenge — figuring out what type of technology training is appropriate for non-MIS employees, and saying no in some cases if a pressing business need isn't being served by a training request.

The forces driving the need are pretty simple. Information systems personnel, like USAir's, are working closely with user groups — and their influence is rubbing off. That's increasing the technical knowledge of users — and whetting their appetites for more.

The problem is that many training units don't have the people or resources to satisfy demand. And even if they did, training must correspond to real business and professional development needs — not to what employees might think would be "cool" to learn. Unfortunately, when it comes to technology, many organizations have not figured out the right mix of information systems skills and business skills needed by employee groups. Until that happens, some trainers may just have to learn to say no. Or make sure that when employees outside the information services department ask to sign up for MIS classes, they have a sound business need to meet. There is also the real danger of letting non-MIS employees develop applications that aren't managed by MIS professionals.

Perhaps the biggest challenge is the sheer difficulty of keeping up with changing training needs when it comes to new technologies. For many employees that requires a basic attitude shift — a willingness to "believe that whatever you need to know, you can learn," says Elliott Masie, a computer training consultant and author of *The Computer Training Handbook*.

Developing confidence in trainers themselves can be surprisingly difficult. Mike Woerner of Wawa has made progress alleviating trainers' fears by working to ensure his staffers are at least as skilled in using com-puter systems and software as his principal audience of store managers. For example, Wawa equipped regional and multi-unit store managers with powerful laptop computers and Microsoft's office automation products three years ago when it closed down some field offices. All the support functions the field offices had provided were in effect loaded onto the laptop computers. Knowing computer training tied specifically to using laptops would be the big need for managers, Woerner equipped his staff with the same hardware/software configuration and put them through the same Executrain course store managers received.

"We want to make sure we stay ahead of the managers' needs," Woerner says, "and that we are just as skilled at using that piece of technology as our customers are."

At USAir, Margaret Weiss has what may be the ideal way of keeping up with training needs. Lotus Notes, a groupware application that lets project team members collaborate electronically, has become an important part of the way the 800-member MIS staff does business. Weiss and her training staff regularly scan Notes discussion databases to see what technical issues and concerns MIS staffers are talking about, and then pose questions on Notes about training needs related to new technologies.

Trainers: Seize These Opportunities for Influence

Masie sees plenty of opportunities for trainers to increase their organizational influence by offering education on current and emerging technologies. For instance:

SURVEY: NEED GROWS FOR CLIENT / SERVER TRAINING

Need more evidence that training functions and management information services (MIS) departments may need to form more collaborative relationships? Recent research indicates 66% of corporations expect client/server developer costs to rise rapidly by 1998. The study, conducted by Cambridge, MA-based Forrester Research Inc. and based on interviews with representatives of 50 *Fortune* 1000 companies, found that only 44% of developers have received any type of client/server training to date. The report found that while many companies have the technology in place, the skills of many veteran application developers are not current when it comes to client/servers.

The study says the skills of many corporate application developers are based primarily in mainframe computer languages. MIS managers surveyed said they anticipate having enough mainframe maintenance to keep these developers busy for the interim, but as the world moves toward client/server, so too must application development. A significant number of respondents also indicated a number of their developers won't make the transition to client/server, or are showing some resistance. Some are on the verge of retirement and comfort-able in the mainframe world, and others just indicate a lack of interest in working in the local area network (LAN) and PC environment.

But the study's authors also say more large companies are starting to retrain. They estimate that initial out-of-pocket client/server training costs will average $9,000 per developer, and that annual skills maintenance training will run about $3,650 per developer.

According to the research, most training dollars are now spent on teaching specific application development tools — but what's needed now is education on designing client/server applications that perform well across networks. The research also found convincing top managers to actually use technology and software — letting their fingers touch the keyboard — is key to unlocking the training bank vault.

The study also found timing to be a big issue. Unless skills acquired in the client/server training programs can be immediately applied to actual development needs, those skills will rapidly begin to fade. Many respondents said most training now is poorly timed, since people will learn a set of skills, then not use them for over a month or so.

- **The Internet and commerical on-line services.** Serving as a conduit for Internet training is one way for training departments to increase their stature. "The next time someone calls asking about Internet training, you should know where to point them," Masie says.

- **E-Mail.** Yes, it's been around forever, but few companies are using it to its utmost capacity, Masie believes. Training departments should be the ones to develop "standards, even rituals" for using e-mail as an effective corporate learning and communication tool. "In most organizations, no one else is doing that."

- **Groupware and collaborative learning.** Companies like Microsoft, Novell, AT&T, and other powerhouses are now introducing electronic teamwork tools similar to the potent Lotus Notes. Learning the software is fairly easy, Masie says, but "getting people to change their work habits to take advantage of it is a challenge uniquely suited to trainers."

- **Desktop videoconferencing.** So far, an expensive "event-based" technology. Now, however, cheaper products are beginning to cascade onto the market that promise to make desktop videoconferencing as ubiquitous as fax modems. Apple already offers the software and a camera (called Quicktime Conferencing) that can connect Macs in a local area network for as little as $200 per machine, he says. Try to envision training where employees can dial-up a 20-minute coaching session on a particular skill set from their desktop workstations, or "attend" a class anywhere without leaving their office chairs.

- **Voice mail.** Another seemingly obvious but often overlooked opportunity for training functions. In many businesses, employees spend up to 45 minutes a day leaving voice mail messages and an hour retrieving them; eight hours a week for an activity that few are ever trained to perform efficiently. "If businesses are truly concerned about productivity, the way employees use voice mail should be a big training issue," Masie says.

- **Seismic shifts in software.** Masie calls the introduction of Windows '95 "the largest single technology change in the history of the world." An overstatement? Maybe not, when you consider that Microsoft's new operating system will eventually require some type of training for every Windows user in the world. The bottom line: This represents an enormous reskilling challenge, one smart training departments ought to be ready to meet.

Notes:

The Myth of Soft Skills Training

Why is it so tough to show concrete results from soft-skills training courses? Maybe it's because no training really happens.

BY JAMES C. GEORGES

Suppose you wanted to become skillful at something. Anything. Golf, karate, selling refrigerators, negotiating, making presentations, being a "leader" instead of just a manager — whatever. The point is, you want to become truly proficient. Your objective is not just to know something about the thing; you want to be able to do the thing, and do it well. Would you:

   a. Read a book?
   b. Watch a video?
   c. Hire a motivational speaker?
   d. Attend a seminar?
   e. Try a few role-plays?
   f. Practice with an expert coach under realistic working conditions until you achieved fluency?

The answer is obvious. Any of the first five choices could provide some useful information about the skill, but only the last choice will turn potential talent into demonstrable competence. Why? Because when you do something repeatedly — trying to perform up to an explicit standard — your mind and body get the "feel" of doing it proficiently.

And the "feel" of doing it is the skill. You can confirm that statement with your whole life's experience. If you don't acquire the feel, you haven't acquired the skill. Further, the feel is acquired only by using the skill to produce a real result: a good golf stroke, a sale, a successful negotiation. Coaching the actual performance shortens the time it takes for an individual to become proficient enough to achieve the desired result repeatedly. Eventually, the new behavior becomes a preferred and self-chosen way of behaving.

So the best way to develop skillfulness is to practice doing the thing you're trying to do, under the expert guidance of someone who knows how. Yet when it comes to interpersonal-skills training in the corporate world — the teaching of so-called "soft skills" such as listening, leadership and teamwork — what's the one choice on the list that is almost never used? You guessed it.

If the student isn't doing it, it isn't training.

Now guess the real reason behind the endless hand-wringing in the corporate training field about how hard it is to get "learned" skills to transfer from the classroom to the job. Guess why trainers find it so terribly difficult to document any measurable business results arising from the soft-skills courses they conduct. Guess why "proving that training makes a difference" has acquired such prominent status as a Big Burning Issue in the training arena.

Here's why: When it comes to soft skills, companies and the "trainers" they employ almost never do any training at all. What they do instead is education. "Soft-skills training" is mostly a myth. The reason it doesn't work is because it doesn't happen.

Training vs. Education
There is a great deal of difference between training and education, though the vast majority of corporate trainers are not aware of it. Educating is not the same as training. For most people, there is no causal relationship between education and performance. There is, indeed, a causal relationship between training and performance.

The reason: Knowledge isn't power. Competence is power. Power is the ability to create a desired effect. And creating desired effects is what we mean by "performance."

To educate is to increase intellectual awareness of a subject. To train is to make someone proficient at the execution of a given task. Many wonderful things can be said about education, but education doesn't cause competence. Only training does.

Try making a youngster competent at riding a bicycle by sitting her down at the kitchen table and explaining how to ride a bicycle. It won't work. It can't work. Because knowing about a skill is not the same as being skillful.

Try taking a one-hour golf lesson from someone who uses typical corporate "training" methods. He'll meet you in a conference room far from the golf course, talk to you about a golf swing for 45 minutes, show you a video for 10 minutes, let you take make-believe swings at an imaginary golf ball for one minute ("Let's role-play!"), then ask you to write an "action plan" describing how you will apply what you've "learned." Absurd? Of course.

Skeptics will protest that some people who receive what I'm calling education in soft-skills areas actually do turn out higher performance as a result; they do, in fact, get better at selling or influencing or working in a team. And this is true — for maybe 10 percent or 15 percent of trainees. Why? Because those people were already skillful before they attended your latest educational offering. If you take anyone who is already competent and add more education, you often will get better performance to some degree.

But what about the other 85 or 90 percent? It's no good pretending that the training department's job is simply to deliver some information about skills ("The Five Key Practices of Famous Leaders," "The 10 Fabulous Values of Team Players"), and then it's the field manager's job actually to make employees proficient. If you accept the title of "trainer," your task is to make people competent, not just more aware. Blaming managers because the "skills" you supposedly imparted in your educational event failed to transfer to the job site is a cop-out and a lie.

Real Training for Real People

How does real training work? Begin by abandoning notions of what people ought to know or what sort of attitudes they ought to have or even how people acquire knowledge. Instead ask, "How does one acquire skillfulness?"

The answer is simple and universal. The most efficient and effective way to acquire skillfulness is the same for everyone: (1) Students are quickly educated about the results they are being asked to achieve and the skills they will have to execute in order to obtain those results. (2) They practice, with a coach who can cut down trial-and-error time, until they achieve fluency.

That's it. All of it. Every time. In the hands of a good trainer or coach,

Step 1 takes up 5 percent to 10 percent of the allotted time. Step 2 takes up the other 90 percent or 95 percent. Step 1 is pure education. Step 2 is training.

Bluntly, if the student isn't doing it, it isn't training. A day spent talking about skills will not make anyone skillful. Nobody gets the "feel" for real execution, done to a specific standard of competence. Toss in a role play or two and they still don't get skillful. You find out only two things from role-plays, games and most sim-

---

IT'S ALL ABOUT BUY-IN

In the accompanying article, you are instructed to prepare for a training session by asking participants to bring business-improvement ideas to a meeting. Then you are supposed to open the meeting by describing the "soft" skills likely to be most useful in gaining support and commitment for those ideas.

The alert reader may have paused at that point, sensing a skunk in the rose bush: "You say this approach can be used to teach all kinds of interpersonal skills, from leadership to selling to teamwork. If I've got 10 or 20 people in the room, and I don't know what ideas they're going to pitch, how do I know in advance which skills they're going to need? And as far as that goes, it sounds as if the only thing anybody will be learning in this session is how to gain followers or commitment or 'buy-in' for a proposal. Maybe that is essentially what leadership and sales skills are about, but teamwork?"

Glad you asked.

I would argue that when it comes to doing business with one another or accomplishing work together, there really is only one set of interpersonal-communication skills that is truly significant. This skill set (or "master skill") is the one that enables us to achieve a state of rapport, trust, accord, mutual commitment — the condition known in the business world as "buy-in."

The skills taught (or talked about) under headings such as listening, influencing and negotiating are all elements of the skill set that leads us to buy-in. So are the interpersonal pieces of the skills taught under the labels of problem-solving and decision-making.

In the business world, very few of our attempts at interpersonal communication are intended merely to achieve understanding or agreement on an intellectual level. What we're after, most of the time, is buy-in.

Buy-in is what you and I get when we are in union both intellectually and emotionally in regard to a given course of action. When we reach that state of mutual commitment on some recommendation, we will act on it without reservation. In a sales situation, I will gladly buy your product. In a "teamwork" situation, we will put forth our best effort. We will keep our prom-ises. We will strive for "quality" performance.

So, yes, you can call it teamwork, as well as leadership or sales or management or anything you like. It all involves the same skill set for the same intended outcome: buy-in.

And these skills are not mysterious or difficult to measure. You can measure my skillfulness at leadership or selling or problem-solving simply by observing my ability to move another person (or people) toward buy-in. You can watch this happen. Whether I'm trying to sell Joe a three-piece suit or enlist his support for my new technology task force, you can watch him move, say, from indifference to hostility to competitiveness to moderate interest to full-fledged commitment.

The skills that move Joe toward buy-in are not only measurable, they are teachable. In bits and pieces, they are taught every day in corporate classrooms. But since the classes take an educational approach rather than a training approach — everyone learns about the skills instead of practicing them — nobody really becomes skillful.

If you want to train people in interpersonal business skills, have them practice gaining support from one another for real proposals, and coach them while they do. Make them practice and repeat each skill until they can perform fluently — with competence and confidence.

What skills are they practicing? Here are the basic ones. I would go so far as to propose that all "soft skills" are derived from these:

• The ability to open a conversation or interaction in a way that elicits open-mindedness.

• The ability to articulate goals.

• The ability to diagnose another person's needs and problems by listening effectively and asking good questions.

• Demonstrating respect for the other's views.

• Obtaining respect for your own views (advocating).

• Raising the conversation "up" the intellectual and emotional ladder in a way that the other person is willing and able to follow (by resolving conflict, forming solutions that meet the other's needs, negotiating for change and so on).

• Carrying the interaction all the way to "buy-in" (the other person is confident and firmly committed to the proposal; she agrees to act on it).

Most people can learn to do these things skillfully and successfully, at a level of conscious competence. But it takes real practice — practice that leads to a successful result that the person really desires. Education won't do the job. It requires training.

—J.G.

---

ulations: whether people grasped the main idea well enough to attempt the task, and whether they are any good at playing make-believe.

Again, if they don't acquire the "feel," they don't acquire the skill. Only training accomplishes that. Training is a lot tougher and can be much more time-consuming than education. Maybe that's why so few "trainers" ever do any of it.

Even readers who agree with these points may say: "Fine, but all of that would have to be done in the field. It can't be done in a classroom. And even if it weren't too expensive and difficult to put that many expert coaches in the field, we don't want our trainees practicing on real customers. So how do we make them proficient before we send them into the real job environment?"

There is a way.

How to Do It

Forget the idea of "classroom." A classroom is a place where education happens. It's a place where people learn about work instead of doing work.

To do real training in soft skills, start by taking a tip from advocates of "action learning": Invite people to a meeting room for a genuine working session — into which some coaching will be added.

The purpose of this working session is to evaluate and make decisions about ideas for improving the business: real ideas for real improvements that will make a real difference to the company. Ask participants to bring

---

HOW TO MAKE A LEVEL 3 EVALUATION OF SOFT-SKILLS TRAINING PAY DIVIDENDS

BY DAVE ZIELINSKI

With all the demands on a training function's time, doing a level 3 or level 4 program evaluation can seem almost masochistic. Few departments without dedicated program evaluation personnel have the luxury of time or dollars to evaluate training transfer to that depth.

But Vickie Shoutz, a human resources planning representative with Hutchinson Technology Inc., a computer components manufacturer, found some long-lasting benefits from a level 3 evaluation she did in a tooling department in her company. Those benefits made the additional time and dollars put toward the evaluation more than worthwhile, she says.

The evaluation was done for an interpersonal skills training program delivered to 150 tool-and-dye makers. The program, Employee Interaction, created by Pittsburgh-based Development Dimensions International (DDI), features modules like communicating effectively, handling conflict and other interpersonal skills. Tooling department managers had requested the training following growing reports from some internal customers that dealings with the tooling department were often strained and marked with miscommunication.

The Pre-Training Work

The important thing is to design evaluation steps into the process as you design the course itself, not after the fact, Shoutz says. She and colleague Julie Page worked with James Robinson of the consulting firm Partners in Change to develop the evaluation protocol. "He worked with us off and on throughout the process, giving us some topnotch advice about when to do level 3 evaluations — and when not to — and how to carry them out," Shoutz says.

Shoutz's program involved two pre-training steps:

1. Administering surveys designed to establish a baseline of interpersonal skill levels. Front-liners, team leaders, and supervisors in the department — and maybe most importantly, the tooling group's internal customers — were all asked to rate the group's interaction skills. There were self-assessment surveys, and assessments of peer, subordinate, and supervisor skills.

Skills rated included two-way communication in one-on-one interactions, clarity of information provided, detail provided in interactions, responding with empathy, ability at dealing with conflict, and team-to-team interaction skills.

2. Holding focus groups to gather more qualitative data. In this step, Shoutz interviewed another set of front-liners, supervisors, and internal customers. "This information was critical — it rounded out the picture, and gave us some concrete examples of interaction problems and their causes," Shoutz says.

The Post-Training Work

Some three to four months after the training ended, the same groups were asked to rate the group's interaction skills on paper surveys and in focus groups. Using a scale of 0% to 100%, the pre-training surveys had shown the tooling group used the required interaction skills only 50% of the time. The post-training surveys showed employees were using those skills approximately 75% of the time, Shoutz says.

Training also followed up with supervisors six months after training to reinforce use of those skills, and to inquire how they believed the training had paid off. "Managers were still talking up the program results six and nine months following it," she claims.

Total tab for the effort? About $110,000, including needs analysis, program customization, survey design and data collection, consultant fees, trainer costs, and participant costs. Shoutz estimates she, Page, and some others spent about 800 hours on the evaluation.

The discovery of work environment problems was an unexpected benefit of the process. The tooling department works in two separate buildings. Those in one building complained in evaluation focus groups that its shadowy, cramped nature made the environment depressing, and affected their ability to be model communicators. The folks in the other building, working with more natural light, high ceilings, and more ample work space, reported no such problem. Management has since addressed the problem with building design changes.

---

their own ideas to the meeting. Stipulate that these ideas must meet two criteria. First, the people in the meeting must be capable of implementing them; that is, someone in the room must have the authority to give a real yes or no to the idea. Second, if adopted, the improvement must be both measurable and capable of producing financial consequences for the business within 90 days.

In other words, you don't want ideas such as, "Let's change the cafeteria's vending machines." That might be an improvement, all right, but it's unlikely to produce a measurable roi within three months.

Ideas that would fit the criteria should sound more like these:

• "Suppose that instead of having a single sales rep call on the ABC Co., we put together a sales team of reps and technical specialists. I believe that this team could get ABC's business within 90 days."

• "I think we could achieve 50 percent faster turnaround on customer orders if we combined credit checking and warehouse dispatch under a single management function. We'd be more competitive, and I believe we'd start getting more orders within 90 days."

• "I think we could reduce breakage and waste on the Illinois plant production line if we changed suppliers. Let's use a local company instead of shipping from Detroit."

Explain to the participants that they are gathered in the room to make decisions about issues like these and to execute the ideas they like — or at least to set the execution wheels in motion. They are not just there to "learn stuff."

Now, give them a quick educational overview of the skills that would most likely help them gain the commitment and support they'll need to implement their ideas (see box page 54). You must also clearly define what "skillful" means — not just what the skills are. For instance, you are skillful

at "showing respect" if you can acknowledge another person's point of view so well that the person begins to feel better — you can see more positive emotions emanating from the person — within 20 seconds. You are skillful at "leadership" if you can obtain a following of committed supporters who actually will show up and work on a task force to achieve the goals of Project X.

Make this introduction as succinct as possible. Then put everyone to work on the task of trying to gain commitment and support from one another. Coach them while they do so. (At the same time, you can teach them how to coach one another.) Make them do it over and over again

---

Knowledge isn't power. Competence is power.

---

until at least 85 percent of them have become proficient at the skills and have achieved concrete, desirable results.

An obvious "desirable result" is that a participant gains the needed support and approval for a good idea. A less-obvious but no-less-acceptable result is that the participant becomes persuaded that his idea is a stinker, but accepts this with no hard feelings; that is, the participant and his "adversary" agree that the idea is a nonstarter, and emerge with their relationship undamaged or even strengthened.

Measurements

Everything that happens after that brief educational introduction is training. Measurably defined skills are developed until fluency is observable in the here and now. Further, the out-

comes of these interactions are tangible commitments for actual business initiatives that have measurable financial outcomes — the elusive "Level 4" result that trainers talk about so much but discover so seldom.

And you can stop worrying about "reinforcement." Why? Because we all naturally keep doing what works. We only need the goading or encouragement or reminding of managers when we can't produce the results we want.

Doing real training is perfectly feasible, even with large groups of people. This approach — educate briefly, then train at length — is the method of martial arts trainers. It's the method of sports teams. It's the method of coaches in the performing arts. It works. The formula once again:

1. Clearly define the measure of skillfulness required. What does the performance look like when it's done right?

2. Clearly define the measurable outcome desired. What is the intended result of the performance?

3. "Educate" quickly and precisely.

4. Then train, via coached repetition, until the measurable performance level and the desired result are consistently achieved.

This formula almost always achieves measurable success, regardless of the skills you're trying to develop: selling, leadership, teamwork, customer service, problem-solving and so on. Instead of seeing slight improvements in the performance of those 15 percent of trainees who were already capable, you'll send 85 percent out the door with genuine skillfulness instead of mere awareness.

Because the group is producing real initiatives that will make or save money, your company can expect a very healthy return on investment within three months. And nobody will have to ask you again if your training actually makes a difference.

Making Competencies Pay Off

Are you busy drawing up lists of 'competencies' for every job in your organization? Hold the phone. Here's how to use the strategy more effectively.

BY TIMM J. ESQUE AND
THOMAS F. GILBERT

The notion of "competencies" has gained a great deal of currency in the training world. Some advocates go so far as to suggest that it should be the basis for all human resource management. The idea is to define a set of competencies for each job in the organization — a list of things that the jobholder must be able to do. These job-specific competencies become the basis for hiring, developing and compensating employees within those jobs.

The danger here is that the term competencies can lead people to err by focusing on behaviors instead of on accomplishments. It is really the accomplishments of the job performer — the results the person produces — that have value to the organization. The specific behaviors that go into producing those accomplishments are important, but they are a secondary concern. Unless we begin our analysis of a job by determining the valuable accomplishments we want the performer to produce, we're likely to make mistakes about which behaviors are really important (see box p. 58).

Since competencies have become a popular tool, let's see if we can clarify how to use them productively for employee development. Specifically, how can we use the notion of competencies to improve the current and future performance of employees? Before we can answer that question, we'll need to clarify what we understand to be the purpose of developing lists of competencies.

The Purpose

Regarding current performance, the purpose of defining competencies is to give people information about what they need to do to prepare themselves to succeed at their current jobs. Employees are provided with a list of competencies associated with their jobs. They are expected to work with their supervisors or peers to determine which of the defined competencies they already possess and which they need to acquire. Presumably, if they acquire all of the competencies associated with their jobs (or at least the "right" ones), they will succeed and the organization will benefit.

> **We are only interested in outcomes that are necessary and sufficient to achieve the mission.**

Regarding future performance, competencies are supposed to serve a similar purpose. "Future performance" can refer to continued success in the same job when the requirements for that job are changing, or simply to performance in a different job that the individual plans to hold in the future. Theoretically, an organization that does a good job identifying emerging competencies will benefit because its employees will be better prepared to succeed when their jobs change or when they change jobs.

In either case, present or future, the point of defining competencies is to provide information to help a person prepare to be successful in a job.

Now we can be clear about the effective use of competencies. Competencies are being used effectively when individuals continually succeed at their jobs and, as a result, the entire organization benefits.

Drawing up lists of competencies for each job in an organization is not very difficult, but how can we be sure that because these lists are provided, individuals will succeed in their jobs and the organization will benefit? What really has to happen in order for competencies to have an impact on the organization's performance? We suggest that the following requirements need to be met:

1. The information conveyed by competencies must accurately describe how individuals can prepare to succeed at their (current or future) jobs.

2. Individuals must, in fact, acquire the competencies needed to succeed at their jobs.

3. Individuals must be able to exhibit these acquired competencies in the appropriate sequence at the right times.

4. Individual success on the job must be defined by the requirements for success of the organization. In other words, if the organization is not succeeding, then individuals by definition are not succeeding either.

When a list of competencies is defined and put to use, and it meets all four of those requirements, we can say that the organization is using competencies effectively. But we still haven't defined exactly what competencies are. So let us suggest the following operational definition: Competencies are behaviors that assist the performer to overcome known barriers to achieving the performance standards.

The question becomes, how do we identify competencies that meet our requirements and fit that operational definition?

Developing Effective Competencies

The table on p. 58 describes a process for identifying competencies that, if acquired, will help overcome known barriers to successful performance. Next to each step in the process are some questions that need to be answered.

Let's apply the steps in the table to a simplified industry example. Suppose we were going to identify competencies for the design engineers at a paper clip company. We begin by asking: What is the mission of these engineers?

Design engineers do a variety of things, but their ultimate output, for contributing to organizational goals, is new (or modified) products. They produce paper clip designs — and in order for the designs to contribute to the company's goals, the paper clips probably need to be easily manufacturable, meet customers' quality requirements, and be ready for production according to some schedule. We have just defined the mission of the design engineers and some criteria to evaluate their success.

The next step is to identify major outcomes (or accomplishments) that result in achieving the mission. We're not talking about a list of tasks here; we want to know the subproducts that lead to the ultimate product. Some of the things the engineers produce are design specifications, product test plans, product performance reports and so on. We are only interested in outcomes that are necessary and sufficient to achieve the mission.

For each of these things the engineers produce, we need to be specific about how we would know if an engineer (or team) had produced it, and if it was any good. Let's look at design specifications as an example.

Several people are going to use the design specs later, so the document needs to include the information needed by all of the different users. It has to be written so that each of those users interprets it the way the design engineer intended. It also probably needs to provide evidence for the customers that the resulting product will meet their stated requirements — and how that will be demonstrated.

Next we want to establish how we can tell, when evaluating design specs, if each of the requirements has been met. For example, we know who will use the specs later, so they can help us design a checklist of the types of information the specs must contain.

How will we know if each user interprets the specs as intended? One way we'll know is if somebody uses the specs to do something that the design engineer didn't intend. That won't prevent the problem but it will tell us, after the fact, if a requirement was met. It might be better to have a specs review meeting, where the users ask questions of the design engineers whenever anything is not crystal clear.

The length of these meetings and the number of spec rewrites required afterward might be an excellent measure of this "interpretation" requirement. It is best to be as clear as possible about how success will be measured for every single requirement.

Experienced design engineers and their managers should have some idea about how well these requirements have been met in the past. A performance standard should be identified for each measure of an outcome requirement. The standard should represent how well the best performers have met the requirements of each outcome.

That standard, derived from the very best performers, becomes a realistic goal for every design engineer. Why? Because this process we are going through is meant to remove the barriers that prevent achievement of the desired standards every time a product is designed.

No.	Step	Questions to be Answered
	A PROCESS FOR IDENTIFYING COMPETENCIES THAT REALLY MATTER	
1	Define the mission of the job.	a. What is the ultimate product or service that results from this job?
		b. Is this the product or service that best describes how this job contributes to the goals of the organization?
		c. How would I know if the mission had been achieved (what are the success criteria for achieving the mission)?
2	Describe the major outcomes (accomplishments) required to achieve the mission.	a. What are the necessary and sufficient outcomes that result in achieving the mission of the job?
3	Define performance standards for each major outcome.	a. What are the requirements of success for this outcome?
		b. How can each requirement be measured?
		c. How well do the best performers perform against these measures today?
4	Identify known barriers to achieving the performance standards.	a. What has prevented people from achieving the standards in the past?
		b. Which barriers, if overcome, will provide the greatest performance improvements?
5	Determine which barriers will be best overcome by training the performer.	a. Would the barrier best be addressed by:
		• clarifying performance expectations?
		• providing performance feedback?
		• providing better tools (or job aids)?
		• teaching the performer certain behaviors that will assist in overcoming known barriers to achieving the performance standards?
6	Develop (or buy) and deliver training	a. What is the briefest training that will allow the performer to overcome the targeted barrier?
		b. Could a job aid be provided instead of training?

That brings us to barrier identification. Why is it that some design specs get interpreted differently from the original intent? Maybe different design engineers use different language to describe the same things. Maybe some users of the specs have their own ideas about how the product should be made, and they choose to ignore parts of the specs. Maybe every design spec document looks so different that the users don't learn anything from one to the next.

By discussing these issues with the design engineers and the users of the specs, and by reviewing some of the specs, we can generate a list of potential barriers.

It is a good idea to go through some process to shorten the list to those few barriers that people seem to agree on. Eventually you will have identified barriers pertaining to each outcome (or even each requirement). It probably isn't possible (or desirable) to act on every barrier at once, so you want to identify the ones likely to provide the biggest bang for the buck.

Those barriers identified as needing immediate attention should then be examined in light of the questions in Step 5 of the table. Not every barrier means that design engineers lack a competency. In the case of interpreting the design specs, it is possible that design engineers have never had the chance to receive input or feedback from the users of the specs. All that may be needed is a review meeting to give design engineers the opportunity to hear how the users interpret their work.

Then again, maybe the design engineers have gotten this feedback, but they all have their own personal style for developing specs and that is causing a problem for the users. In this case we might want to get the engineers to behave more uniformly in regard to the format and language they use.

This would seem to be a competency issue for design engineers, as we've operationally defined competencies. But even in this case, we don't want to jump to the conclusion that training courses are warranted. If some simple rules for formatting the specs were clearly stated, would the design engineers really need training, or would they just need to review those rules before they write their next spec document? This general line of thinking should be applied to each

continued on p. 61

COMPETENCIES VS. ACCOMPLISHMENTS

BY THOMAS GILBERT

In a 1978 book called *Human Competence: Engineering Worthy Performance*, I defined competence as the worthy outputs of behavior. I asserted that competence has to do with the accomplishments that certain behaviors enable us to produce, and not with the behaviors themselves.

Recently there seems to be more discussion about "competencies" than competence. The word competency typically implies "behaviors exhibited when the performer is performing well." But what does it mean to perform well? Organizations are primarily interested in behaviors or activities that have value — that are worthy. The only way to tell if activities are worthy is to look at the outputs that result from them: a well-made product, a big sale, an excellent safety record, a delighted customer.

Thus, worthy performance is evidenced by people's accomplishments, not by their behaviors. Unfortunately, the use of the term competencies seems to be putting the focus on behaviors at the expense of accomplishments.

It is argued that in order to achieve valued accomplishments a person must exhibit a certain set of correct behaviors (or competencies). This is most certainly what you will be told if you begin analyzing a job by asking experts how they do it.

But in 30 years of observing exemplary (and nonexemplary) performers, I have not found this to be the case. In fact, I have found a surprisingly low consistency in how exemplary performers do their jobs. In other words, two exemplars are likely to exhibit quite different behaviors in the course of producing their masterful results.

I came upon a classic example in a company that sold forklifts. One exemplary forklift sales representative spent much of his time cruising through the countryside looking for abandoned warehouses that might be open-

ing in the future. Another spent his mornings on the phone tracking down leads. Still another top sales rep (who hated phones) sorted through all manner of paperwork — building codes and the like — looking for prospects.

All three were distinguished from the rest of the sales representatives by one thing: Their prospecting was excellent, and it led to sales, an accomplishment highly valued by this company — and most others.

The best way to improve performance is to begin by observing it: Determine which performers are really achieving worthy accomplishments and understand why. But for a variety of reasons, it is often difficult to make direct observations of performance the first step of a job analysis.

When this is the case, the method described in the accompanying article is the next best thing; you are still beginning by identifying the valued accomplishments and focusing on overcoming barriers to those accomplishments.

The popularity of "competencies" (and loose definitions) seems to lead many organizations to focus solely on behaviors when analyzing performance. This can greatly reduce the effectiveness of training and other performance interventions.

We are not suggesting abolishing the term competencies. Training professionals need to be ready and able to communicate in the language of their clients, and many clients are using the C-word these days. The process we present here is described in terms of competencies so that you can respond to clients who ask for competencies. Obviously, the same method can be used without anyone ever mentioning the term — whenever your client is simply looking to improve performance in a way that really matters.

Just remember: To be effective, accomplishments first; behaviors second.

GIVE LEADER COMPETENCIES SOME BITE —
TIE THEM TO NEAR-TERM GOALS

BY DAVE ZIELINSKI

There's no greater incentive for managers to change or build new leadership skills than knowledge that they'll need to do so to meet near-term business goals. That essential truth remains lost on a lot of training efforts, says John Murphy of The Executive Edge consulting firm, particularly when it comes to creating management competencies.

Murphy, a long-time HRD manager with GTE and later Northeast Utilities, says companies should dismantle traditional approaches to competency models. Most competencies focus too much on behaviors at the expense of results, Murphy claims.

He says trainers should shun what many popular vendor competency models promise: a shotgun approach to building multiple competencies with no real tie to business goals. "We shouldn't want to address the total range of skills managers need to become some theoretical 'ideal' manager. Our development efforts are already too scattershot."

The answer, Murphy says, is to first identify a handful — three or four — key business goals for managers to strive for in a year or two, and then identify competencies to get to those goals. He calls this a "results first, change second" approach.

How It Worked at Northeast Utilities

At Northeast Utilities in Berlin, CT, where Murphy served as HRD director, he had a chance to put his system into practice. The year before he arrived, senior officers were assessed in performance appraisals largely on 10 competencies, with some 70 supporting behaviors. "In theory, they could be 'called' by their bosses on any of those 10," he says. He finally convinced them to toss out that model, renaming competencies "management actions" and creating goals around only three "actions": performance management/developing people, strategy, and implementation. Then, Murphy and his staff asked senior managers a question: "If it turns out you don't meet these business goals, what do you think the reasons might be?" In other words, begin by identifying valued results you want, then focus managers on how they can overcome barriers to those accomplishments.

Murphy tested the system with a pilot program in a nuclear division that had a history of failed HRD efforts. He asked managers in the division for their top three "make or break" goals for the next two years. The $100,000 pilot was completely funded by HRD.

The performance challenge: The head of the division admitted his managers could probably achieve the goals the old way, "by managers simply overworking and riding their people," Murphy says. "But he knew there wasn't much mileage left in that approach. And we told him if nothing else at all comes of this HRD project, at a minimum we would help him accomplish those three goals. The 'gravy' would be his people would develop new management processes and team skills in the process."

The three goals:

1. Achieve 90% schedule adherence in the plant. Each day there are a series of events — safety checks, maintenance, etc. — scheduled to happen at specific times. Current performance: 70% adherence.

2. Boost performance of staff that supports operators of a $3 million control panel for the nuclear reactor. Too often the operators, who already had their hands full, had to do the jobs of support staff themselves.

3. Reduce the time for shutdowns from an average 54 days to 30 days, which would save millions. Nuclear plants undergo regular shutdowns for refueling and repair. Typically plans for such a shutdown are completed 90 days in advance. The goal was to have a plan ready by Dec. 31, 1996 — for a March 1998 shutdown. In other words, managers wanted a shutdown plan completed in three months, rather than the typical 15 months.

HRD's response: Line managers had a good idea of what needed to be changed, but not how to do it. That's where Murphy and Co. came in. Three teams in the division began working toward the goals, with an HRD rep on each team. "We stated up-front we had no silver bullet," Murphy says. "We told them the way they would meet these goals would be by improving their management performance which, by the way, would result in their being better managers when they were done."

Team members first benchmarked other nuclear plants to find out how they set and met similar goals. "We filled a situation room with flip charts listing goals and upcoming deadlines, and discussed what was keeping us from performing. The idea was to set clear and enforceable ground rules." HRD helped managers examine root causes of performance gaps. Then, maybe most importantly, they helped managers lay out specific actions the teams would take in week one, week two, and down the line to work toward the three goals.

"Much of it was management 101 stuff," Murphy says, "except we were using an urgent need to meet goals in 90 days as a way to motivate people" and create a change template managers could use again to meet other goals — without HRD's help.

When Training Helps Managers Act
Behaviors Change Quickly

Two months into the project, the unit director asked Murphy to stop by his office. "He told me he was very skeptical about the project going in, and had I not come to him with the CEO's stamp of approval, he wouldn't have let me in the door.

"But then he said it was the quickest achievement of results, and the fastest change in his managers' behavior, he had ever seen in the division. He said the action plans we helped develop were simple, but they had never used them before. He said his managers would have never made these changes had they gone through a classroom course, then come back to their jobs and wondered how to apply the knowledge. They had to have that result stake first."

continued from p. 59

barrier to determine the most effective (and cost-effective) way to remove it.

Out of this analysis, a plan emerges for overcoming the barriers that limit performance. To remove some of these barriers, the design engineers will have to acquire certain competencies. But now it will be clear exactly how acquiring each competency will lead to the achievement of organizational goals. Using this process, we are able to identify competencies that are linked to important business goals; therefore, they are measurably worth the effort expended to develop and apply them.

Tips for Developing Useful Competencies

Generating a list of competencies is easy. Identifying a set of useful competencies is harder. Here's how to avoid a few of the most common pitfalls.

The first obstacle to a successful analysis is defining the mission. Through decades of conditioning, most of us have learned to analyze work in terms of jobs. But when you try to paint a picture of a job, you are likely to include lots of work (or activities) that do not directly result in valuable outcomes; that is, most jobs involve a lot of tasks that don't really contribute to organizational goals.

Useful mission statements are usually associated more with specific business processes than with whole jobs. Invariably you find that more

than one job contributes to the success of a mission.

Returning to the paper clip example, the mission of producing a paper clip design that is easily manufacturable, meets customer requirements, and is completed on schedule is largely the responsibility of design engineers. However, responsibility for designing a product is often shared by a team of design engineers, and many other jobs play a role in the success of this mission.

For example, for every new paper clip design, one or more people from marketing will interrogate the customers who define the requirements for that product. People from manufacturing may also play a role in the design process to ensure that the end design is manufacturable (in very measurable ways).

When we set out to find a clear mission, we are more likely to find it in a process than in a job (in this case, design engineering or product development as opposed to "design engineer"). It is the process with a clearly stated mission that provides our link to organizational objectives and, ultimately, business impact.

You will probably begin this whole analysis by focusing on a specific job, and that's fine. But if you are proceeding correctly, it is likely that you will soon find yourself describing a process — and that other jobs will come into play. In fact, some of the key barriers to success that you identify will likely involve these other jobs in addition to or instead of the one

you started with. Avoid getting hung up trying to remain focused on a particular job. That several jobs play a role in the process just means there are more opportunities to identify and overcome barriers to success.

The other major consideration for a successful analysis involves the training professional's role in the effort. Because this analysis is going to identify more than training issues, you would like your clients — the people who perform the jobs you're analyzing, and their managers — to feel as much ownership for the initiative as possible.

The clients need your help to do this analysis, because it requires discipline to focus on outcomes and measures before jumping to conclusions about barriers and solutions. But in the end, you will be better off if they consider the end product their own work.

The analysis allows the clients to discover that there are lots of barriers to success that are not under the direct control of the performers (design engineers in our example). As they make these discoveries, it is imperative that they seek ownership for these barriers from people who can do something about them. In most cases, that means line managers and executives, not the training professional.

Keeping those two considerations in mind will greatly enhance your chances of developing useful competencies.

Notes:

Deciding Who to Train

Strategic management of human resources requires admitting not all employees are created equal.

BY BRIAN MCDERMOTT

Training professionals, as a group, don't like to make discriminatory judgments or comparisons about people, according to George Odiorne, management professor at Eckerd College. But lumping employees into a few broad categories can be an effective strategy for managing human resources, he told attendees at a Training Directors' Forum Conference.

Odiorne, who pioneered the development of Management By Objectives (MBO), says, "Not every training dollar you spend gives you the same return." Some training offers an immediate return but is not an investment in human capital; sales training is an example. By contrast, some training is almost purely an investment in a company's people. By classifying workers according to their job performance and potential, Odiorne says, it's possible to make strategic decisions about managing and training personnel in order to effectively develop their strongest assets for the company.

Shining Stars

Odiorne's model is based on the Boston Consulting Group's (BCG) design for categorizing a business's products or divisions according to their profitability. Employees with high job performance and high potential are stars; those with high job performance and low potential are workhorses; those with low performance and high potential are the problem children; and those with low performance and low potential are the deadwood.

"This is an oversimplification, but it's a conceptual idea that can help in thinking about human resources strategy." Stars, Odiorne says, should be trained to assume general management positions. He recommends spending approximately 10 percent of a training budget for this purpose, and he suggests using mentoring as a primary source of training for this group. Another 10 percent should be spent on the problem children.

The remaining 80 percent of the budget, he says, should be used to train the workhorses; they do the bulk of the work, and therefore, they need and deserve the most training. Workhorses, Odiorne says, make good bureaucrats for running a company's cash cows, which, according to the BCG model, are the divisions that have high market shares, large profits, but low potential for growth.

Effective training interventions for the workhorses include quality circles, team building, selling techniques, work simplification, value engineering and profit improvement. Many organizations get into trouble training their workhorses, Odiorne says, because they set people's expectations toward promotions rather than toward learning to do their present jobs better. It's generally agreed that due to shifts in work force demographics, promotions are — and will be — more difficult to earn for the current working generation.

Training Strategies

During small-group sessions, attendees at the Forum developed the following training strategies and ideas based on Odiorne's model:

- Mentors might be found outside an organization, possibly from among a company's board of directors.
- The deadwood should be confronted about making self-assessments about their future with their companies.
- Problem children might respond favorably to relocation or counseling.
- Consider these six factors when assessing potential: performance in current job; desire to move upward; level of education; level of intelligence; specific experience; availability for promotion.
- Gather and present background information on mentoring programs to your company's top management. Identify your stars and mentors, then work with mentors to come up with developmental activities, special jobs and other tactics for training those high-potential people.
- When dealing with problem children, decide why these people are problem employees. Some stars may be ex-problem employees who have been mellowed by tough experiences in other organizations. It may be possible to turn troubled employees around before they move to another company and blossom.
- Train all employees "how to do things around this organization" so they can avoid appearing as troublemakers.
- Work to eliminate the perception that if you get more training you will earn more promotions.
- Coaching could be an effective strategy for working with problem children. Determine if it is the situation or the individual causing the turmoil. Identify where these people would fit best in your organization.
- Determine what the ideal mix of stars, workhorses and problem children is for your organization. Does the company need more stars? Could a few strategically placed problem children create favorable results?
- Stars are highly motivated to learn, but typically are moving quickly within an organization and unwilling or unavailable to participate in training programs. On-the-job training will be most critical for this group.
- Competition among stars is likely to be high, and therefore, team building is essential.
- Stars have a strong bias for action. As a result, they are more likely to make mistakes. An organization must tolerate these failure/learning experiences.
- The glamour and allure of working with stars or saving problem children can be very attractive for trainers. Don't let it distract you from your main job — training the workhorses.

Assessments

Odiorne suggests there are at least three techniques for assessing and categorizing employees: using assessment centers; having meetings for managers to identify from their experiences the performance levels and potential of employees; and having the training staff conduct tests.

Companies that make a constant and unremitting investment in their people are likely to be among the leaders in their fields, but not every employee needs or deserves the same kind of training, Odiorne says. Although training executives may be reluctant to make those judgments, he says, it doesn't mean those judgments aren't being made somehow.

"Not everybody can be a company president. Some will make it, some won't." The challenge for training directors, Odiorne says, is to make strategic decisions about training that will help employees to be rewarded appropriately and to help a company increase profits.

Notes:

The Care and Breeding of Global Managers

Global companies need global managers. But what is such a creature — and how do you develop one?

BY BEVERLY GEBER

Years ago an overseas assignment for an ambitious manager in a U.S. company meant exciting challenges, an intriguing new culture to explore, and the opportunity to stretch oneself personally and professionally. In most cases, it also meant the guillotine for his career.

Considering the times, it was understandable. In the post-World War II era, most American companies were so busy mining their own huge, affluent domestic market that selling their wares in another country was merely a profitable afterthought. Products were designed for the U.S. market; if consumers in other countries happened to like those products, they were welcome to buy them. If foreign sales were strong, it was easy enough to set up a small sales and marketing office in another country, staff it with a manager whose absence wouldn't hurt the company, and wait for the gravy to flow.

The trouble — from the perspective of the expatriate manager — was that out of sight meant out of mind. Because executives devoted little time or attention to overseas markets, they tended to forget about the guy stuck in a foreign post.

Some companies found it easy to develop "foreign corps" of managers who spent their careers moving from country to country. If an expatriate complained loudly enough about being pigeonholed or forgotten, he might be moved back to the States, but not necessarily into a higher-level position. After all, executives reasoned, a manager may have worked miracles in Sweden, but why would that qualify him for a promotion back home? It wasn't as if Swedish exper-

tise could help him sell merchandise in Nevada or Okla-homa.

It didn't help the visibility of those expatriate managers that their numbers were steadily dwindling. Under pressure from foreign governments, many U.S.-based multinationals steadily cut back the number of American managers assigned overseas so that foreign nationals could be developed for top spots in satellite offices.

In most companies that maintain a strong international presence today, things have changed. Credit "globalism," perhaps the hottest business buzzword around. It's not enough to say that today's multinationals recognize that the U.S. market isn't the only one in the world. Some perceive that their efforts in Singapore or Brazil are *at least* as important as their activities at home. Even companies that compete only domestically must stay abreast of developments in their industries around the world if they want to compete successfully with foreign firms that are storming into the U.S. market.

"Whether companies like it or not, they're competing globally," says John Garrison, manager of recruitment and development for Colgate-Palmolive Co. in New York. Smart companies recognize this, he adds, and are trying to fill their executive ranks with managers who have international experience. Procter & Gamble CEO Edwin Artzt, for instance, was head of the company's international operations for nine years before winning the top spot.

That's no longer a remarkable path into a corner office, says David Weeks, head of Weeks and Associates Inc., a Bridgewater, NJ, consulting firm. Recently, while working for The

Conference Board, a New York City business research firm, Weeks studied the efforts of 130 companies to recruit and develop "global" managers.

It's a rare multinational that hasn't devoted considerable thought to the question of developing global managers. But there is more consensus on what the animal is than on how to breed it. Most companies would not argue too much with this definition: A "global manager" is someone with a strong interest in and tolerance for other cultures and who understands how a particular decision might affect a company's many markets or competitors around the world.

"If you develop a product in your market, you have to be thinking if this will play in Korea. It's understanding the linkages between countries," says John Fulkerson, vice president of organization and management development for Pepsi-Cola International in Somers, NY.

How does one create such understanding? Some companies believe that the only way to cultivate a global manager is to let her conduct business in as many foreign milieus as possible. Others think a global manager is merely a person with a "global perspective," which can be developed almost as easily in a training class as in a foreign outpost.

Fulkerson belongs to the camp that says you can't grow real global managers in a cultural vacuum. "It's difficult to have that understanding without living in another culture. You can have some understanding by reading, but you can't have that gut-level understanding without working across borders," he says.

Managers at work in other countries experience things they never will at home. The mere act of dealing with a foreign government can be an immensely eye-opening experience. Often, foreign branches are just starting up, so they offer lessons in entrepreneurship unavailable on the home turf of an established corporation. And there's no question that day-to-day life is...educational.

"Once you take an offshore assignment, you're going to be 'marred' for the rest of your life because you're going to look at things differently," Fulkerson says. "You don't get upset about not being able to get a call through for 10 minutes, when it used to take two hours in another country."

Starting Early

In order to develop a global perspective in employees, organizations have made some significant changes in their approach to international job assignments, according to The Conference Board's study. Among the 130 companies surveyed, 112 were U.S.-based multinationals, 12 were based in Europe and six in Asia.

Researcher Weeks found some interesting differences between U.S.-based and non-U.S. multinationals. For one thing, non-U.S. companies are more likely to have top managers with international experience.

A main finding about U.S. firms was that companies are giving employees international experience much earlier than they used to. In the past, an international assignment may have hinted that the midcareer manager was being kicked off the fast track. Today, an overseas assignment is likely to be an indication that the person is a "high-potential" employee being given a developmental assignment as a route to a top spot.

Shrewd companies collar fast-trackers very early in their careers — sometimes right out of college — and tell them what they can expect in the way of international assignments during their rise within the company. In some global companies, a refusal to take an overseas assignment may well mean a derailed career.

According to Weeks and other observers, few companies nurture global managers better than Colgate-Palmolive. The company has been truly "global" much longer than most corporations. Colgate earns about two-thirds of its $6 billion annual revenue from overseas operations. If anything, says Garrison, the company needs to concentrate on doing better in the U.S. market, where it faces its stiffest competition.

Because overseas markets have been the company's sustenance for years, international assignments are prized, and most senior managers have had some foreign experience, Garrison says.

Even so, in 1987 the company decided to fine-tune its approach to recruiting and developing future stars. It draws off the cream of the college crop and offers graduates the choice of two tracks. Those who are eager for international assignments can get one within 18 months, after they have been properly inculcated into Colgate's operations. The U.S.

track allows new employees to begin their careers in the States, moving to an international assignment some five or six years hence. So sought after are these putative "high-potential" positions that the company gets about 15,000 applications annually for a maximum of 30 spots.

Candidates for both tracks are counseled about what they could expect for a career path along either of those avenues. Not only does the system lend rigor to the employee-development process, it also gives potential employees some flexibility. International experience may be necessary for a top-level career at Colgate, but the company doesn't want to lose promising, high-potential candidates who are unwilling to move self and family overseas at that point in their lives.

In some global companies, a refusal to take an overseas assignment may mean a derailed career.

Family is one reason Pepsi-Cola tries to send its employees overseas early in their careers. The company has found that managers are more willing to move their families if the children are quite young rather than after the kids have reached adolescence.

Still, although there is a clear trend toward giving foreign assignments earlier in a manager's career, there is no cookie-cutter approach. 3M, for instance, uses a formal process to identify the top talent in the organization and make sure those people get overseas assignments during their careers. Almost always, these candidates will have spent some years at home before being dispatched abroad. "We believe that a person can best come into 3M and learn the culture, processes and philosophy. Then he or she would be better able to represent our businesses," says Bruce Hoeffel, 3M's executive director of international human resources.

Johnson & Johnson isn't necessarily sending its managers abroad any earlier than before, but the company is increasing the number of overseas

assignments — and making sure that its "high-potential" people fill them. Michael Longua, director of international recruiting and personnel development, says the company used to staff its foreign offices mostly with indigenous managers, who would be brought to this country for developmental stints. But J&J recently has begun to weave its American fast-trackers into those overseas offices as a way to give the young people a global perspective. It asks U.S. managers to identify candidates whose absence would "hurt," Longua says. "That's how we know it's really a high-potential person."

In The Conference Board's study, Weeks found that not all people chosen for these assignments are managers. Increasingly, companies are sending technical professionals and even support staff for these broadening experiences.

Steve Powell, manager of the North American task group for Honda of America in Marysville, OH, oversees a new program that is sending a broad cross section of U.S. employees to Japan on assignment. In the past, Japanese employees came to the United States for managerial stints, but U.S. employees went to Japan only for training or on short business trips.

Now, not only do U.S. employees gain direct knowledge of technological advances and of how business is conducted in another culture, but Honda has found this to be an efficient method for diffusing good ideas throughout the company. For instance, Powell says, the Marysville plant is one of the first to use a water-borne paint system in mass production. Japanese plants aren't using it — yet. But who knows what will happen if you throw the technical experts together? "If you take the experience of both sides, you can develop something that didn't exist before," Powell says.

That's another reason for the short overseas stints The Conference Board found to be more common. Employees may be sent somewhere on a specific project for a period of months. Sometimes, an ulterior motive of the short-term project is to prepare the traveler for a longer stay someplace overseas later on. A six-month stay in a place like Singapore can indicate whether a person tolerates other cultures well. For other employees, especially technical professionals, these short trips may constitute the only overseas experience of their careers.

Not only do short-term projects give the traveler a dose of another culture, they often enable the company's finest minds to connect. In addition, short stints reduce or eliminate the need to bring along the family; that saves the company a lot of money. And short assignments make it much more likely that employees will agree to go in the first place. It's tough to persuade an employee with a career-minded spouse to accept a lengthy offshore assignment.

How Tolerant Are You?

Overseas assignments may breed global managers, but that's seldom the primary reason they're sent abroad. The assignments are driven by the needs of the business. A manager may believe her high-potential subordinate ought to get some overseas experience, but that doesn't mean the organization has a suitable opening. Also, a company usually must balance its desire to develop global managers with its need to hire and promote people in the country in which it operates.

Few global companies are haphazard about selection and promotion. The Conference Board found that nearly three-fourths of the companies studied use formal succession plans — and not just for the handful of top positions in the company. Motorola Inc., based in Schaumburg, IL, uses a complicated system that identifies two or three people to succeed each employee. Bill Faust, program manager for leadership development at Motorola University, says the system looks for the best person for the job, but also takes into account the kinds of experiences an individual might need if he is on a fast track into upper management.

Overseas assignments are not automatic for fast-trackers. A person may have the skills to fill an open position and the need to gain the experience, but that doesn't mean she's ready for the challenge. Pepsi looks carefully at the candidate's background, perhaps to see if she has vacationed offshore extensively. There are also exhaustive interviews with the employee and spouse to make sure she understands the markets she's going to, and they begin to understand how different the culture is.

Fulkerson says Pepsi also gives the employee a special test. "It's a mea-sure of your ability and flexibility to live and work with people of a different culture," he says. Among the attributes it examines: tolerance, patience, flexibility and a sense of humor about strange situations. Later, the employee and spouse will visit the country for a "look-see," Fulkerson says.

Sometimes, the assessment or the visit will reveal that the assignment isn't right for the candidate. The company hopes the employee will recog-

---

"If you take a look at our organizational chart, it's star-studded with people who have had assignments outside the United States."

---

nize this on her own, during the interviewing process, and take herself out of contention. "Some people may decide that it would be too much travel or they may not want to live in that part of the world. We want them to have a very clear sense of what they are getting into," Fulkerson says.

Does a reticent candidate bump himself off the fast track with that decision? Not necessarily. "We don't have a penalty box," Fulkerson says. "There are lots of ways to have a great career [at Pepsi]."

Global companies are spending more time these days trying to figure out what attributes produce the kind of employee who can succeed in another culture. When The Conference Board surveyed companies on this question, it found a certain uniformity among U.S. and non-U.S. companies. The two success factors that tied for top place were knowledge of the business, and a high degree of tolerance and flexibility.

The third success factor on the list was the ability to work with people. Interestingly, The Conference Board found that non-U.S. companies were much more likely to consider this a crucial factor. Researcher Weeks speculates that European executives, to a greater extent than their U.S. counterparts, expect their expatriate managers to be aware of the foreign business climate and to cultivate contacts in the countries where they do business.

Tolerance and flexibility, so crucial to success in a foreign locale, are of considerable interest to multinational companies. One reason that Colgate spends so much time in college recruiting is that it wants to find candidates who already have those qualities at a young age. The company looks for four things in potential candidates: work or education overseas, proficiency in a language other than English, computer skills, and some marketing, sales or entrepreneurial experience.

Garrison discounts a candidate who spent two weeks in Italy with her 10th grade class: "We're talking at least six months and preferably a couple of years [overseas]. If we had someone who lived in Brazil for awhile, we wouldn't hesitate to send that person to Italy."

When Colgate looks for potential global managers, management or sales experience is secondary to that elusive characteristic, adaptability. "Skills can be developed. It's harder to develop that adaptability. We want to get as much of it at the gate as possible," Garrison says.

Weeks believes that while tolerance can be developed, adaptability can't — at least not easily. He distinguishes between the two with a simple example. An expatriate manager in a South American country may have no objection to his workers eating their main meal at midday and knocking off work for a couple of hours afterward to rest. He may even think it's quaint. That's tolerance. But if in the entire two years he lives there he never alters his own work and eating habits to match those of the country, he's not very adaptable.

The fact that adaptability is considered hard to develop doesn't mean that organizations don't try. More commonly, however, they aim at boosting tolerance, hoping that adaptability will follow serendipitously. In addition to the usual pre-departure orientation and cultural familiarization sessions that most organizations have conducted for years ("Never make this gesture in France." "Always study business cards carefully in Japan; it's a mark of respect."), some companies now try to develop tolerance and a global perspective among employees in training classes.

How? Weeks cites a couple of common approaches. For some time, for

continued on p. 69

AT&T GROOMS MIDDLE MANAGERS WITH NEW-LOOK LEADERSHIP PROGRAM

BY DAVE ZIELINSKI

AT&T's leadership training for high-potential middle managers has emerged as something of a model for management development in the 1990s — particularly for managers in large, decentralized companies.

The thinking behind the redesigned program is this, says Dick Sethi, AT&T's assistant director of executive education: general managers increasingly need the knowledge and skills to help them think more like entrepreneurs and get closer to AT&T customers. Rather than just help managers do specific jobs, training is designed to help them adapt to constant change. It focuses almost exclusively on real-world problems but also encourages introspection, with the idea that for managers to act more accountable for their own piece of the business, they need to be able to reflect with skill on past experiences.

The program is in-house designed and delivered, says Sethi, with the belief that trainees can learn more from candid give-and-take with AT&T peers than they can from almost any other resource.

In 1989 the company realized its leadership training for promising middle managers was no longer relevant to AT&T's new infrastructure and changing market conditions. The catalyst was the arrival of new CEO Bob Allen, who decided to divide the company into 22 decentralized business units in order to get employees closer to customers, make the huge company quicker on its feet, and get managers thinking like business owners. Executives also knew they had to start grooming managers who could lead challenging cultural change.

More peer-to-peer learning was seen as one path toward that end. "We realized we were underutilizing each other as learning tools," says Sethi. "Getting managers from different units together also helps us avoid reinventing the wheel. "

How the Program Works

About eight weeks before the course starts, the 45 managers nominated by their superiors are asked to document the key business issue challenging them.

The two-week program is held at AT&T's new headquarters learning center.

Step 1: Small "Gap" groups. Participants are first placed in "Gap" groups of seven — "gap" signaling the difference between where they are with management skills and where they need to be — who meet every morning of the program. Every day a different group member takes a turn discussing his or her most pressing business challenge — dealing with subordinates' requests for promotions, cutting costs, or developing new products — for about 30 minutes. The other group members act as a team of consultants, offering advice and feedback. Sethi and an outside consultant act as roaming facilitators, jump-starting groups where needed.

There are three objectives to this exercise, Sethi says: (1) to use group feedback to better define individual business challenges. "If they don't frame the question or problem correctly, the solution is likely to be off base," says Sethi; (2) for group members to come up with creative action plans to address challenges; and (3) to do the groundwork for a follow-up "learning laboratory" where trainees experiment with new leadership styles.

Step 2: "Big picture" discussion. This is a dialogue with a business school professor or a leading consultant on a mix of "hard and soft" subjects ranging from dealing with growing competition, trends in information technology, change management, understanding finance, and creating values in business units. The idea is for experts to help participants see the big picture and view problems in a multidisciplinary way.

Step 3: Learning circles. Sethi borrowed these from Peter Senge, author of *The Fifth Discipline*. Trainees are put in small groups different from the gap groups. "The idea is to help them extract and clarify nuggets of learning that have happened during the day and see how applicable they are to the real world," Sethi says. Honesty is strongly encouraged. One participant, for instance, recently felt comfortable enough to tell to a peer that her body language was shutting off discussion.

Step 4: Leadership "laboratories." These include a heavy dose of experiential learning.

In one exercise, two groups line up facing each other, are blindfolded, and given one long rope to fasten loosely around their hands. Then they're asked to form two geometric shapes — usually a square and a triangle. Finally, they're asked to collapse the two forms into the shape of one house. All the movements have a time limit.

In the debrief, trainees discuss whether the groups did the right amount of planning before executing, who took on leadership roles and how they performed, and how team communication worked.

Step 5: Holistic issues. AT&T views the program as holistic, so participants perform hour-long activities that serve as "a metaphor for taking care of your body and mind," Sethi says, and energize them for the rest of the day. Activities include stretching, mild aerobics, and talk about nutrition and balancing work and family.

Step 6: Discussion with AT&T executives and customers. Trainees have dinner together, and following meals an AT&T executive or an AT&T customer holds a dialogue with the group. Sethi and others brief the customers, encouraging them to be as candid as possible about their perceptions of the company. "Because we're such a large company, some managers in the room have never engaged the customer on that level," he says.

A Lasting Sounding Board

The program's most lasting benefit may be that the "gap" workgroups continue to meet and counsel one another long after the training program ends, says Sethi. Other reinforcement includes post-training meetings with supervisors to discuss training transfer, follow-up calls from Sethi months after the program ends, and a formal survey to measure whether the trainees' subordinates, peers, and supervisors have seen any change in leadership style as a result of training.

continued from p. 67

instance, many organizations have made sure that courses held in the United States include a healthy percentage of trainees from overseas locations. It's a nonthreatening way to expose U.S. managers to other cultures and other viewpoints.

Lately, however, some companies have taken that philosophy a step further. They are holding training courses overseas and taking U.S. managers there. Motorola's Faust says the company does this for middle managers as well as top managers. It's another small chance for exposure to another culture.

Another approach some companies take is to incorporate cross-cultural awareness exercises into the usual slate of management training courses. Serge Ogranovitch, a partner in Potomack Partnership of Vienna, VA, says demand for his consulting services has risen recently, as would-be global companies try to make their employees tolerant of other cultures.

Ogranovitch uses a model based on research done by Geert Hofstede, a former IBM employee who studied the cultural values of more than 160,000 people in countries around the world. He then ranked each country on five dimensions. For instance, the power/distance dimension involves the degree to which people in a given culture accept that certain individuals are entitled to power and privilege. France would rank much higher on the scale than a place like Sweden, where collectivism is more prominent.

The Hofstede model is used in training courses to push the message that no cultural system is "good" or "bad"—just different.

Still, even companies that use classes to try to develop a global outlook among employees recognize that success is limited. "There is no substitute for living in another culture," Faust says.

¿Habla Español?

Does that mean global companies are making sure that departing employees can speak the language of their destination countries? One would assume, after all, that this would be the primary avenue for adapting to the culture. But it doesn't necessarily work that way. Some companies indeed consider language training crucial, but others argue that it's not essential.

At one end of the spectrum is Colgate, which believes that the ability to speak the language is a necessary ingredient for an expatriate's success. While it's true that most employees will be working in an office where English is the primary language, Garrison says, the office is not an isolette. Employees may need to talk with local suppliers or customers. Winning sales from a local competitor may be impossible if the expatriate hasn't bothered to learn the language. Such a lapse will strike some natives as imperious or insulting.

In the two or three months before a Colgate employee goes to another country, she and her family go through a Berlitz language course. Learning the language is the employee's "No. 1 priority," Garrison says.

Weeks believes that language gives an expatriate an extra chance at success. "If you have a good knowledge of a language, you can converse with people. And in that conversation, you can pick up a tremendous amount of business-related knowledge," he says. It's swell to have a "global viewpoint," but inability to speak the language causes you to miss a lot of the nuance and business intelligence that could produce breakthroughs rather than mediocrity.

Nevertheless, The Conference Board's study found that most companies do not require employees to learn a foreign language. Human resources directors who were surveyed reason that since business will be carried on in the office in English, and the expatriate spends most of his time in the office, there is not a pressing need to learn the language before he goes.

Weeks suspects that a more truthful answer is that companies want to limit the cost and time spent in pre-departure training. They're also afraid that candidates for overseas assignments will be scared off if too many demands are placed upon them ("I have to learn a whole *language?*").

Pepsi claims the middle ground on this issue. Is it necessary for an employee to learn the language before he goes? It depends, says Fulkerson. Sometimes, English is so pervasive in a country that proficiency may not be necessary before the bon voyage. In other cases, particularly if the destination is the Orient, Pepsi may insist on some language training before the departure.

3M encourages, but does not require, its employees to learn the language. The company takes the position that the international language of business is English. But things are changing, Hoeffel says. He predicts that 3M, as well as other global companies, will soon acknowledge a greater role for language in an expatriate's success overseas. "In years to come, it will become more important as our people do more dealing with customers rather than let-ting the foreign nationals do it," Hoeffel says.

Companies commonly send employees overseas for stints lasting anywhere from two to five years. Increasingly, organizations that are trying to raise their global profiles make sure the experience isn't wasted, and that returning expatriates are boosted up the career ladder. But is there any evidence that companies value overseas experience where it counts: at the top levels of the organization?

Yes indeed, says Weeks. The Conference Board's study discovered that among U.S. companies, about 42 percent of the highest echelon — CEOs, presidents and executive vice presidents — had worked abroad at some point. More tellingly, among the cohort directly below those people, about two-thirds had had overseas assignments.

Anecdotal evidence appears everywhere, and employees have begun to notice. "If you take a look at our organizational chart, it's star-studded with people who have had assignments outside the United States," 3M's Hoeffel says. "It's an agreed-upon philosophy today that you need to have that experience to get to the top."

The change at Motorola has been apparent too. Currently, about half the company's officers have had international experience, Faust says. Ten or 15 years ago, that number would have been about zero.

Faust himself worked in the company's international division from 1979 to 1985. "I knew how valuable [international experience] would be," he says, "but I wasn't seeing how it was rewarded in the organization. Now, there's little doubt that this is experience you want to have."

That is, if you want to be a fast-tracker in a global organization.

Avoiding Copyright Traps: It Pays to Know the Rules

BY DAVE ZIELINSKI

Many trainers ignore or remain unaware that "public performance" or duplication of purchased training materials without permission — including videos, off-the-shelf CBT, and music — is illegal, and increasingly prosecuted.

It's something many trainers still do without enough of a second thought: make a handful of copies of a dynamite new video they've just bought for distribution to field offices, use that five-minute film clip that so perfectly complements a training concept, download training-related clip-art or graphics from the Internet, or play music from a favorite CD during session breaks.

Trouble is, without written permission or special agreements from copyright owners, most of those seemingly benign practices violate copyright law, and increasingly are leading to some big fines for companies.

According to Bob Gehrke, executive director of the Training Media Association (TMA), which represents producers of training films and fights such piracy, there are two basic rules you need to know to avoid violations and possible legal action:

(1) No duplication of any kind is legal without the written permission of the copyright owner.

(2) No public performance of purchased training materials is permitted without written approval from the copyright owner. Gehrke defines public performance as "any use that would involve the possibility of commercial gain." For instance, if you're showing a legally purchased film clip to help improve the performance of your own employees, that ultimately can give your company commercial gain," he says, and is illegal without written permission.

To get around this, most companies arrange to pay copyright owners a fee for public performance rights, or for site licenses to create duplicate copies.

Some trainers find it's not always that easy, however. It can sometimes be difficult to identify holders of copyright, and at times when the owner is identified, they don't have a policy or set fee for public performance or they don't return correspondence quickly. In these cases, Gehrke suggests trainers call the TMA in Frederick, MD, for help (301-662-4268).

More Than a Slap on the Wrist

Lest you think it's nearly impossible to get caught in a copyright violation, Gehrke points out that the TMA settled two big cases involving violations in just the last two months. In one, a large Midwestern retail chain with 90 stores purchased copies of off-the-shelf programs from two different vendors, "and they liked them so much they decided they should be used by all their stores," says Gehrke. So the chain made copies — illegally — of five different titles and sent them out to each store. "That's 450 titles. Potential statutory damages are $100,000 per illegal copy made in this case," he says. If the violation is deemed willful, damages could go even higher.

In the other case, an electric utility in Milwaukee purchased a 13-module training program for about $10,000. "But they decided they needed more than one copy, so they sent it out to a duplicating house," Gehrke says. The utility assured the duplicator in writing that it would assume full responsibility for the duplication, but the duplicating house was suspicious and called the TMA — largely because of a $5,000 reward sticker placed on the materials — and there was an investigation. Turns out they hadn't asked for permission. It cost them about $250,000 in fines after we filed a complaint in district court."

In past years, the TMA has estimated that its member companies lose up to a third of their sales to illegal copying.

Create a Company Policy on Copyright Issues

Most cases of violation aren't willful. "It's usually someone trying to save some money or time, or simply being ignorant of copyright law," he says. "We understand its often impractical to get copyright permission when you're trying to get information out quickly, but the reality is it's also illegal."

The TMA strongly suggests companies develop a formal copyright policy, and make sure all employees are aware of it, or have easy access to it when questions arise.

The biggest violation the TMA continues to see is illegally using small clips or vignettes from films or videos in training sessions, which violates the "public performance" standard.

• **CBT and computer networks.** The growth of CBT and both wide and local area networks (WANs and LANs) has created new problems, too. It's illegal, without permission, to put a purchased copy of a vendor's program on a network for sharing with satellite offices, as is broadcasting or "cablecasting" protected work without permission.

Some CBT authoring packages allow you to develop at will but then specify that if you intend to distribute your work, you must pay the owners of the authoring language a license fee for every copy you create — even if you are going to distribute your program internally.

• **Downloading clip-art or cartoons from the Internet.** Beware of copyright infringement on clip art and cartoons. Often those materials aren't "free" but protected by copyright.

• **Using pre-recorded music.** In its strictest interpretation, using music during session breaks — from a pre-recorded CD or tape, not the radio — without copyright owner's permission is considered a "public performance" violation. But that violation falls under the domain of ASCAP, the primary defender of copyright law in the music industry, not the TMA.

Dos and Don'ts of Questionnaire Design

Try these tips to make sure your next one doesn't bomb.

BY DEAN SPITZER

Questionnaires are the most frequently used method of data collection among educators and trainers. Yet few questionnaire designers heed the simple "dos" and "don'ts" that can make a good questionnaire. A few errors in design can go a long way toward invalidating an otherwise well-conceptualized research effort. Therefore, it is especially important for trainers to consider these simple guidelines — along with content considerations — the next time a questionnaire effort is proposed.

'Do' Guidelines

• **Begin with a few nonthreatening and easy-to-answer items.** This ensures that respondents will continue to complete the questionnaire with a positive attitude. Threatening items at the beginning of a questionnaire can cause defensive — and frequently invalid — responses.

• **Use simple and direct language.** The major cause of invalid questionnaire results is misinterpreted items. Avoid this pitfall by making sure that your items will communicate adequately to your respondents.

• **Make your items as brief as possible.** Filling out questionnaires can be a bore. Sometimes respondents will automatically "turn off," when they encounter tediously long items.

• **Emphasize the crucial words in each item.** If certain words might change the entire meaning of the item if misinterpreted, italicize or underscore them.

• **Leave adequate space for respondents to make comments.** Although unstructured comments are often difficult to analyze, they can provide valuable information that might not otherwise be collected. Plenty of "white space" also makes the form appear less cluttered and more professional.

• **Group items into coherent categories.** This makes the respondent's job easier because he or she won't constantly shift mental gears, become fatigued and make a mistake. Categories don't have to be labeled, but similar items should be grouped together.

• **Provide some variety in the type of items used.** This keeps respondents from becoming fatigued and bored and is particularly important for long questionnaires. Alternative types include: multiple choice, true/false, short answer, open-ended items, ranking items, and items that are contingent upon previous responses.

• **Include clear, concise instructions on how to complete the questionnaire.** Heed Murphy's Law here, too. Be sure that your instructions will inhibit any attempts (conscious or otherwise) to complete the questionnaire incorrectly.

• **Make sure that there are clear instructions on what to do with the completed questionnaire.** The return address should be clearly identified on the cover letter and on the form itself. Should the questionnaire be returned in a self-addressed envelope? What's the deadline for completing it? By the way, deadlines increase questionnaire response rates. Make sure that all relevant information related to the disposition of the completed questionnaire is clearly specified.

• **Provide incentives as a motivation for a promptly completed questionnaire.** This doesn't mean that you should "bribe" respondents, just that you should make every effort to motivate them to respond. Help respondents realize the importance of collecting this information, and how it will be used to benefit them. Sometimes the responsibility of a questionnaire signed by a highly credible person can promote responses. This device should be weighed against that of an anonymous questionnaire, one that will encourage more candor on controversial items.

• **Use professional production methods.** The more professional your questionnaire looks, the more likely you will get a high response rate. A printed questionnaire is easier to read and respond to.

• **Provide a well-written personal cover letter.** Questionnaires should always be sent with cover letters explaining their purpose and the reasons respondents were selected. Personal letters are best, but if this isn't feasible, have the letter printed to match the type in the address and salutation. Never use a form letter.

• **Include other experts and relevant decision-makers in your questionnaire design.** This helps assure that your questionnaire is comprehensive and technically correct. It will add credibility to the project and will provide you with a head start toward utilizing the completed data.

• **Plan how to analyze and use the data when designing the questionnaire.** Consider the analysis and use of data from the start. What might be a good question can result in meaningless data. Consider the nature of responses as carefully as you design the questions.

• **Be prepared to handle missing data.** Invariably, there will be incomplete responses and missing data on the returned questionnaires. Unless you have a plan for dealing with this missing data, you'll be stymied. Anyone who has used a five-point (or seven-point) rating scale knows that missing data cannot always be treated as if they were three's or five's (the midpoints of the scale).

• **Test your questionnaire on representatives of the target audience.** You may be surprised how many serious errors went undetected during the most careful and systematic design process. Perhaps the best way to test a questionnaire (without involving complex statistics) is to watch a few respondents complete it. If they're having difficulties, question

SAVE TIME BY ASKING TRAINEES TO DO OWN
NEEDS ANALYSIS WITH DATABASE TOOL

BY DAVE ZIELINSKI

More training managers are finding the most efficient and effective way to conduct a needs analysis is to turn more of the process over to line workers. And new technology and software makes that transition easier than ever before.

At the Insurance Corp. of British Columbia in North Vancouver, BC, Kevin Savage and his staff have created a new needs assessment process using Microsoft Access software. The program's database allows for automated self-assessments of skills gaps, and generates individual training plans for the 450 workers in the information services division where Savage is director of education.

Accessing Competency Sets Online

In the past, Savage identified skills gaps mainly through interviewing focus groups of representative employees, and compiling that information in Microsoft Word documents. But that process was inefficient and didn't always yield dependable data. So Savage hired a local outside contractor to help build a needs assessment database in Access. Now, for instance, a systems analyst can access the database at her computer, call up the competency skill set for "systems analyst" — the skills are ranked by importance to the job — then do her own skills gap analysis. Both interpersonal and technical skill competencies are listed and rated, along with specific supporting behaviors. The analyst rates her proficiency in the target skill areas, and the system automatically calculates where the biggest skill gaps are, printing out a report.

At that point, the analyst meets with her boss to discuss the report results and any skill rankings the boss may think questionable. The two then reach some consensus on possible training options and schedules. The systems analyst then goes back into the system to review internal training courses listed on-line, gets her boss to sign off on those courses, and registers online. She will typically take those courses over an 18-month span, Savage says.

Savage monitors all the training requests in the pro-gram, so he can track what courses employees are asking for and plan accordingly. There is a necessary degree of confidentiality built in, he says. "We don't make records of the fact John Q. Smith has indicated this or that skills deficiency — it's important some confidentiality be maintained, so people don't think any of the information might be used against them and are more willing to participate."

Savage estimates he invested about $60,000 to create the program, including the outside contractor's services and the training staff's time. "It may sound expensive, but what we have now is something very tailored to our company that speaks to the unique skill needs of our employees."

Savage says the program has helped his education planning process immensely, and aided his efforts to sell training to upper management.

"After you've been training in a company for awhile, you tend to have a good gut feel for where the real needs are. But having the data gives me even more credibility with top managers. Instead of using intuition, I can show senior leaders during the budgeting process this data — empirical feedback from the line — that says we have real corporate skill gaps in these key areas, and that we need more dollars for development."

A Version for Leaders

The program is so successful that a similar competency database is now being rolled out for the 40 managers in the IS division. The managers will be able to access a skills database listing competency sets unique to their positions and weighted for importance, and peruse training options to help shore up the gaps. Originally a paper model, Savage felt the system could easily be converted into an Access function.

One tool for identifying managers' skill shortages is a 360-degree assessment survey Savage and his staff help administer. Skills rated on those surveys include customer focus, innovation and creativity, commitment to employees, teamwork, financial management, aligning people to a vision, effective dialogue, and planning change.

---

them in detail to determine the source. Questionnaire designers frequently find that a single, ambiguous word can invalidate even the best questionnaire item. A little time spent in pilot testing can eliminate lots of problems later on.

• **Number and include some identifying data on each page.** It's possible that the pages of the questionnaire may come apart, causing problems for the respondent. Avoid this by numbering and identifying each page.

Don't Guidelines

• **Don't use ambiguous, bureaucratic, technical or colloquial language.** It can confuse or "turn off", respondents. Don't give Murphy's Law an opportunity to sabotage your study. Pilot testing the questionnaire can help avoid this error.

• **Don't use negatively worded questions unless absolutely necessary.** Negatively worded items can easily be misinterpreted or clue respondents into a "desired" response. Most negative items can easily be worded positively.

• **Don't use "double-barreled" items.** Don't use items that ask respondents to respond to more than one statement or question. Such items can be confusing, especially when the respondent feels differently about each part. Instead, make each item a simple, discrete question or statement. "When in doubt, make two items out of one."

• **Don't bias respondents by hinting at a "desired" response.** For questionnaire results to be valid, respondents must not be biased by the way the items have been written.

Again, pilot testing is the best way to avoid inadvertently biasing respondents.

• **Don't ask questions to which you already know the answers.** Don't waste respondents' time — and your own — by including items with only one realistic response. The inclusion of such items will bore respondents, needlessly increase the length of the questionnaire and cause more work for those analyzing the data. The only exception to this rule is when you need documentation for the item in question.

• **Don't include any extraneous or unnecessary items.** Make sure all the items on your questionnaire will yield useful data. Otherwise, you may overwhelm or unnecessarily fatigue the respondent. The best cure for this error is to practice tabulating and analyzing the data yourself.

• **Don't put important items at the end.** Items at the end of a questionnaire rarely get the same kind of attention that earlier items get. Save the least significant items for the end.

• **Don't allow respondents to fall into "response sets."** When a great many questionnaire items call for similar responses, there is the tendency for respondents to continue responding in the same way. Item variety will counteract this tendency, as will a conscious decision to vary response formats and probable responses for consecutive items.

Following these simple "dos" and "don'ts" will enable you to design questionnaires that will yield better responses. If you use them, I think you'll find that both your response rate and results validity will increase considerably.

Notes:

Constructing Tests that Work

Here's a refresher course on how to construct tests that measure whether trainees learned what they were supposed to learn from your training program.

BY MARC J. ROSENBERG
AND WILLIAM SMITLEY

When the objectives of a training course demand a pencil-and-paper test of knowledge or appropriate job-like performance, the trainer confronts a deceptively difficult challenge: How do you write test items that effectively and accurately measure the extent to which trainees have learned the material you've been teaching them?

Like so many training tasks, this one looks easy until you try to do it. Constructing effective tests requires subject-matter expertise, clear and concise writing, and considerable time and effort. Above all, it requires that each test item be designed so that every student interprets it in exactly the way the designer intends.

The four most common types of written tests — multiple choice, dichotomous, matching, and short-answer completion — are all variations of the same basic, two-part format: first a stem, which is a statement or question that provides the stimulus to the student; then two or more alternatives, often called distracters, from which the correct response to the stem is selected. The alternatives may be provided directly, as in the case of multiple choice, dichotomous or matching items, or, as in the case of short answer-completion questions, they may be implied. In the latter case, the "distracters" are all of the imaginable answer choices the student must filter out in order to provide the correct response.

By looking at the four types of questions as variations of this universal format, our discussion of each type, including definitions, advantages and limitations can be simplified. We should note at the start, however, that the advantages and limitations of each format in a general sense will not indicate which is best for a given testing situation. The format you choose should reflect your analysis of the specific content you wish to test and the learning objectives of the training course.

Multiple Choice

A multiple-choice test item consists of a stem, in the form of a statement or question, followed by more than two distracters. A key point in the design of multiple-choice questions is that all distracters should be plausible. Here are three acceptable examples:

Question format: What cartoon character was Walt Disney's first commercial success?
a. Donald Duck
b. Goofy
c. Jiminy Cricket
d. Mickey Mouse

Incomplete statement format: Walt Disney's first commercially successful cartoon character was:
a. Donald Duck
b. Goofy
c. Jiminy Cricket
d. Mickey Mouse

Incomplete statement format 2: The cartoon character was Walt Disney's first commercial success.
a. Donald Duck
b. Goofy
c. Jiminy Cricket
d. Mickey Mouse

Major advantages of the multiple-choice format include:

1. Test scoring is simplified because possible bias by the test administrator cannot influence a student's score. And because all distracters are provided in the item, an answer key can be developed to allow anyone to grade the tests — you don't need a subject-matter expert to do the grading.

2. When more than two distracters are provided for each item, the trainees' chances of guessing the correct answer are reduced.

3. When enough plausible alternatives are available to be used as distracters, multiple-choice items are relatively easy to construct.

Major limitations of the multiple-choice format:

1. Since the answer is provided among the distracters, it can be guessed; you can't be certain that the student really knew the answer to a given question.

2. The format relies on recognition, rather than "production" of the answer by the student. It is generally agreed that recognition reflects a lower level of learning than does production.

3. When enough plausible distracters cannot be identified the development of quality multiple-choice items can become very difficult.

4. Since several distracters must be provided for each item, the format uses more space than some of the others.

Dichotomous Test Items

The stem of a dichotomous, or alternative-response, test item is typically a declarative statement but can be in the form of a question. The stem is followed by only two mutually exclusive distracters (yes/no, true/false, right/wrong, cold/warm).

Major advantages:

1. The dichotomous format is useful for distinguishing fact from opinion, right from wrong, or in any other situation where there are two, and only two, mutually exclusive alternatives.

2. As with multiple-choice items, scoring is simplified and unbiased.

Major limitations:

1. Since only two choices are provided, the student has a 50% chance of guessing the correct answer. Therefore, the dichotomous format usually requires more test items than

TEST ITEM CHECKLIST

_____ _____
Reviewer's Name   Date

Directions: Indicate whether *all* test items meet each criterion by placing a check mark [ ] in the appropriate box. Write the number of any items that did not meet the criterion in the space marked "REVISIONS." Use only those criteria which apply to each particular item or test type.

Revisions: If any test item receives a NO, revise that item as needed.

I. GENERAL CRITERIA

	YES	NO	REVISIONS
1. Is the item grammatically correct?	[ ]	[ ]	_____
2. Have ambiguous statements/terms been avoided?	[ ]	[ ]	_____
3. Is the item written at the trainee's language level?	[ ]	[ ]	_____
4. Does it avoid giving clues that can be used to answer another item?	[ ]	[ ]	_____
5. Does the item contain only a single idea?	[ ]	[ ]	_____
6. Is only relevant information included?	[ ]	[ ]	_____
7. Has the use of a correct answer from another item as part of the stem for this item been avoided?	[ ]	[ ]	_____
8. Is there only one correct answer for the item?	[ ]	[ ]	_____
9. Are all parts of the item on the same page?	[ ]	[ ]	_____

II. MULTIPLE CHOICE TEST ITEMS

	YES	NO	REVISIONS
10. Have negative and double negative stems been avoided?	[ ]	[ ]	_____
11. Have grammatical clues been avoided?	[ ]	[ ]	_____
12. Is as much of the wording as possible in the stem rather than in the distractor?	[ ]	[ ]	_____
13. Are all distractors approximately the same length?	[ ]	[ ]	_____
14. Are all distractors plausible?	[ ]	[ ]	_____
15. Are enough distractors present in each item (4-5) to reduce guessing?	[ ]	[ ]	_____
16. Are distractors arranged in an orderly manner (alphabetically, numerically, logically)?	[ ]	[ ]	_____
17. Have distractors such as "none of the above," "all of the above," "A & B only," etc., been avoided?	[ ]	[ ]	_____

III. DICHOTOMOUS TEST ITEMS

	YES	NO	REVISIONS
18. Is the statement worded so precisely that it can be judged unequivocally?	[ ]	[ ]	_____
19. Have negative and double			

negative stems been avoided? [ ] [ ] _____

	YES	NO	REVISIONS
20. Have clues which tend to qualify the "absoluteness" of the stem been avoided?	[ ]	[ ]	_____

IV. MATCHING TEST ITEMS

	YES	NO	REVISIONS
21. Are there more distractors than premises?	[ ]	[ ]	_____
22. Is the premise list short?	[ ]	[ ]	_____
23. Are distractors more concise than premises so that reading load is reduced?	[ ]	[ ]	_____
24. Are the distractor and premise lists related to the same central theme, concept or idea?	[ ]	[ ]	_____
25. Are all premises, distractors and matching rationale on one page?	[ ]	[ ]	_____
26. Are premises and distractors arranged in an orderly manner (alphabetically, numerically, logically)?	[ ]	[ ]	_____
27. Is there only one answer match for each premise?	[ ]	[ ]	_____
28. Have grammatical clues been avoided?	[ ]	[ ]	_____

V. SHORT ANSWER/COMPLETION TEST ITEMS

	YES	NO	REVISIONS
29. Is the item constructed so that only one briefly written answer is possible?	[ ]	[ ]	_____
30. For incomplete sentence items, does enough of the statement remain to convey the intent to the trainee?	[ ]	[ ]	_____
31. Does the main idea of the incomplete sentence precede the blank?	[ ]	[ ]	_____
32. Is the only omission a significant word, symbol or number?	[ ]	[ ]	_____
33. For numerical answers, has the degree of precision been included in the stem?	[ ]	[ ]	_____
34. Have negative and double negative stems been avoided?	[ ]	[ ]	_____
35. Has a list of acceptable responses (variations of the answer that are acceptable as correct) been specified?	[ ]	[ ]	_____

---

other formats to measure the student's knowledge accurately.

2. Few important statements are absolutely right or wrong, true or false. Therefore, dichotomous test items can be difficult to construct. It usually is a mistake to try to "qualify" the stem with words such as "always," "usually," "never" and so forth; such qualifiers provide clues to the correct answer, as in these examples:

__T __F An open style of supervision is always the better way to deal with subordinates.

__T __F It never rains in California between the months of June and September.

If the test item doesn't fit the dichotomous format, don't force it;

choose another format.

3. As with multiple-choice questions, the dichotomous format does not force the student to "produce" the correct answer.

Matching Test Items

In the matching format, a series of stems, usually called "premises," is listed in a single column, while the possible distracters are listed in a second column. All of the distracters in a matching series should be plausible answers for each stem or premise. All the premises and the answer choices must be similar, or homogeneous.

In a matching exercise, stems should contain the majority of the information to be tested, while each distracter should be short, containing only a key word, number or phrase. This reduces the burden on the student of repeated reading of a long list of distracters.

Example of a matching format:
Match the type of frame joint with the correct method of nailing that should be used.

Frame Joint	Nailing Method
Soleplate to joist	a. Blind
Rafter to valley	b. Edge
Rafter to rafter	c. End
Header to joist	d. Face
	e. Toe

Major advantages:
1. Since the matching format allows all the distracters to be used as possible answers for all of the stems, a lot of test items can be covered on a single page. Matching tests also can be completed more quickly than tests using other formats.
2. The format measures factual knowledge and the student's ability to recognize relationships and make associations.
3. As with multiple-choice and dichotomous items, scoring is simplified and unbiased.

Major limitations:
1. As students complete the items they know to be correct, the possibility of making a correct guess increases through the process of elimination. This limitation can be reduced by providing more distracters than stems.
2. Stems and distracters in a matching group must be homogeneous. That is, they must relate to the

USING 'DAILIES' TO KEEP TRAINING ON TARGET

O ur organization has sunk a lot of money into this training program — design time, material and logistical expenses, perhaps travel and lodging expenses for the trainees, not to mention lost work time. As with any investment, you want to know whether or not this one is working out, and you want to know soon enough to correct any mistakes.

To protect your investment, one instructional designer recommends borrowing a technique from another fast-paced, high-budget industry: the movies. Kenneth A. Lawrence, chief of instructional design at the Veterans' Administration Medical Center in Washington, DC, points out that the film industry avoids expensive return trips to remote locations by processing film samples each day, so that any necessary reshooting can be done immediately.

Those film samples are called "dailies." If Steven Spielberg were a corporate trainer, he might refer to dailies as a type of formative evaluation. That idea occurred to Lawrence a few years ago when the VA switched from local to centrally conducted training for its medical center procurement specialists nationwide. The new arrangement called for eight to 10 five-day training sessions a year. Each session would cost more than $10,000. No room for second chances there.

Lawrence and his associates decided that what they needed was an evaluation form they could pass out at the end of each day's training — a form that would give them results they could process and interpret overnight. They rejected a daily content quiz as cumbersome to create and administer. Instead, they settled on an instrument very much like your standard, end-of-session evaluation form. It asks trainees to rate the program on such dimensions as relevance to their jobs, clarity and pace. It also asks them to list the most important things they learned in the session, and to make any other comments they wish.

The difference is that instead of filling out the questionnaire only at the end of the course, trainees are asked to complete it at the end of each of the first three days

and occasionally on the fourth day — "for example, when a new or revised course is being tested, or when a new instructor is presenting training," says Lawrence.

The form uses Likert-scale questions ("Rate this characteristic from 1 to 5"). After each class, an evaluator plots the response distribution for each question, and categorizes the write-in comments by frequency. Then the evaluator reviews the results with the instructor.

They're looking for the usual things. For example, the distribution on "relevance," (1 = all the material was highly relevant, 5 = little or no relevance) should be toward the left end of the continuum. For "pace," rated from 1 (too fast) to 5 (too slow), the responses should be grouped near the center, with outliers evenly balanced between the two extremes. Trainees' comments about the most important things they learned should bear a reasonable resemblance to the intended content of the course.

Not long ago, Lawrence says, the usefulness of gathering this sort of data daily instead of only at course's end was illustrated when an instructor got sick on the third day of a session and had to be replaced. The day's subject — analyzing bidders' projected overhead costs — was one that often gave participants trouble anyway.

The evaluation showed that one of the classes taught by the substitute instructor had a particularly hard time with the lesson. For example, the "clarity" item, which normally turned up a leftward distribution (meaning most of the day's instruction was understandable), showed a nearly flat distribution for this particular class. That night the trainers developed a review sequence. The instructor presented it first thing the next morning. According to Lawrence, that day's evaluation indicated that the problem had been resolved.

One additional benefit of dailies, Lawrence adds, is that their cumulative information can be very helpful in evaluating an entire course. It may not be as glamorous as a Hollywood screening, he concludes, but it does the job.

— Marc J. Rosenberg and William Smitley

same concept and must be phrased in basically the same way. If the designer isn't careful, students will be able to reduce the number of plausible distracters.

3. Again, the matching format relies on recognition rather than production of the answer by the student.

Short answer-completion:

Short-answer test items, also referred to as "completion" or "fill-in-the-blank" questions, have stems constructed in the same manner as multiple-choice items. But, instead of choosing from distracters supplied by the designer, students must come up with a specific word, number or symbol on their own.

Major advantages:

1. Short-answer items are relatively easy to construct since distracters do not have to be created.

2. They are very effective in measuring recall.

3. Unlike other formats, the short-answer item requires the student to produce the correct response rather than simply to recognize it. Thus, the possibility of guessing the correct answer is drastically reduced.

Major limitations:

1. The range of distracters depends upon the "mind-set" of the student at the time of testing. This mind-set may be different from the trainer's without being "wrong." Thus, the student might produce an unanticipated response which is arguably correct.

2. Scoring is more difficult due to potential subjectivity in the interpretation of responses. A subject-matter expert may be required to determine whether the response is correct.

3. A short-answer format should be used only when the correct response is, indeed, a significant word, number, symbol or short phrase. Here

are two inappropriate items:
1. A telescope is_____.
2. A tool used by astronomers to observe planets and ___ is a telescope.

Here is how the item might be improved:
3. A tool used by astronomers to observe planets and stars is a/an ___.
4. Short-answer items that are poorly developed may measure the wrong things — by asking the student to recall an insignificant aspect of some important concept, for example, organization.

Another important concern in the test-design process is that of layout. The organization of a written test centers around four major areas: (1) the cover page, (2) general test directions, (3) specific directions and (4) item groupings.

(1) The cover page: At least two matters should be addressed clearly and concisely on the cover page of any written test: the purpose of the test itself and a reminder of the objectives of the lesson or course which the test covers.

(2) General test directions: These give the student any information necessary to complete the test. General directions should include: total time allowed; any resources the student is permitted to use during the test; whether any group work will be allowed; how to complete a separate answer sheet, if necessary; suggestions to help the student complete the test efficiently; scoring procedures and values for each test item; and instructions about what the student is to do at the conclusion of the test.

(3) Specific directions: Each set of test items, multiple-choice, matching, dichotomous or completion, requires specific directions as to how the student is to respond. It also may be appropriate to provide practice

items. If the procedures by which students indicate answers vary throughout the test (e.g., circle the letter, write in a number or write in an answer), those procedures must be explained.

Whenever possible, however, construct tests in a manner that relies on as few differing procedures as possible. Don't forget to repeat your directions if the same types of questions appear in more than one place in the test or if a given format continues on following pages.

(4) Item groupings: The placement and grouping of test items is an important consideration. Some general recommendations:
1. If possible, group all items according to content.
2. Within each content area, group all items according to type (i.e., keep all multiple-choice items together, etc.).
3. Provide more space between items than within items.
4. Try to disperse the easier test items uniformly throughout the test.

Test Item Checklist

After your test has been constructed, a careful review by content and training specialists can identify potential problems, such as items that are ambiguous, poorly worded or incorrect. The accompanying checklist provides assistance in this process.

You also may save time and effort by reviewing the checklist before you begin writing test items. Remember, however, that the best "test of a test" is to try it out with typical students. Even the most knowledgeable reviewers cannot foresee all possible problems, since their "mind-sets" are inherently different from those of the students for whom the test is designed.

Notes:

CHAPTER 2
STAFFING ISSUES

The New Trainer

Remember 'stand and deliver'? Well, forget it.
That was then, this is now.

BY MARC HEQUET

When Jeanne Hartley worked as staff trainer at the *Los Angeles Daily News* in the early 1980s, a manager came to her with a routine request. "Teach my people how to deal with angry customers," said the manager.

Hartley's first thought was: "Why are customers angry? How can we make customers less angry?"

But that first reaction was also minor heresy, and her mentor warned her off. In those days, trainers trained. It was the customer service manager's job to worry about what steams customers. If Hartley wanted to presume to investigate such problems, she'd better have an advanced degree in organization development, at least, her mentor told her.

So Hartley got one. And now, with her OD master's, Hartley works at the *Daily News'* crosstown rival *Los Angeles Times* as manager of training and organization development. Her job: Work with line management to help introduce and manage change in the organization.

This, says Hartley, is the direction all trainers should be heading today.

Why? Because in organizations intent on improving performance, the accustomed practice of delivering courses scattershot helps little or not at all. To be sure, some have long advocated that training should be very specific to business needs. What's different now is that more companies are paying attention.

"When I was hired here five years ago, this was a state-of-the-art training department," says Hartley. "Its main output was a catalog of classes. Good training. Top-notch trainers. The catalog came out a couple of times a year and people would clamor to get into classes."

And now? *The Times* — staid, old,

successful — is morphing into a performance-oriented organization. You keep your job if you perform at a high level. Training is specific to business issues. If there's a class you really want to take, and you're first in line to sign up — you still might not get in. Instead of first-come, first-served as in the old days, employees go to the head of the line for a class when their performance review says they need it.

But aside from delivering courses, the emerging priority for Hartley's

---

Is the role of the trainer under transformation to the point where the job as we know it will vanish altogether?

---

department is to help manage the corporate transformation — facilitating teams, redesigning work processes, rolling up sleeves and getting out on the line where the real work happens.

What Choice?

When Hartley's department decided to changed its name to "Training and Organization Development" to reflect its OD responsibilities, Hartley says, "We didn't get rid of 'training' — because that's how people identify us." But all her trainers now have skills in organization development so they can serve as internal consultants to the change process.

What's happening at the *Times* is happening elsewhere — but not fast enough to suit some who are intent on corporate makeovers. Training and development pros in such settings are confronted with a decision: Keep doing what they know best — traditional, stand-up training — or change

to a strange new job that might best be described as change manager.

Which to choose? "To me," says Ellen Kamp, learning and development vice president with New York City-based Chase Manhattan Corp.'s card services unit, "it's not a choice."

The evolution in trainers' jobs has to do with the difference between activity and results. The traditional approach valued trainees' backsides in training-room chairs. The more backsides, the better your training department was doing.

The more recent approach looks beyond the training room. Do things to and for the workers that contribute directly to better productivity, improved sales, more profits — the things that matter to the business.

Conceptually, none of this is really new. Many of the most respected gurus in the training field have contended for decades that performance improvement should be the focus of all training. But more trainers and more organizations now appear to be taking that seriously. And training appears to be inching toward a place at the strategic heart of the corporation.

So — what's a trainer supposed to do in 1996? "Other than become relevant?" deadpans Michael Lyden, education and training director in the human resources department with University Hospitals of Cleveland.

Trainers? Lose 'em

"Training is an Industrial Age kind of concept," says Mark Copeland, based in Independence, OH, as a regional training manager for McDonald's Corp. "I think we've gone beyond that. We're more into a whole different way of educating employees."

Is the role of the trainer under transformation to the point where the job as we know it will vanish altogether? Probably not. But that would be all right, some say.

"Trainers' roles aren't just changing," thunders Alan Weiss, president of Summit Consulting Group Inc. in East Greenwich, RI, in an e-mail exchange with training, "they ought to be vanishing. Increasingly, companies are looking for 'trainers' from line areas, to combine the learning with the pragmatism of real-time business needs. Some trainers can make the switch, but most isolate themselves behind rubrics like 'servant leadership' and 'learning organization' or large-program superstructures, such as TQM and business-process reengineering."

Rather than caving, some trainers fight for their old job as they have known it, Weiss continued in a subsequent interview. "You find a lot of trainers either retreating into their silos or saying things like, 'Total quality is the way of the future and we are the high priests of that particular faith.' Training becomes an end, not a means."

If training is, in fact, being pushed out to managers, supervisors and subject matter experts, what does that leave for trainers to do?

Let's take a look at job descriptions. How's this for a trainer's old job description:
- Assess training needs.
- Design training.
- Deliver training.
- Measure impact of training.
And how's this for the new:
- Grill executives about strategic direction.
- Stay in touch with workers and work processes to be aware of skill needs.
- Broker training delivered by internal and external suppliers.
- Teach line managers how to train.
- Facilitate process improvement, and/or teach line managers how to do it.
- Know learning styles.
- Know the nature of your organization's business.
- Know information technology.
- Author interactive multimedia training programs.
- Go on line to access electronic training opportunities, both internally and on the Internet.
- Help managers think through performance problems and find solutions, whether the solution is training or something else.
- Make big-picture observations of work processes for problems or potential improvements that people in the trenches might not see.
- Facilitate problem-solving teams.
- Push training upstream, so that it's planned into the front end of a business initiative (a new plant, an overseas expansion) instead of hung on as an afterthought.
- Bring about change that, yes, wrings workers out of jobs and stretches others all over the plant, but nevertheless pushes dollars to the bottom line and so helps the company.

That's the new model, based on interviews with trainers living it. Notice that there's room for the old-fashioned, stand-and-deliver trainer —but not much. "If they're good at it, they go in there and razzle-dazzle 'em and then go home and sleep," says the *Times'* Hartley. But a good night's sleep isn't always the lot of the new trainer. "No," Hartley sighs. "I wake up a lot at night. But I love the work."

Define 'Lousy'

Where do trainers go if they can't stand in a classroom and teach? Federal Express Corp. of Memphis says its instructors now spend less than 50 percent of their time in the classroom. The balance of their time they're in the field, working with managers on performance issues.

For example: A manager says a courier is doing a lousy job. Define

---

There's room for the old-fashioned, stand-and-deliver trainer — but too much.

"lousy," demands the trainer. Is the courier not filling out the form correctly? In what way? Has the courier been trained properly? If so, is the courier listening to a more experienced courier who's telling him to do it the wrong way? Maybe that used to be the right way. Things are changing fast enough with FedEx — and with many companies — so that last year's way of doing things may no longer be this year's, or yesterday's today's.

That makes the trainer a kind of performance troubleshooter. Track down the subpar performers. Find out what's wrong. And fix it.

As recently as three years ago, FedEx's top management used to rely on seat counts to measure the efficacy of the training function. "That's ridiculous," says Peter Addicott, senior manager in training and development with FedEx. "That is no longer, and never really has been, a good indicator. Our instructors are moving more from instruction to human-performance technology. In doing that, we're really saying the instructor is no longer just responsible for teaching in a classroom."

When not in the classroom or the field, the new prototype trainer may go to the computer. Some argue that the trainer's role has become one of selecting and applying educational material already available with information technology. The job now, the argument goes, is to identify and access the best material and programs from a horde of choices, and figure out what learning approaches are best for a particular organization.

That goes beyond just learning a few computer tricks, though. It reshapes the entire job of training. When you layer business literacy and computer know-how atop the old-fashioned andragogy, is it a three-layer job? Or is it a new job entirely? Diane Gayeski, a partner with Omni-Com Associates, a consulting firm in Ithaca, NY, argues the latter.

Gayeski sees the transformed trainer as the curator of a company-wide skills collection. "Stop thinking of yourself as a trainer," says Gayeski. "Start thinking of yourself as the manager of the communications infrastructure of your organization."

Get Businesslike

But don't only think of yourself as a performance troubleshooter who is also in the communications-infrastructure racket. Think of yourself as being in the same business as the organization for which you work.

When Ann Meier lost her training job in a department store shutdown a few years ago, a co-worker tried to cheer her up by saying: "This is no big deal for you. You're not a part of this industry. You can go anywhere."

That, suggests Meier, is a widespread notion that trainers themselves share to an extent greater than they ought. Rather, says Meier, trainers should identify closely with the business they serve. Her well-meaning friend was wrong. Meier's heart and soul were in that department store business.

Today, Meier, now a training program designer with Orlando, FL-based Darden Restaurants Inc., again lives and breathes her company's business. "Don't go out to lunch with a restaurant person," she warns. "They just pick, pick, pick. 'The temperature of the food is wrong. The plate isn't attractive. A manager isn't visible in the dining room.' Then all of a sudden you realize — you're doing it too."

Darden Restaurants, a recent General Mills Inc. spinoff whose properties include Red Lobster, has sacrificed the efficiencies of a centralized training function to be able to keep training directors close to individual restaurant chains.

Within General Mills, the restaurant unit's training had been centralized. Trainers were sent where they were needed when they were available. With the spinoff, Darden reorganized by assigning a training director to each of its restaurant chains to tie training more closely to the chain's strategic stronghold.

Forays toward the strategic heart of the business they serve have risks for the trainer too long cloistered in the training department and in the jargon of adult-learning theory. They have to learn to speak business.

"We proposed a $500,000 program to do action-reflection learning for about 30 people," a trainer from a consumer paper products company told *Management Review* magazine earlier this year. "The chairman did not know what 'action reflection' meant. I told him that it's keeping a daily journal of your normal work and learning from that journal. The chairman said, 'Oh, I see, we'd pay a half-million dollars for 30 spiral notebooks.'"

Fast Movers and Short-Cutters

Ouch. So forget the terminology you use to impress peers at conferences. Instead, consider this example of rough-and-ready language from *Supervisory Management* magazine. The subject is how to pick people from the plant floor to be trainers. The article does explain eventually what it means by each of the following types. But for our purposes, merely appreciate the workmanlike simplicity: "Individuals who should be avoided when selecting potential trainers are know-it-alls, carefree types, fast movers and shortcutters." That's how business talks. Are you taking notes, here?

Getting top-management's ear doesn't mean you have to go cold-calling on the boss of all bosses in your organization. Rather, you can proceed stepwise. "We integrate ourselves into the business and become resources to them and partners with them," says Ruth Loyd, manager of Texas Instruments Inc.'s Performance Enhancement Center in Plano, TX, a Dallas suburb. "We become more in tune with what top-management's priorities are. And as we become more in tune, they tend to notice us more."

Or, if you have had a dazzling success, make sure top management finds out about it, suggests Gerald Jones, executive vice president with Forum Corp., a Boston-based training firm.

Some make the case that it falls to the training department to keep upper management in touch with reality. John Humphrey, Forum's chairman, recalls with glee the senior marketing vice president at a client company who described his company's executive row as the place "where the rubber meets the air." Execs were determined to hit the ground running with every new idea, but their legs didn't reach that far. That is, their big ideas weren't suited to the reality of the front-line worker's job.

A case in point would be the fast-food chain Humphrey describes, where senior management wanted more variety in the menu — while front-line workers were delayed fill-

---

UP CLOSE AND PERSONAL AT ARM'S LENGTH

What's the function of a training department? And how well does it work? One way to find answers is to extract the department from its mother corporation, and run it as a separate entity.

That's what E.I. du Pont de Nemours and Co. did by farming out its employee-training function to Forum Corp. The Wilmington, DE, chemical giant and the big Boston training firm linked up two years ago in a partnership in which Forum essentially acts as DuPont's corporate training department.

Under the arrangement, Forum delivers all training and development services worldwide except operator mechanic training (done by community colleges and technical schools), and safety and diversity training — both of which DuPont has kept in-house as part of its corporate "heritage."

Forum does needs assessments for DuPont and delivers training from Forum's own curriculum, from internal DuPont sources, or from other vendors. DuPont gets better-managed purchases and volume discounts.

DuPont says it's happy with results so far. Prior to the partnership, DuPont used a completely catalog-based, open-enrollment training strategy. Now the company provides just 34 percent of its course offerings on an open-enrollment basis; the remaining two-thirds of all training addresses specific business needs.

Meanwhile, DuPont's fixed costs for training taken over by Forum plunged from more than $8 million annually to virtually zero. Meanwhile, the unit cost for train-

ing — what it costs to deliver one unit of training to one person — dropped 30 percent.

Forum manages the load by spinning off some courses to about 50 other training organizations — including some firms that compete directly with Forum on other fronts. Forum fences off those prickly situations with what it calls "Chinese walls" — essentially, agreements not to talk about pricing and terms in settings where a sometime competitor could use the information.

As for the relationship between Forum and DuPont — well, it's a little like dating vs. marriage. When you see each other day after day, there's a kind of unwritten accountability. "A vendor will come in and work with you and then they'll leave," says Ed Trolley, DuPont training and education manager. "If they did a decent job, you might call them back — or you might never call them again. Forum does something today, they're here tomorrow, walking the halls with the people they worked with the day before."

Companies are watching the so-called "insourcing" deal with DuPont. Forum expects more such deals.

The alliance appears to be making it — running itself like a business, which, some argue, is what a training department should do. Others are cautious about such an approach. Is your training department a profit center delivering bang for the buck? Or is it the heart and soul of your organization? If so, can you hold your heart and soul at arm's length? Stay tuned.

— *M.H.*

---

ing orders as customers puzzled over a menu that was too detailed already.

Who's in a position to set top management straight on that one? Arguably, the trainers who would have to teach workers to cope with the new menu.

Performance Prophets

Can trainers grow into the role of companywide performance prophets, predictors of what works and what doesn't, banging with impunity on the chief executive's iron portcullis to set the Big Guy straight? This sounds like a tall order for the meek, gets-no-respect, flip chart-scrawling drone in the training room.

Not necessarily. "It's a natural extension of the skills we have," shrugs TI's Loyd. "The needs-analysis work we've been doing is a natural transition into performance analysis."

Meanwhile, some managers are learning to ask the right questions. "We don't hear, 'We want sales training' from our customers," says Forum Corp.'s Jones. "We hear, 'We want growth.'"

Are you ready for that kind of request? That would mean the new trainer can't just know how to do sales training. The new trainer has to know sales, and the business as a whole. "The old paradigm of training (client request, follow ISD model, build course, offer course) is impossible and ineffective," consultant Gayeski e-mailed in an exchange with training. "Organizations need to set up learning systems, not course-building departments, and integrate learning with other communication systems."

It sounds like a tough transition for traditional trainers who got where they are by knowing the classic routine of assessment, design, delivery and evaluation. Many probably don't want to change.

Texas Instruments, for one, has doubled its budget for traditional training in the past four years — but has expanded the role of trainers to other functions, including organization development and multimedia.

Get a Job

McDonald's Copeland says the role of the trainer has expanded within the classroom too. When he asks his restaurant-manager trainees about their biggest barricade to success, and they respond "frustration" — it becomes the trainer's job to help them figure out what it is that frustrates

them. In other words, he suggests, he teaches his charges how to think. "The thought process is going to make the difference," Copeland says, "for them and for the company and for society."

But if you want to grow from the old trainer model to the new, how do you get from here to there? At one extreme on the option chart is the career move. "Joining HR as a career

---

THE NEW TRAINER'S SKILL CHECKLIST

Training and development professionals we talked to say the new trainer needs skills in:

- Listening.
- Negotiating.
- Coaching.
- Facilitating small-group interaction. (Spend less time talking.)
- Awareness of different learning styles.
- Testing and measurement.
- Business processes. (Know how things get done in business.)
- Strategic planning.
- Problem-solving.
- Facilitating organizational change.

If you have all of those skills, give yourself a pat on the back—and go find somebody to practice on.

— M.H.

---

and building your way up to manager or vice president of HR — that's a dinosaur," says consultant Weiss. "Companies don't want people who don't have line experience. If you love training, if you love helping people learn, go out and get a line job as a salesperson or customer service rep. Spend several years out on the line, preferably moving up through supervisor or management."

Wait a minute. Someone who has already invested 20 years in a training career should drop it and start over in sales? Weiss relents. "In that case, develop close alliances with line partners and at least through osmosis start gaining some of the knowledge they have," he says. "One reason HR and training [departments] lose credibility is that top management looks over there and sees people who don't have a clue, who don't know what return on equity or attrition mean, or who can't tell what's the latest problem on the custom lines."

The New Trainer

If that's the case, many trainers face an uphill battle to gain some respect. They can get started by looking for people to help, people who are working on real business problems. The new trainer finds ways to become indispensable. "My mission is to help the people at TI do their jobs better," says Loyd. "If that means getting them specific skills, we'll do that. If it means helping them study a manufacturing process, we'll do that. If it means providing them information they can't find, we'll do that. If it means helping them better define where they want to be five years from now, we'll do that — anything to help them do their job."

The let-me-help approach also works for external training vendors. Dave Vollmer is an instructor at Chippewa Valley Technical College in Eau Claire, WI, who works with area companies as a training consultant. Vollmer positions himself with prospective clients as the guy who may not know the answer — but knows how to find it. "'If you have a question about quality,' says Vollmer, 'call Dave. He'll make a commitment to find the answer.' That's how I built my credibility. I was offering free services."

The new trainer thinks big. "My mission," says Jan Howard, assistant vice president and quality officer with The Mutual of New York (MONY), "is to liberate the potential of everyone with whom I associate." Compare those sentiments to those communicated by her old mission: "Train and teach and share information with other people."

New trainers make themselves valuable to customers. What do customers value? They value that to which many trainers pay least attention: the front end and the back end, says Forum's Jones. That is, clients want a good, sharp, businesslike assessment of needs on the front end and, on the back end, businesslike dialogue about what happened and whether or not it helped.

The new trainer is a lifelong learner. "Stay on top of your field so you know what's going on constantly in research and education," says the *Times'* Hartley. "The minute you think you know something — you don't know it."

Giving It Away

The new trainer gives away training skills to line workers and subject matter experts, says David Peterson, vice president with Minneapolis-based consulting firm Personnel Decisions Inc. "If [trainers] aren't giving it away and staying ahead of the curve and reengineering themselves," Peterson warns, "their training business is going to go to video-based or software-based training."

All right. So what does the new trainer look like in action?

"I spent my morning with one of the businesses, meeting with a quality-improvement team on organizational effectiveness, scoping our '96 priorities," says TI's Loyd. "We talked about what we wanted to rededicate resources to and spent our time monitoring and supporting. Five years ago, as the training manager, I would not have been an integral part of that process."

At MONY, trainers facilitate twice-a-year, seven-day, peer-to-peer sessions for the company's commissioned salespeople. The sales reps train each other, with trainers guiding the session.

A utility client faced with the spreading deregulation in that industry asked Gayeski's help in restructuring its marketing department. Her needs analysis asked the marketers what they needed to learn. Their responses pointed to a total of nearly 40 courses, each of which would take two or three days. "These marketing reps would be doing nothing but sitting in training for a year," says Gayeski. "They'd never get any work done."

Gayeski helped alter the two-person training department's mission to one of brokering professional- development resources. The trainers did develop some courses, but she also helped them build a database of skills already available within the company. Employees experienced in, say, structuring bids on providing electrical power to major customers could share those skills one-on-one or in brown-bag sessions with small groups.

Turbo Training

Working overseas in 1991, Robert Laney — now head of the Tall Man Group, a Littleton, CO, training-video producer — was faced with the need to train Television New Zealand news production workers to run a microwave truck for live TV news remotes. That was a tall order, considering the demands on TV newspeople's time.

Laney sat down for an hour at a time with the one man who knew how

---

"Stop thinking of yourself as a trainer. Start thinking of yourself as the manager of the communications infrastructure of your organization."

---

to run the truck's equipment, and took notes. Laney calls it a "brain dump." He did seven such hour-long dumps with his expert. Laney then wrote up his notes and organized them into a readable training plan. Then the expert coached the other technicians one-on-one, using the written training plan to prompt him. "I've adopted the word 'adequate' as a good word," says Laney. "I want the best. But for a lot of people in particular situations, adequate might be the best."

At the *Times*, Hartley helped compress three newspaper production processes — inserting, bundling and delivering — into one, a classic case of work-process improvement. Training-department operatives helped develop teams and get them rolling on process-improvement analysis. Result: Success, from a business point of view. The compressed process is faster. But jobs disappeared. "That's a painful part of this work," Hartley broods.

This is as much about the new worker as it is about the new trainer. Where the old trainer taught workers to do, some say, the new trainer teaches them to think. That means trainers have their work cut out for them.

Hartley regrets the *Times* job cuts but glories in the new worker ideal she feels she's helping to build with employees at the newspaper. "We've taken them out of the Industrial Age, the way business has been done for years," says Hartley. "Now we tell them, 'This is what a budget looks like. We need more than your hands. Now we need your heads.'"

If this is the direction you're taking, where to begin? There's the irony. Get some training.

"Trainers should spend a lot of time learning new skill sets," says MONY's Howard. "Starting with the whole cadre of communication skills. We need to educate ourselves to become superior facilitators and to understand what the word 'catalyst' means."

Copeland says: "There is growth on both sides of my mission. I want to continue to grow on the intellectual level. I challenge myself and challenge my people."

In short, to change, learn. That's what trainers have been espousing all along. Shouldn't be a problem. Physician, heal thyself.

How One Training Leader Is Turning His Staff into 21st-Century Trainers

BY DAVE ZIELINSKI

Steve Jensen is bucking the trend. At a time when an increasing number of training leaders are saying, "Why bother developing the expertise to create multimedia-based training in-house?," Jensen is among those looking for the best way to get a training staff with limited technical experience up to speed on those new competencies.

A recent study done by *TRAINING Magazine*, in conjunction with the marketing strategy firm OmniTech, reflects on the trend. The results, based on responses from managers in charge of multimedia-based training in 146 *Fortune* 1000 companies, show a majority of them will be hiring "highly experienced" personnel from the outside to develop multimedia-based training in the future. One reason why: When asked how many of their current classroom trainers and instructional designers could "successfully transition to multimedia development roles," respondents answered just 40%.

Jensen, national training manager with Value Rent-A-Car in Boca Raton, FL, is intent on building that expertise internally, in his own staff of five — who, incidentally, had zero experience with in-depth performance analysis or multimedia authoring. Jensen's goal: to include these skills as part of building high-level performance consulting expertise in his staff so they can help develop people in whatever ways are most appropriate. Here's how he's making it happen.

New Management Imperatives

The process started with Jensen locking all the top brass in his company in a room for a day "to put down on paper what they want the company to become — their vision for competitive advantage into the future." An urgent need emerged to become more customer-focused. That meant middle managers and car-rental agents in the field would need new incentives — and a radically new performance orientation.

Jensen knew his staff of traditional trainers needed new skills to help the company get there; his vision was to use better performance analysis and more technology-assisted instruction to help fuel the change.

Step one was to reduce the size of his staff — yep, you're reading right — from 12 to five. Those who had been working in a help-desk function were relocated to the information services department. Also, three field sales training manager jobs were eliminated, because much of their work had been subsumed by line managers, Jensen says.

That left two field training managers, two instructional designers at corporate headquarters — one a systems worker who was completely new to training — and a newly hired OD expert with a specialty in management development.

"I said I was going to cut my staff in half and at the same time do more, and that wasn't easy. But the shift to more technology and less classroom-delivered training makes it possible for us," he says.

'True' Performance Analysis

Following the new management decree for better customer service, "People in the field were screaming for training for middle managers," Jensen says. But he wasn't at all convinced training was the answer. He conducted a "performance-gap analysis," using the model popularized by Dana Gaines Robinson, to help determine true needs and problems. "And that created a need for a whole new set of skills on my staff right away," he says.

To indoctrinate his streamlined staff in the principles of performance analysis, Jensen held a three-day, off-site meeting to redefine their new roles.

"It was 'Performance Consulting 101' — basically the difference between traditional training design and performance consulting," he says. "It represented a whole new way for us to gather information that goes into training design."

Then, however, the trainer boot camp became mostly trial by fire, or what Jensen likes to call "learning by doing."

The staff began with two-hour interviews of top performers — as nominated by Value's field managers — in each job category. Because of his earlier gap analysis, Jensen knew this identification step was critical. The commission structure for car-rental agents had been identified as an "organizational barrier" to changing service-related behavior.

"Agents were paid solely on incremental sales brought in, not necessarily customer service performance. In other words, customer complaints after the sale had little effect on agents' commissions." So Jensen and staff made sure they interviewed top performers "who weren't just making record sales numbers, but who also were known to be very customer oriented," he says.

His two designers were nervous about conducting the interviews.

"It was so different from what they were used to," Jensen says. He modeled a few rounds of interviews himself as the designers looked on and took notes. Then it was their turn in the barrel, using established interview questions.

"The real skill here comes in identifying environmental obstacles and company structures that are barriers to performance," Jensen says. "That's the biggest difference from our old needs-analysis process. It's the difference between someone saying, 'I have a training need' and taking it at face value vs. probing further — and with tact — for a more well-rounded analysis."

The interviews were followed with on-site observation. The designers' mission was to look for specific behaviors — or lack thereof — that came out of the interview process: execution of the sales process, cus-

COMMUNITY COLLEGES OFFER HIGH-TECH RESOURCES FOR TRAINING YOUR TRAINERS

There are plenty of options for helping your staff acquire skills to design and manage multimedia training projects. Most large authoring-software vendors, for instance, offer packaged training. But one training manager has yet to find anyone who can beat a nearby community college when it comes to providing cost-efficient, reality-based training for his staff.

John Nolan, director of technical instruction at VISA International in San Mateo, CA, contracted with the nearby College of San Mateo (CSM) to help his staff — which had zero experience in building self-paced multimedia training — acquire new skills sets using an "action learning" format.

The staff had created some basic text-based CBT courses, but Nolan wanted to move to the next level to update some long-running technical courses.

"We wanted to get into multimedia courseware, both building our own and using off-the-shelf titles," he says.

He first evaluated three authoring platforms before making his final choice. The next step was deciding how the staff would learn to use it.

"There are classes out there for thousands of dollars a head with set curriculum, but more often than not people come back from those kinds of sessions and beat their heads against the wall trying to figure out how to apply the training to their unique situations," he says. "Standard off-the-shelf training didn't seem like it would be effective for us. We needed to customize training, and do it cost efficiently."

Nolan had previously worked with the college — which has a division devoted to conducting training for corporations — to deliver customized technical-writing training and had confidence in its abilities. And it just so happened the college also had a multimedia development lab. But Nolan's training request was a bit unusual.

"I wanted the training to be the actual development of our own project," he says, "so they needed fundamental design concepts of multimedia, modules on managing multimedia projects, and hands-on development of the training. The upshot: not only would my get people trained, but we would get a completed project we could put out on the floor right off the bat."

The training was very cost effective, he says: "To train five people through the usual means in the typical four-day multimedia training would have cost roughly $1,500 to $2,000 per head," he says. "Through the college, it has cost me less than $5,000 for training all five of my folks."

A Welcome By-Product: Training Builds Team Skills

Because of the unique nature of the training, Nolan interviewed the college instructor at length before agreeing to the training contract.

"We would not be following a strict curriculum, and our team would need a good deal of leeway during the training," he says. "Sometimes decisions our people would make about the project would contradict the instructor's recommendations, but our people needed freedom to make up their own minds, incorporating the feedback."

Nolan's five staffers went through the training as a group, with the unexpected benefit that "it was a positive team-building experience because they were not used to working collaboratively on an extended project," he says.

"We coordinate with each other regularly, but rarely do we all work together on the same project."

The entire training/multimedia project development took about six months, and the college proved quite flexible in adapting to the training staff's often-unpredictable work schedule.

"Because of workloads and commitments here, we often had to reschedule classes, but the college has been very accommodating," he says. "And the training was designed in a way that the whole staff didn't have to be off site for an entire week at a time."

— D.Z.

---

tomer service behaviors, operational knowledge, and so on. Designers shadowed rental agents and managers, working behind the counter, watching the day unfold, and taking notes.

"That was very new for them too," Jensen says. "Under our old model, instructional designers maybe talked to a few subject-matter experts, then would dive right into design. Face-to-face contact with line workers was rare. We wanted to change the old lament that trainers don't have credibility because they haven't been in the trenches."

Using 'Action Learning' to Develop Authoring Skills

The information gleaned from that performance analysis was then fed into development of a new training CD-ROM for field employees. And once again, Jensen's staff needed new skill sets — in a hurry.

The only way to truly develop authoring skills in novices, he believes, is via action learning, or hands-on involvement in a real project, not by attending "just-in-case" outside courses. The group first purchased authoring tools from IconAuthor and CBT Express, which provided an early lesson.

"We had a trainer from IconAuthor come in and do 'Authoring 101' training right after we purchased the tool," he says. "But it was months before we were actually going to do the multimedia project, so much of that knowledge was lost."

When it was time to actually author the CD-ROM, Jensen brought in Eric Parks from the consulting firm Ask International in Long Beach, CA. Over the next six months, Jensen and his designers worked hand-in-hand with Ask in the development of storyboards and content for the CD-ROM. "We didn't just feed the consultant content and say, 'Go design this,'" Jensen says. "They spent weeks out here teaching and working with us."

Once storyboards were approved and it was time to program or "author" the training, the consultant and Jensen's team continued to furiously swap e-mail. "As Ask was developing things we were reviewing them, and I was beta testing with my staff. Although we didn't handle the bulk of the authoring, we were playing around with code, getting an idea of how it was structured," he says.

The final result was a CD, with about 10 hours of computer run time, integrated with on-the-job activities. But the education didn't end there for Jensen's staff.

In a debriefing phase, the consultant returned to Jensen's office, "to open the code to the finished program so we could examine how it is structured so we would be able to do maintenance of the program." He now feels his staff is equipped to author another multimedia project from A to Z.

The CD-ROM contains four training modules on customer service behaviors, product knowledge, the new sales process, and contract processing. Testing on content in the CD has two parts: (1) an online test measuring knowledge acquired in all modules, plus information learned off-line via on-the-job training activities; and; (2) a rental simulation, where trainees are faced with a "video couple" they have to take through all the proper rental steps using new behaviors.

The incentive for mastering the content: Rental agents need a minimum score of 85% on the final exam to receive a "log on" to access the real computer system and to begin generating commissions.

To reinforce the new training on the job — and at least partly as a result of Jensen's staff's recommendations — Value's top management committee is phasing in a new set of customer service incentives and recognition programs. The sales commission program already has been replaced by a program that rewards agents based more on overall, not individual, revenue. And top management's bonus structure is being altered in 1997 to reward attention to customer service and employee development.

Notes:

How to Hire the Right Trainer

The effort you put into the process determines the quality of your results.

BY CHRIS LEE

Whether you've been a manager for 10 years or six months, you know the standard hiring routine: You advertise and/or post the position, get deluged by résumés, sort/grade/rate potential candidates, interview anywhere from six to a few dozen eager applicants and offer the job to the person you decide is "right." In the best of all possible worlds, the successful candidate accepts the job and proceeds to prove that you made an excellent decision.

In the real world, of course, the hiring process often doesn't go quite this smoothly. Maybe you get loads of résumés, but none quite fit what you have in mind. At the other extreme, your ideal candidate declines the offer. Or, you may hire Mr./Ms. Right only to find that not only do they not "fit" with your team, they are subtly undercutting the camaraderie that once characterized it.

Most training managers would agree that hiring decisions are critical — make the wrong choice too often and you can permanently damage the training function's credibility in your organization. The question is, are you willing to put in the time and effort required to make your selection procedures more than a crapshoot?

"A funny thing goes on in selection situations," says Patricia McLagan, president of McLagan & Associates, Inc., a St. Paul, MN, consulting firm. "The people hiring are usually in a hurry and they'll take the first good thing that comes along. They will present an image of the company that isn't strictly accurate and the new employee will be unhappy as a result."

That isn't a one-way street either,

she points out. Job applicants obviously present the image they think the employer wants — and can end up in the wrong job in the wrong company. "Both the company and the candidate should be open about their strengths and weaknesses," McLagan adds. "Everybody has a stake in a good match — without it, everybody loses. It's not a failure to be turned down; you should be looking for a fit."

Stacking the Deck

The wisdom of those experienced in hiring trainers and human resources development (HRD) professionals can be summarized succinctly: Know what you want and why. Careful consideration and thought invested up-front, they agree, will pay off exponentially when it comes down to the actual selection decision.

"The training and development field has become measurably more sophisticated and diversified over the last 10 years," says David Brinkerhoff, president of Abbott-Smith Associates, an employment firm that specializes in HRD personnel. "You've got everything from human resources planners to quality-circle trainers — who'd heard of that 10 years ago? Training managers have got to know what the hell they want.

"The whole process of recruiting is becoming more professional," he says. "Hiring managers are more sophisticated about what they want. Rather than 'someone who has a good image' — who doesn't have a good corporate image? — they want a specific background, or someone who comes out of a specific industry. And they are clear about it."

Training managers who are unfamiliar with the nuances of the growing number of new specialties in the field are going to get into trouble,

Brinkerhoff adds. He cites a case where a manager started out offering $33,000 for a position and ended up paying $48,000 after a six-month search. Say, for example, an HRD manager is suddenly asked to get a human resources planner on board. If that manager doesn't happen to be up to speed on HR planning, some quick scrambling may be in order.

"They've got a learning curve themselves," Brinkerhoff points out. "I don't envy a new HRD manager in a large company. It's a tough job. And they had better know what's going on or they're going to get eaten alive."

One tool that can help training managers sail through these shark-infested waters is "Models for Excellence," the competency study published last year by the American Society for Training and Development (ASTD). The study defines 15 roles — functions, not job titles — that comprise the training and development field. It also lists the "outputs" that result from performing these functions successfully and the key "competencies" (tied to specific behaviors) that are required in order to produce those outputs.

How can it help? McLagan, who directed the competency study for ASTD, recommends first taking a step backward. "It's important to see the systems issue, to back up and take a strategic look at the mission of the training function in the company," she explains. "Given that strategy, you can ask, 'What are the roles that give us the most leverage?' If 'strategist' is a critical role or if 'trainer/facilitator' is an important role, you can aim for people who have developed a high level of competence in those roles.

"The 'outputs' list is a powerful part of the study," McLagan continues. "From the list of 102 outputs, you can pull out what you expect this person to produce and develop a job description from that." During this process, the outputs you want from an individual job tend to fall into clusters — that is, they define the role of instructor, evaluator, needs analyst and so on. "If you end up with 13 of the 15 roles," she says, "you might want to think about restructuring the job."

The competency study also can serve as a guide throughout the selection process. "It can give you a framework for looking at résumés and structuring an interview. You can set up a job application that asks questions that get at the competencies and roles in question. You can ask applicants to rate themselves on skills, which gives you anchors for the interview — 'Tell me why you gave yourself a 3 on that.' You can pick the competencies you want to zero in on in a reference check," McLagan suggests.

If sorting through hundreds of roles, outputs, competencies, behavioral anchors and the like strikes you as overkill, think of the process as akin to deciding on the specifications for a new motor, suggests Lynne Tyson, vice president of the Institute for Business & Industry, Inc. in Cornwell Heights, PA. "You have specs to make sure the motor would be able to perform certain functions. You may require that the candidate has a masters degree and so many years of experience, but is that what you need?"

Concentrating on the actual tasks (the "specs") the person will perform will prevent you from overlooking qualified candidates, and at the same time allow you to narrow your scope of candidates, Tyson explains. And once you have developed specs, you're prepared to decide on selection criteria.

Sidestep

Methods for setting selection criteria are as idiosyncratic as taste in lamp shades, but create your criteria before you identify likely candidates to avoid skewing them to a particular applicant, Tyson urges. "Once you have decided on your 'must haves,' 'nice to haves' and 'wish I hads,' you can objectively and fairly hire the best person for the job," she says.

According to Brinkerhoff, most training managers want someone with three to five years of corporate experience, and the key word here is corporate. "They're looking for someone with a business head, someone with business sense. They say, 'Give me someone who knows business, and, I can take them the rest of the way.

Many training managers have successfully sidestepped that issue by hiring trainers exclusively or primarily from inside their organizations — that is, by selecting people with subject-matter expertise rather than training expertise — yet they still have devised an effective basis for their selection decisions.

Tom Hartley, manager of sales-

education services at Union Carbide's sales-training headquarters in Tarrytown, NY, has designed the job of sales trainer as a "flow-through" position for field salespeople. "It's a tremendous developmental experience for them," he says, "while we get people who have skills we can build on."

Since they provide hundreds of training sessions each year for each Carbide division, Hartley and his staff have the opportunity to scan the field sales force continuously for likely candidates. "We see them go through training so we have a sense of who we think would be good," he says. "We also get vibrations from people who we think would be interested."

Although he characterizes human resources planning as a practice that "sounds great, but is hard to do," Hartley has created a process that allows him to select potential trainers years in advance. "We have a list of people who are ready now, those who will be ready soon (in about one year) and those who will be ready in the future (about four years)."

Hartley's criteria for selecting a trainer include:

• **Interest.** "That's the biggest thing: They have to be interested in coming out of the field to Tarrytown for two or two-and-a-half years," he says.

• **Career stage.** Field employees who have a minimum of four years experience, but probably not more than eight, are likely candidates. After a stint in training, they are likely to return to the field as sales managers or to accept a promotion elsewhere in the company.

• **Reputation.** They don't necessarily have to be "super-duper" salespeople, Hartley explains, but they must have credibility among their peers — and with management.

• **Experience.** Since Hartley's staff provides training on a wide range of products, new trainers need expertise that complements that of the existing staff.

Managers who hire trainers from inside their companies have to be careful to avoid the classic tendency of organizations to use the training department as an elephant burial ground — to staff it with people who can't be fired but whose usefulness elsewhere is pretty much exhausted. That isn't a problem at NCR Corp., where a stint as a trainer in the technical-education organization is a recognized career step for field engi-

neers, partly because director John E. Marohl chooses carefully from the ranks.

"We're looking for someone with an interest, a bent toward education. We're not looking for someone who's seeking a hiding place from the field," he emphasizes. "We want someone who wants to help. We want to know what motivated them, what their long- and short-term goals are, why they applied for the job in the first place."

Although Marohl does not hire exclusively from inside NCR's ranks, in many instances he and his staff have the advantage of knowing the pool of potential trainers from first-hand experience — they train the field engineers. Which trainees are they likely to conclude have a "bent" toward education? Those who are critical of training they have gone through, but who come up with good suggestions for changes.

An additional "quality-control check" built into NCR's technical-education system: Field managers have a vested interest in seeing good people become trainers because they are part of the process. "Training is important and expensive — and they have to pay for it," Marohl says.

"This is a strenuous position. We get our pound of flesh. And we're looking for people who want that kind of challenge," he adds.

Eliminating Them

If you believe in going the opposite route — hiring training specialists and teaching them the ropes in your organization, rather than teaching insiders to be trainers — you have a number of options. You might hire a search firm; advertise the position in professional journals, specialty magazines, or newspapers; or use the job listings of ASTD and other associations to publicize your opening. Thus, the next activity on your hiring agenda will be to sort through piles of résumés. But if you've decided upon the criteria the job demands, the task may not be as arduous as it appears.

Carnie Ives Lincoln's experience in the training and development field ranges from 26 years as a training manager at Connecticut General Life Insurance Co. to a stint in a placement firm to independent HRD consulting. According to her, an advertisement in, say, *The Wall Street Journal* for a good job in the HRD field can easily produce a torrent of 1,500 résumés. But,

Lincoln points out, "you use résumés to eliminate applicants, not to select them. You often can automatically reject a large stack of résumés."

It's best to make extensive notes on the resumes of likely prospects Lincoln advises, so that you can follow up with a phone interview to clarify the experience listed and question missing information before you set up a personal interview.

Some managers have perfected the art of résumé reading (at least for their own purposes) to the point where key phrases immediately clue them to prospects worth further consideration. Jack Zigon, manager of human resources development at Yellow Freight Systems, Inc. in Overland Park, KS, wants to see very specific and measurable evidence of performance improvement when he hires "performance engineers."

"I want to see performance-improvement programs that helped management improve quality, saved the company X dollars, reduced overtime by X, etc.," Zigon says. "I want to know if they bothered to evaluate a training program's effect on employee performance."

Alan Pickering, national training director for the YMCA, admits to a personal prejudice against "mass résumés," the professionally printed variety only vaguely targeted at the job in question. "That tells me a lot about someone," he says. "If they are interested in my job, their résumé should be directed to my specific job requirements. The way one prepares to secure a job indicates how one prepares to do a job. Since targeting is what education is all about, the person who sends me a mass résumé is not the kind of craftsperson I want."

Pickering also uses résumés to gauge written communication skills, including use of punctuation and spelling. "I look at them very carefully, and I want them to be 'perfect.'"

The Interview

The personal interview is, of course, the only really effective way to judge the important, but rather nebulous quality of "fit" — the question of whether this person will function effectively as a member of your team. Carnie Ives Lincoln says flatly that final hiring decisions are always based on chemistry — the rapport between the hiring manager and the candidate.

"That's the bottom line. If I were

going to teach someone how to get a job, I would emphasize how to establish rapport," she adds. (See accompanying article, "How to Find the Right Training Job.")

William Swan, whose New York City-based company, Swan Consultants, Inc., specializes in training interviewers, says the effective interview begins with preparation: "Know what you want."

Swan joins the chorus urging careful up-front preparation. His shorthand for selection criteria are "can-do factors" (skills, abilities), "will-do factors" (initiative, willingness to take responsibility) and "fit factors" (attitudes, values). Determine what you want in these areas, he says, and you will be able to draw moment-to-moment impressions of the candidate throughout the interview, instead of waiting for an impression to form at the end.

His "tripod" model for an effective interview goes like this:

• **Build the proper atmosphere.** Greeting candidates pleasantly, calling them by name, occasionally reacting to what they say instead of interrogating them are not merely social niceties, Swan says. If you want to foster spontaneity, you must create a relaxed, comfortable atmosphere. "A 'stress' interview only tells you how the candidate handles pressure in an interview," he cautions.

• **Structure the encounter.** "The objective of an interview," Swan points out, "is to be able to validly predict performance. Interviewers tend to focus on the most recent full-time professional job, education and on-the-job training."

That's a mistake, he says, because the information solicited will be too narrow to enable you to see patterns of behavior. If you go further back into the candidate's seemingly less relevant work and educational experience, you will be better prepared to see patterns and, therefore, better able to predict performance.

"Despite their best intentions, most interviewers focus on the 'can-do' factors, and neglect the 'will-do' and 'fit' factors," he adds. "Yet 75% of unsatisfactory hires are due to those critical issues."

Swan also advises structuring interviews around a fixed, though not necessarily locked-step, set of questions. "If you ask three candidates whatever questions come to mind, you will not be able to compare and

contrast them. You need recognizably similar databases." And if you use more than one interviewer, it is even more crucial they ask candidates similar questions. Otherwise, they will lack coherent information and will be arguing apples and oranges when they attempt to compare candidates.

• **Ask probing questions.** This is elementary, Swan admits, but even interviewers who know better have the bad habit of asking closed — yes or no — questions. This kind of question produces three consequences: a single-word answer, i.e., exactly what you asked for; a brief answer with no spontaneity; or a brief answer that sets the stage for a prepared speech, which the candidate promptly delivers.

A good probing method, he says, is to accept the answer and then ask "How?" or "Why?" to get more detail and the facts below the surface. "People don't bring accomplishments with them from another job, they bring how they did it. That's why you want to ask them to account for their successes."

A fifth step that Swan says is often neglected by interviewers is selling the candidate on the job. "If you give the candidate five minutes of information, tailored and adapted to the person's specific needs and interests [which you know from the probing interview you have just conducted], they are more likely to say, 'This is the place for me.'"

To Swan's interviewing advice, Diane Gutierrez, a director of personnel at Burroughs Wellcome Co. in Kansas City, would add, "Avoid theoretical questions. Always ask questions in the past tense — instead of asking 'What would?' or 'What should?,' ask 'What did you do?' and 'How did you do it?' "In this way, you get an answer based on a candidate's experience — what they actually have done — rather than on knowledge.

Simulations

Asking a candidate to demonstrate the expertise you expect to see on the job is nothing new: In a sense, the age-old practice of auditioning covers everything from a theatrical tryout to a typing test. The obvious advantage is that the potential employer actually gets a chance to see candidates "show their stuff."

Many organizations hiring trainers ask candidates to design and/or deliver a training session as part of the application procedure — often the final step. One legal precaution here: Since a simulation is a "test," each candidate who progresses to a certain level in the selection procedure must be offered the chance to take it, and the task must be set up in exactly the same way for each individual.

Assessment Designs, Inc., a Florida-based consulting firm, not only has helped clients such as the Federal Aviation Administration and Gulf Oil set up simulation procedures to select trainers, it uses the same process to hire its own employees. "When we hire a facilitator or senior training consultant," says Stephen Cohen, ADI's executive vice president, "we'll give data to candidates and ask them to piece together a training program — the synopsis of a film and lecturette.

Then we'll interview them on the 'whys.' "The idea, he explains, is to sample candidates' analytical skills to see how they might respond to a client's needs.

ADI also asks candidates to conduct an hour-long exercise on the topic of their choice to see their organizational, communication and group-process skills in action. People who look good on paper — who have all the right qualifications — are thus put to the test, Cohen says, "and sometimes they don't have the level of skill their credentials would indicate." Simulations do work as a selection device, he adds, but they don't stand alone. "A simulation can't assess motivation, but it does tell you if they have the basic skills to do what you want on the job."

Yellow Freight's Zigon is a firm believer in the efficacy of simulations, which he uses to complement an extensive nine-step application process.

"We set up an obstacle course that includes live ammunition," he says. And he's not stretching too far for that metaphor.

When Zigon hires a "performance engineer" (who must be able to analyze problems, design training and nontraining solutions, implement the solution, deliver training and/or train trainers to deliver it, and evaluate and report the results), he begins by scrutinizing résumés. If he likes what he sees, he sends the candidate a standard Yellow Freight application and position questionnaire.

The questionnaire covers analyzing performance problems, developing training materials, delivering training, evaluating performance-improvement programs and consulting with management. "It asks three questions about each of these activities," Zigon explains. "What experi-

---

HOW TO FIND THE RIGHT TRAINING JOB

BY CHRIS LEE

Advice on breaking into the training and development field abounds: Most seminars on the topic suggest strategies like attending local chapter meetings of the American Society for Training and Development (ASTD), conducting informational interviews with working trainers, and concentrating on informal networking among your business contacts. But if you've been in the field for, say, five years, how do you go about finding a position that will offer you a new challenge?

Abbott Smith Associates, Inc., the New York-based recruiting firm that specializes in HRD personnel, also publishes "Finding and Getting a Better Position in Human Resource Development," a pamphlet designed to help those already in the field in their job-changing search. Its advice, in a nutshell, centers on doing your homework: Decide if you are committed to a change; know what you are looking for; know what you have to offer; know your priorities; and research prospective companies carefully beforehand so that you can interview intelligently. A systematic and organized preparation strategy is the most important phase of the job search.

Although serendipity certainly can play a hand in landing a desirable position, people who undertake a systematic job search obviously have an edge over those who trust to dumb luck. We happen to know a veteran trainer who was willing to talk, anonymously, about the ups and downs of his recent quest for that "perfect" job.

"Oh, I had a strategy, but I have a better thought-out strategy now than I did when I started," he says. In fact, he sees the whole process as an excellent learning experience. "I spent 18 months looking, and I feel that I got the kind of position I was looking for."

Frustration prompted his search for a better job. "I felt like I was in an outpost, like the world was passing me by," he says of his former position in a small Midwestern town. "I decided to find out what kind of opportunities were out there — and that's a posture you should take all the time or you get out of practice and your sources dry up. You need to rub shoulders with the people in the field."

He employed a carefully plotted strategy to gain visibility: He attended and spoke at professional conferences, wrote for professional journals and cultivated relationships with colleagues. He also registered with a search firm that specializes in the human resources development field, and would recommend that approach to others.

"I went to three different search firms, but the others didn't specialize in HRD and that was a problem. We just didn't communicate very well — they were not familiar with the field. They would send me on interviews for positions that were entirely different than what I was led to believe," he says. "The search firm needs to act as a middleman — they need to understand your desires and what the organization is looking for — and I didn't feel that kind of intimacy with [general] executive recruiters."

Regardless of whether you decide to use a recruiting firm, leave no stone unturned in your search for a better job, our source advises. "Answer ads — always look at the Tuesday edition of *The Wall Street Journal* with all the career stuff in the back. Use ASTD's referral service, and network like mad," he says. "You've got to keep 12 different balls in the air all the time."

More tips from our successful job seeker:

• Tailor your résumé to the job you're applying for. "I had three different résumés, emphasizing different skills. Development and delivery are different, but a lot of people are equally adroit at either. It's just a matter of emphasis...."

---

ence do you have doing this? How do you know you did a good job? What training do you want from Yellow Freight or some outside source to help you develop in this area?

"The questionnaire allows the candidates to organize their experience around these areas, and they can put their best foot forward," he continues.

"It also helps me because if they don't have anything good, they don't return the questionnaire. That's 50% [of the applicants] gone."

He knows this approach doesn't sit well with some potential candidates.

"I've heard [through the grapevine] some people say, 'Who the hell does he think he is?' That's fine. I don't want them. This is a logical, straightforward process — it tells people, 'here's what I'm looking for, tell me what you've done and how well you've done it.'

Zigon peruses the returned questionnaires and then interviews the most promising candidates by phone, basically asking them to expand on their written answers. He goes through a structured list of questions, then turns the tables and asks the candidate to question him on any aspect of the job or the company.

After a reference check, candidates still in the running go through a formal selection-center process. First they submit sample products — self-paced training, group-based training and job aids — they have created, which are evaluated on the basis of instructional design, structure and writing skills. Zigon also puts candidates through two simulations: one tests problem-solving skills in a one-on-one simulation with a former line manager, the other tests delivery skills in a one-hour session with current line managers.

This combination, Zigon says, allows him to see a sample of applicants' analysis, interpersonal and organizational skills in the first simulation, and platform and design skills in the second. Another bonus he sees in this process: "After the simulations, I give them feedback, which also gives me a chance to see how they handle feedback."

After this grueling morning of "auditioning," the candidate goes through a series of interviews with Zigon and his staff. "At this point, we know they are competent, but do they 'fit'? Do we like them? Do they like us?"

In Zigon's words, his selection process is "stressful, but functional." It not only creates a certain camaraderie in the department, he says, but shows him a lot more about a new staffer's strengths and weaknesses than a tra-

• Especially if you're using a head hunter, come up with a list of questions you want answered before you will agree to an interview. "Know what you're looking for and get answers to questions like what is the name of the company, the title of the job, the reporting structure, the staff that will report to you, the location, the salary range, the percent of travel required. That way you won't waste the company's money and your time on an interview for a position you don't want."

• Reserve judgment on a position until you have enough information to make an intelligent decision. "You may see an aspect of the job you don't like during the interview. Your tendency will be to spill your guts to the interviewer — and that's the wrong time to do it. The point is to get an offer. You'll find that the company will make all kinds of concessions once they've made you an offer. That's the time to negotiate."

• To prepare for an interview, come up with the worst question an interviewer can ask you. "In my case, I didn't have a traditional management position, yet that's what I was looking for. I knew they'd ask me about it." His solution: "I get other people to do things for me through 'informal influencing skills.' In other words, I pointed out that I had developed the ability to get things done through other people when they didn't have to do things for me.

Also anticipate the old standard, "What are your strengths and weaknesses?" Pointing out your strengths may not be a problem, but acknowledging weaknesses is a bit stickier for most people. "One good answer is, 'I tend to be a perfectionist.' Then elaborate by explaining 'I work long hours and take things home because every project has to be the best I can produce.'"

• When it comes to salary, talk ranges. "Interviews often end with 'If we were to decide on you, what salary would we need to offer you?' Don't state a dollar amount — you may have cut your throat by going either too high or too low."

A better approach: "Counter with another question. 'Because we're talking about salary, can I assume you're ready to make me an offer?' If the answer is 'yes,' then ask 'What is the range?' If the answer is 'you have more interviews to go through before we get to that point,' ask, 'Can we talk about salary when you are ready to make an offer?' "If you absolutely cannot avoid talking dollars, he recommends, only name your range.

• After an interview, indicate your interest with a follow-up letter. "Always send a letter, but don't beg. Like a courtship, if you're too interested, the other party turns off. It's an art to show your interest without appearing to be desperate."

• Don't jump at the first offer. "If you come back with a counter offer, chances are they will sweeten the pot. Since they have made a decision, they won't withdraw if you come back with a reasonable offer.

"Turning down offers is difficult," says our source, who turned down one attractive job before the position he really wanted was formally offered. "You tend to want to reward them for making you an offer, for reconfirming your value." Any job is going to involve making certain trade-offs — responsibilities, geographic location, potential advancement, pay — so knowing your priorities is essential to sorting offers.

A network of people in HRD helps too. "They can act as a sounding board to help you make a major decision and can sometimes get additional information for you."

• If possible, talk to the incumbent. "At least try to talk to someone who used to work for the company." Here, again, your network of colleagues may come in handy.

• Be discrete. "If your company knows you're looking, you can stifle your career advancement. Schedule interviews for Saturday, if possible. And exercise discretion in your choice of a confidant within your organization. I'd say a maximum of one — if too many people know, it begins to mushroom."

ditional interview could do. "I've observed them in action," he explains, "and I can pair them up with someone in the department with complementary skills so that they can contribute immediately and develop specific skills."

Isn't all this a bit much to ask of a job-seeker?

Early in his career, Zigon replies, he was asked to teach a session as part of an application procedure. His reaction: "I loved it. I thought 'This is great. I can just stand up and do it and let my actions speak for themselves.' Of course I was nervous — the sweat was pouring down my legs — but I decided that from then on, I would do the same thing myself. It's not unfair.

If someone is really competent, they welcome the opportunity to demonstrate their expertise."

Happy Endings

The care you put into each phase of your selection process is insurance. If you have designed a job that meets the strategic needs of your organization's training function, drawn up specs that clarify what you expect the employee to produce, screened résumés carefully, structured your interviews around your selection criteria and, perhaps, asked your top candidates to demonstrate what they can do, you have covered your bases well.

Any selection process, of course, can fail you. There is no such thing as an ironclad guarantee that your new star won't somehow turn out to be a lemon. But that's another....

Notes:

The Care and Feeding of Trainers

It's not that trainers are always the last to get any training. But developing them and keeping them happy do present special problems.

BY BEVERLY GEBER

Nineteen training directors sprawl in a ragged circle around a couple of tables in a Florida resort and ponder a question: "What one thing would make a career in training more satisfying to you or your subordinates?" They give it all of four seconds thought, and no one wrinkles a brow or gazes reflexively into space. 'A bigger office," one director says quickly. His joke a success, he quiets the laughter with his real answer: more respect and recognition by line managers.

Most of the others sober up and nod agreement. Nobody mentions money and nobody seriously pines for the trappings of success. True, it may be a mistake to extrapolate from that, since these are undoubtedly some of the best-compensated human resources development (HRD) people in their organizations. But it appears that the need for recognition never abates, even for many people at the top of the corporate-training pyramid. It's a need that drives some very good trainers out of the field altogether. And it helps explain why others, convinced that they cannot be prophets in their own land, seek respect by leaving salaried HRD jobs to become consultants.

Training directors know that they know that the care and feeding of their own subordinates is one of the trickier challenges they face. It's also sometimes among the most neglected ones. In a recent survey of subscribers to the newsletter "Training Directors' Forum," 45 percent of the 172 respondents disagreed — 11 percent of them strongly — with the statement that "development of my training staff is given high priority." Too often the Cadillac ideal becomes the Yugo reality that there may not be enough time and money to give those staffers as much training as they need.

It's hard enough to come up with an efficient development plan for "pass-through" trainers who come in from the line to spend a few years in HRD before moving on. The problems are often more acute with "career" trainers. If a company does employ career trainers, and if those professionals do get regular, high-quality training that lets them continue to hone their skills, the HRD director still is left with the problem of keeping them satisfied when promotion opportunities and pay hikes fizzle out.

Sometimes ambitious trainers are even frozen out of the top jobs within their own departments. One director of a 700-person corporate training function says bluntly that none of his subordinates will succeed him by advancing within the training department. In fact, say many training directors, the only promising career paths for an ambitious trainer lie beyond the training department's door.

What a depressing thought for career trainers, the ones who invariably say they became trainers because they wanted to make a difference. Granted, their plights may not be measurably more severe than those of professionals in many other specialties; a technical writer at IBM, for instance, will climb the ladder only so far in his company, too. But if you want skillful trainers to turn down other opportunities in order to cling to their calling, you have to give them some reasons. They want fulfilling work. They want to be respected. They want to learn and grow. Hence the challenge for training directors.

Robert Saunders Jr., a vice president of the Northern Trust Co. in Chicago, is one training director who admits that there is a gap between the ideal and the reality of developing his staff. "We ought to do for ourselves what we do for other people [in the company]. But it's tough. I can see as a manager how easy it is to let those things slide," he says. He tries to send his subordinates through training as much as time and money allow — often to the neglect of his own continuing education. His attendance at the Training Directors' Forum in Boca Raton, FL, was his first formal attempt at self-development in two years.

The career-development issue sometimes influences the very structure of training departments. It's a factor that weighs in the basic choice between staffing the HRD function mostly with training careerists or with pass-through people.

Saunders intimately understands the difficulty of keeping career trainers satisfied in their jobs. He recently revised the department's hiring philosophy precisely because its design was making it difficult to keep people happy. Under his predecessors, the plan was to hire seasoned career trainers, individuals with experience in lecturing, group facilitation and instructional design, who would need minimal training and could immerse themselves in the work immediately "You can't go out and get experienced, highly paid individuals because if you don't have the resources to back them up, their satisfaction is going to run out very quickly," he says. "It's a problem, and I don't think it's unusual."

Now he hires only entry-level people, who tend to stay longer as they acquire skills and become proficient. Of course, when Saunders traded away experience, the result was a need to spend much more time on training those new trainers. He has created a formal development plan that includes orientation and outside courses in instructional design. Then the new employee observes expert trainers and undergoes a self-study course to become certified to teach his assigned courses. The next step is team-teaching, before he finally teaches solo. It's a laborious process.

"With somebody who's really green, it could take six to nine months. That's tough in a small group," Saunders admits. In the meantime, the novice is producing minimally, and the others are sacrificing some of their own productive time to coach the newcomer along.

Then Again...

There is, of course, a paucity of universal truisms in the training business. Edward Zobeck takes exactly the opposite tack in his HRD department and argues its wisdom strenuously. When he became manager of training and development for AAA Michigan in Dearborn, three-fourths of his trainers were subject-matter experts from line operations who had come into the training department, liked it and stayed.

For many training functions, that wouldn't be a problem. Early on, subject-matter experts contribute their specialized knowledge. Later, after training, they couple that knowledge with teaching skills and become valuable as experienced, stand-up trainers. But Zobeck found some of his subject-matter experts lacking instructional-design skills at the precise time that his company was decentralizing. It was a bad combination. "I'd like to reduce classroom time by about 50 percent in the next couple of years," Zobeck says. "So we need to find other, more cost-effective methods of getting the training out to the people. And that's dependent on tight instructional-design expertise."

His ultimate goal is to have a department that consults on specific training problems and designs courses that would be facilitated in the field by subject-matter experts. So, he says, he'll only hire experienced, career trainers in the future.

But in the meantime, his staff of subject-matter experts is getting a big dose of training to meet the immediate need. Since it would have been too expensive to send them all away for training, Zobeck looked for something that could be done in-house. He selected a course on criterion-referenced instruction. "This one course won't make an instructional designer out of everyone, but at least we'll all be speaking the same language," he says.

With the help of additional training and practice, Zobeck's trainers should be able to cut the time they spend designing programs. He also hopes to see an increase in the quality of the programs.

Once the immediate need is met and the flurry of train-the-trainer instruction is finished, Zobeck isn't sure what the normal routine of trainer training will look like. He admits that he is limited by his budget and by the need to serve clients first, even if his own staff's development suffers.

He doesn't consider that an unusual dilemma. "In my experience, there's very little done for trainers. I came from a government background. We did zero for staff development; it was left up to the individual. My experience with talking to my peers is that that's not always the case. But we do concentrate more on our clients than on ourselves"' he says.

Generally, the people who get the most developmental attention are pass-through trainers. Their time is so short in the HRD function that it must be carefully planned if it's to be meaningful at all. In fact, if they don't learn quickly they're liable to be millstones for their entire stints.

John Purcell, director of training at Ameritech Publishing in Southfield, MI, has a model for developing trainers who are pulled in from the line

---

> ## "We did zero for staff development; it was left up to the individual."

---

and kept for two to three years before he shoots them back out again. He calls it "seeding" the organization with people who, he hopes, have become adept at developing others and will retain fond memories of the training department as they become more influential in the company

Before he recruits them, Purcell carefully describes the training skills they'll acquire progressively. In the first year, they learn to be evaluators, group facilitators, instructors and individual development counselors. The second year finds them practicing instructional development, marketing, needs analysis and media development. The best ones stay for a third year and learn skills needed to be a lead trainer, program administrator and program designer.

Purcell admits that expecting people to learn all those skills — in essence, to become a well-rounded HRD professional — in three years is an imposing goal. Not all of his candidates succeed. But enough do to make the program an attractive career-development move at Ameritech. At least they're not bored in the HRD department, he says,

Off-he-Shelf vs. Customized

In the first year, Purcell's new trainers usually teach courses that relate directly to their previous experience. Salespeople, for instance, teach sales training. Also in that first year, Purcell sends them to an outside train-the-trainer course to learn platform skills and methodologies. In the second year, they do more instructional design and attend an outside course to learn related skills. In the final year, they may attend a national trainers' conference.

The flow of neophytes through the department puts a strain on the career trainers, who are expected to be coaches and to deliver on-the-job training, since there is no formal train-the-trainer instruction on-site. Three career trainers serve as team leaders for the rest, and an additional three are full-time course developers. The remaining 16 are rotational trainers. "It's tough to manage," admits Purcell, "but it's a working model and it's better than going at it willy-nilly."

Those career trainers don't get the same kind of development attention that the pass-throughs receive. But Purcell says that doesn't mean that the careerists have fewer opportunities to sharpen their skills. The pass-through trainers, he says, need a rigid format to adapt to new duties that might seem foreign. The difference between training for the pass-throughs and training for the careerists is akin to the difference between off-the-shelf programs and customized programs, he says. "You analyze their own needs," says Purcell of career trainers.

Unlike Northern Trust's Saunders, Purcell is satisfied with the training his subordinates receive. "I believe I'm doing as much as I want to do, and I really don't have trouble getting money for it," he says.

Michael Goodman, director of network operations education and training for AT&T in Bedminster, NJ, also uses a structured approach. He is trying to turn his function into one that is primarily rotational, and he is in the midst of revising the trainer-development program to make it more uniform across the company. The new plan will be based on specific competencies that the trainers must master. Currently, novices receive training in a stepped approach that calls for them to attend train-the-trainer courses, watch an experienced trainer teach a course, co-teach a course with an experienced trainer, then teach the course alone.

As for career trainers, Goodman aims to limit their numbers to just a small percentage of his 700 subordinates. That means forcing some people to leave, and Goodman is candid about the need for it. He says that during AT&T's pre-divestiture days, some deadwood types were dumped into training and retired there on the job. So he has drawn up some guidelines to determine their fates. From now on, those who are judged average on performance appraisals will be encouraged to leave the training department after three years. Those who are above average will be asked to stay for five years.

In most cases, five years should be the maximum stint, Goodman says. "If you're going to stay in training in this organization for more than five years, you'd better be one of the top people in your job or you better have a particular skill that's difficult to find on the outside."

The corollary to Goodman's philosophy is that there will be no appealing career path for training specialists. In fact, the transitory nature of the job makes it hard to argue that training is a legitimate profession within the company. HRD professionals at AT&T can't even reach the top of their own department.

"I don't think anybody will move into my position by staying in the training organization," says Goodman, whose one year in his current position equals his tenure in the HRD field. (It's telling, too, that there are no vice presidents of HRD at the company.) "I'm running a line organization, and the skills I need in my job are management skills, not training skills. We tell people who want to move forward in the company that they will find it tough to move to middle management and impossible to move beyond middle management by staying in a training job."

That sends a fairly brutal message to career trainers: The skills they acquire and the challenges they face in their chosen field are not the ones the organization values when it comes to advancement and compensation. But depressing or not, many training directors agree that the message holds truth.

In his 22-year career in the training industry, Arlan Tietel, a training manager at 3M Co. in St. Paul, MN, did some zigzagging back and forth between the training function and other departments as he sought to advance. But he kept returning to training because it involved the kind of work he most liked to do.

The lack of advancement opportunities — and in most cases, the lack of a "dual career ladder" to provide status and fatter paychecks to key specialists, instead of just to managers — leads some career trainers to jump out of the corporation. They land in what they hope will be the greener pastures of the consulting world, where the money can be much better and respect is usually greater.

Tietel says a major allure of consulting is that consultants are often regarded as instant experts, who lend a fresh perspective and specific skills and knowledge the organization lacks. Deserved or not, that kind of respect suggests greater job satisfaction than trainers can glean in the corporation, butting their heads against a status ceiling.

Careers in training don't have to stagnate, of course. Zobeck, for one, considers it his responsibility to develop his people and groom someone to take his spot eventually. That means giving his subordinates as much management experience as possible within the training department. Yet, he concedes that in many organizations, advancement means leaving the HRD world behind.

So how do you persuade good trainers to stay as long as possible? How do you keep them happy? One possibility, of course, is to follow the advice that HRD professionals sometimes give to managers of other departments that face the same sorts of problems: Create a dual career ladder. This is an arrangement that allows high-performing technical experts to receive perquisites and salary increases roughly parallel to those they'd get if they were moving up in the management ranks. The idea is to reward valuable performers who don't want to become managers, or who can't move into management because their organizations' hierarchies are flattening, or whose technical expertise the company doesn't want to lose by turning them into administrators.

Zobeck likes the idea but sees no mass rush to enact such systems. He thinks the ideal arrangement for developing trainers and keeping them happy would couple a dual career ladder with a developmental program based on the instructional design competencies prepared by the International Board of Standards for Training, Performance and Instruction. The former would provide satisfaction; the latter would provide specificity and uniformity in training.

Never Enough TLC

Aside from a structured approach such as that, there probably aren't many special strategies training directors can use to keep their subordinates happy that wouldn't work equally well in any other department. Keep job assignments varied, for instance. And above all, give trainers strokes. Training specialists are probably little different from their bosses who attended the session in Boca Raton and voiced an overwhelming desire for greater recognition and appreciation, especially from line managers. The best way to get that respect, according to Saunders, is to make sure the department is perceived not as a supplier of training events but as an organizational problem-solver.

Another important goal is to make sure trainers have the resources and authority to solve problems. "They should see themselves as contributing on an even par with other people in the organization," Saunders says. Eventually, "they have people coming back to them and considering them an expert."

David Brinkerhoff, president of Abbott-Smith Associates, a Millbrook, NY-based executive recruitment firm specializing in the human resources field, says he knew a training director who stumbled upon a useful trick for boosting morale among her 30 to 40 subordinates. She would pick trainers in turn to attend and evaluate a commercial training program. They would then report on it and recommend whether to buy the program for the organization. Within the department, the trainer would be viewed by colleagues as the expert on that particular program or subject.

The importance to the trainer of respect and recognition from colleagues or clients can't be underestimated, says Tietel. "I'm doing what I like to do and I'm getting feedback that matches my value set," he says of his own word. When he gets a thank-you from someone who was helped by his training he feels as though he's accomplishing the goal that prompted him to enter the training field: to make a difference. At times like that, money — or lack of it — doesn't matter as much, he adds.

But recognition alone does not job satisfaction make. One thing training directors can do is to ensure that job duties are rotated enough to provide challenge and limit ennui. "Nobody wants to keep doing the same thing over and over again," Purcell says. His department is fortunate in that it is constantly consumed by special projects.

To some trainers, it doesn't matter much if they aren't compensated lavishly and the training department is perceived as merely a funnel to another, more important place. There are those who understand their company's reward system and simply ignore it. These are the kind of people who get their satisfaction from internal reinforcers, rather than external reinforcers, says Tietel. They're the people who turn down promotions just to stay in the training department. And they aren't all that rare. Tietel suspects most training directors could cite at least one such lifer they've known.

Zobeck has one on his staff now. She has reached the top of her salary range. He can't give her a raise and was worried that he'd lose her. But when he sat down to talk to her, she said she had no interest in going into management. Her goal was to learn more about training'

Goodman says he has one subordinate who asked for a downgrade to a lower salary level because she misses hands-on work in her new position as a training manager. Another asked Goodman to take her out of the company's high-potential program because she knew it would mean promotion out of the training department. "She said, 'I like training. I'm making a choice between wealth, power and all this other stuff, and going home at the end of the day and feeling that I've done what I like to do.'"

Notes:

Just Passing Through

In revolving-door training departments, employees from other parts of the company spend a few years as instructors, then move on. How does it work? And how do the visitors view the permanent residents?

BY BOB FILIPCZAK

Call them transient trainers, fly-by facilitators or impermanent instructors. No matter what you call them, it's a popular practice in many training departments to play host to people from other departments who come into the training organization for a two-year stint and then rejoin the fray at the front lines or move on to other careers.

It's worth noting that the training department didn't always attract people from outside the field who saw it as a steppingstone to advancement, or who felt they had a teacher somewhere inside them trying to claw his way out. In a speech at the *TRAINING '96* Conference in Atlanta, consultant Bob Mager of Mager Associates in Carefree, AZ, and a charter member of the HRD Hall of Fame, pointed out that training was often a dumping ground for managers or employees who couldn't cut it elsewhere in the organization. The practice was driven by the adage that those who can, do, while those who can't, teach. Unfortunately, Mager admitted, the practice of dumping ineffective people into the training department isn't just a legacy of the past. It still goes on, though to a lesser extent.

On the other hand, up-and-comers in some companies now see an interval in training as a plum assignment, a smart move that will further their careers. It can bring them to the attention of senior management and build relationships with people they wouldn't normally meet. Morris Jensby, a claims analyst with the St. Paul Cos., an international insurance firm based in St. Paul, MN, spent a couple of years in the training department and built a lot of bridges with senior leaders at the corporate headquarters. Those relationships have continued even after he finished his stay in the training department.

Others echo Jensby's sentiment that doing time in the training department increases their exposure to different areas of the company, giving them a chance to get out of a narrow silo of expertise and see what other people do for a living. Blake Ingram, a national account manager with W.W. Grainger, a tool manufacturer based in Chicago, spent two years doing sales

> **You germinate the company with a support network of people who have seen the training function from the inside.**

training before going back to his former position in San Francisco. Training, he says, exposed him to a national audience of 1,200 salespeople and taught him a great deal about what salespeople were doing across the country and how various markets were changing.

"It was the best experience I've had since I've been with Grainger," says Ingram. "I learned more in that two years about myself and about sales than I did from seven years in the field. It was a major, accelerated-learning curve."

Fresh Meat

From the company's perspective, one obvious advantage to bringing in people from other departments for a training stint is the influx of new ideas

and fresh perspectives. Mike Christie, a national sales trainer for business-equipment maker Pitney Bowes Inc. headquartered in Stamford, CT, is currently in the middle of a two-year rotational assignment in the training department. He feels he brings a healthy pragmatism to the training world from his former incarnation as a sales manager in Orlando, FL. "We're so fresh from the field," says Christie, referring to temporary trainers like himself. "I think that's a great advantage about this rotational program. You're not too theoretical, you're not too conceptual, you're still very much [grounded in] real life."

That real-life experience may be the biggest advantage of bringing in these transient instructors. There is often a certain credibility issue between training departments and their audiences; the training unit is seen as a little too far from the front lines to offer much practical, job-specific advice. Ingram says he was recruited to do sales training because "our training and development department had a certain skill set, a certain expertise, but it was more in terms of general overall knowledge, things like company orientation."

Salespeople, in particular, tend to be a skeptical crew, says Ingram. Sending in a trainer without a sales background to tell them how to treat customers can be a recipe for disaster. Steven Rauschkolb, director of training and communications for Schering-Plough Corp., a pharmaceutical company in Kenilworth, NJ, makes sure all of his sales trainers have some experience in sales. Moreover, he requires all of his trainers to spend at least one day a month out in the field with sales reps. He insists that anyone getting up in front of a classroom of salespeople should have more than an intellectual understanding of the market. Otherwise, says Rauschkolb, "they won't have the same gut feel for what it takes to stand in front of a customer and be able to sell."

Kathy Szymborski, training officer with Meridian Asset Management in Reading, PA, says the credibility she gained from having worked in different areas of the bank is now her greatest strength as a trainer. Szymborski spent most of her career in other departments of the bank, starting as an entry-level clerk and gradually moving into her current position as the firm's one-person training department. She says that being able to face trainees with a real-world background in the skills she is teaching really makes a difference.

Szymborski adds that she can easily spot trainers who only have a background in instruction and not in the skills they are trying to impart. Grainger's Ingram agrees: "I can pick out in a heartbeat when someone stands up in front of a group and they don't have any idea what we do. They're there to present their program, and I have very little tolerance for it anymore."

One very important benefit of drive-through trainers is the links they forge between training and other departments. By having employees rotate into the training department and then go back into the organization, you essentially germinate the company with a support network of people who have seen the training function from the inside, observes Bob Inguagiato, leader of education services with Astra Merck, a pharmaceutical marketing company in Wayne, PA. If their experience was generally positive, these guest trainers can help you market the training department and be advocates for your efforts.

Another Planet

Of course, bringing fresh perspectives into a training department can be a double-edged sword. These new people may expose the soft underbelly of the training unit, seeing flaws in its mind-set that training careerists can't. This can be valuable, but also uncomfortable.

Jensby's stay in the training department of the St. Paul Cos. was eye-opening on many levels. First off, he was struck by how little the training professionals seemed to understand about the insurance business. He remembers meetings where his comments about the actual day-to-day work of the company left his new comrades staring at him as if he came from another planet. While he felt the training department tended to be good with the big picture, it had trouble connecting to what was going on with the people on the front line. "[The trainers] talk in terms of strategy, they talk in terms of broad training issues, and yet when they go out and deliver, they can't get down to the level that says 'This is what you do,'" says Jensby.

Focus was another problem that jarred Jensby. His background in claims taught him to be very results-oriented, because much of his work could be assigned real dollar amounts. The bottom-line thinking behind the training department's activities wasn't always evident in its behavior. "They would spend as much time developing training to save $100,000 on claims paid as they would on training that would save $12 million. They made no distinction between them," says Jensby.

W.W. Grainger's Ingram also suggests that training departments have blind spots. He's particularly critical of what he sees as a programmatic approach to the world. Trainers, he

---

"We no longer could afford to have a revolving door."

---

says, think that for every problem, there must be a program that will provide the solution. "The majority of things that are out there can be affected a lot more easily without putting [employees] through another three-day program," says Ingram.

He also voices a complaint reminiscent of one that many training professionals have leveled at their own field for many years: Trainers tend to evaluate their service in terms of how many people got trained, how many programs were run, or how many hours of training were delivered. Those aren't legitimate ends, Ingram points out, but merely the means toward some end that is supposed to benefit the company.

While they may find plenty to criticize, most interim trainers agree that they personally derived a lot from their tours of duty in the department. Jensby picked up what he discovered to be an important skill: the ability to speak the language of training. When he went back to the claims department of his organization, he could help his peers translate their training needs into terms that the training department could understand. Moreover, he says, his time in the training department dramatically improved his presentation and group-facilitation skills.

Ingram agrees. He credits improved interpersonal skills with making him a better salesperson when he went back to his position as a national accounts manager. Along the same lines, Pitney-Bowes' Christie says that his time in the training department made him focus on his listening skills. He learned that "you need to use the ear muscle more than the jaw muscle" when you are working in a classroom.

License to Train

Having outsiders do a tour of duty in the training department may be beneficial to the individuals involved as well as the larger organization. But what about the trainees? Isn't it hard to imagine that instructors newly acquainted with the field of training can be as effective as professionals?

This raises a long-debated question. Is it true, as some suggest, that it's usually easier to teach a subject-matter expert (SME) how to train than it is to have a professional trainer master an unfamiliar body of skills and knowledge well enough to teach it? Or is the other side right when it argues that a solid background in training and development is the most important asset to consider when you put someone in a classroom, while "content" generally can be supplied by SMEs during the design of the course?

Consultant Mager points out that this so-called dilemma often turns out to be a no-brainer; the answer simply depends on the complexity of what is being taught. If the skills are pretty straightforward — how to use a computer to perform some relatively simple tasks, for instance — then a professional trainer can probably deliver the content effectively. If the course involves more complicated knowledge, like actually programming a computer, then a subject-matter expert with training skills might be a better choice.

But the issue isn't always that simple. Edward Gordon, president of Imperial Corporate Training & Development, a Chicago-based training consulting firm, and author of the upcoming book, *Opportunities in Training and Development Careers*, questions the practice of running a series of temporary instructors through the training department. Without an extensive background in training, he argues, the drive-through trainers are bound to have significant limitations because the body of knowledge in training has increased dramatically. "We've come a long way over the last 20 years," he says. "Can people in the pass-through system be utilized? Of course they can. But the expectations of what they are going to produce [must be lower] than for someone who has exposure to all this knowledge."

One reason professional, permanent trainers are preferable, says Gordon, is the changing nature of the training requests these days. In the past, most requests for training were for hard skills, what he calls behavior-based skills. "Only about 20 percent of what companies want now is behavior-based, while 80 percent is higher-level thinking skills," he says. That is, more training today is devoted to subjects requiring problem-solving, decision-making and critical-thinking skills, as opposed to technical skills. Further, these conceptual skills are often supposed to be applied in interpersonal situations.

When you're dealing with higher-level thinking and less-concrete skills, you really need someone familiar with the whole body of training and development knowledge, says Gordon. Ideally, he argues, a trainer will have a thorough grounding in three areas: business knowledge, educational psychology and training expertise. The temporary trainer wouldn't have time to assimilate all of that knowledge and experience in a two-week train-the-trainer course, and probably should be relegated to more behavior-based, technical-skills training, says Gordon.

The St. Paul Cos.' Jensby disagrees. Though he did technical training, he also conducted management development courses and currently is an internal facilitator for diversity training at his company. Since there is a strong emphasis on connecting diversity issues to the bottom line, Jensby became the logical choice to conduct the training. He argues that the diversity training in particular calls on his intervention skills, something you don't usually develop if you're just doing technical training.

Astra Merck's Inguagiato sides with Gordon on the issue of professional trainers vs. interim people. In fact, since he took over the training department a year and a half ago, Inguagiato has moved away from letting temporary trainers flow through the department. "From a strategic standpoint, we no longer could afford to have a revolving door," he says. In fact, his department is now staffed completely with professional trainers; before he arrived, most instructors were pass-throughs who spent only a year in training.

Inguagiato says that he wanted to build "wisdom" into the training function and he didn't see how to do that when people constantly filed through the department. He also wanted the training department to become more concerned with the long-term ramifications of what it was doing instead of just slogging from project to project.

But how does he deal with the credibility issue? Fortunately that's not a problem because the business is a matrixed organization: Employees report to more than one manager across functions. At Astra Merck, Inguagiato acts as the functional leader of his trainers, but they are permanently deployed on product teams and customer teams. Since his people spend so much time out among the departments, there is less a sense of separation between the front lines and the training department.

Everyone's an Expert

One problem that can arise with temporary trainers is that, because they spend some time in the training department, they begin to assume they are experts in the field. "Anybody who ever wrote on a flip chart thinks they can train," says Schering-Plough's Rauschkolb. "They don't understand that training is more than a flip chart and marker."

But while temporary trainers may not be experts, they do become more astute, and that can lead to another side effect: a population of employees who've had an inside look at training and may become much more critical of the training they get in the future. Meridian's Szymborski says she now watches trainers' techniques closely when she is on the receiving end and isn't always impressed with what she sees. Pitney Bowes' Christie recalls that he was aghast at a train-the-trainer course he took through an outside supplier. The technology was outdated, there was no interaction, and the training techniques were shoddy, he declares.

Finally, if you think you might like to recruit some temporary trainers, what are some of the sales points you might use to lure them to the training department? Most of the people we talked to were drawn to training because they felt their current positions were a bit inert in terms of learning and growing. Christie says he got into training in order to learn as well as to train. And in some corporate cultures, a term in the training department is considered a steppingstone for fast-track managers. In most Japanese companies, two years in training is a prerequisite for those seeking promotion up the ladder. Jensby says that, although he made a lateral move into and out of the training department, the St. Paul Cos. looks favorably on the career of anyone who has spent some time training.

Rauschkolb, however, is a little leery of recruiting people who wish to give training a try simply because their own careers are stagnating, preferring people who have tried out training others and caught the bug. "I want somebody who says, 'Look, I love training. This is what it does for me. This is how I feel when I train someone. This is the satisfaction it gives me and here's how I see this two-year rotation helping my career.'"

Using Subject-Matter Experts in Training

A training director's guide to mining the lode of specialized information your program needs.

BY TOM GOAD

Almost everything trainers do for the learning process requires working with or consulting the people who know most about the subject being taught — subject-matter experts. You may be part of a formal training unit within your organization, but the whole organization should be viewed as a pool of training talent in which every member is potentially a consulting or participating expert. Their roles can range from advisors to temporary staff members to long-term trainers. They can operate within the full span of training functions.

Experts often possess technical knowledge or skills too complex and specialized to be packaged and presented by a lone trainer. And for the numerous training projects that are short-term, straightforward and prepared on short notice, subject-matter experts can be invaluable.

These days it bears repeating that every minute is precious; a day or week is comparatively priceless. Unless you and your staff are unusually versed in technical fields, it is likely that you can use the help experts can provide. If the training is going to be automated, individualized or long-term, there is even more reason to rely on experts: The more control learners have over the instructional process, the more technically on-target the training must be.

How important is expert input? Take the case in which expert pilots were developing, under a training specialist's guidance, a curriculum for jet-pilot training. The trainer's idea was to place qualifications for night aircraft-carrier landing early in the curriculum. The prerequisite skills were there — on paper — and if feasi-ble, the tactic would have made the curriculum more desirable than the competition's. But the experts pointed out an objection that had nothing to do with learning principles or training methods. A tremendous amount of pure, gut fear comes into play the first time a pilot tries to set an airplane down on a tiny, bouncing island in the middle of the ocean — in the dark. The more time "behind the stick," the easier it is to overcome this fear and do what has to be done. Night-carrier landings were assigned later in the curriculum.

In another case, a sales training course had to be developed and delivered in too little time for things to be done "right." The program had to be successful, of course, success being measured by how quickly the learners could get into the field and secure qualified leads. The training specialist's natural desire to take the time to do a task analysis to identify and prioritize the program's key elements was thwarted. The demand was to get on with developing materials and do a dry run. Using their intuition and experience, expert salespeople came up with the handful of items they considered most important, and the course was born.

It isn't a question of whether the subject-matter expert or the trainer is more vital to training. Both are important. The point is that, as "facilitators," we are continually called upon to facilitate through experts. Much of the training we do is classroom-ori-ented — an instructor interacting with learners — and it helps if the instructor knows more than the students. This places the expert in the most visible training element.

Experience has led me to believe that three steps can be decisive in making the most effective use of sub-ject-matter experts — in helping them help you turn out good training.

1 Welcome yourself to the team. Some experts may be more extensively trained in their areas than you are in yours. Often their work is highly specialized. Recognize the pride and mind-set that may accompany the experts when they step in.

The work they are about to do is an extension of their regular work. You may have to do a lot of convincing in some cases, but most will accept this notion readily. Help your experts see the training tasks as important in their own right — as important as work on the assembly line, in the field, behind the counter or in the cockpit. Their supervisors can help make the mission clear when the experts are initially recruited.

Serve up some positive strokes; let them know you value their expertise and that you are happy to have them as part of the training team. Why are you happy to have them? Consider this:

• They have been trained — presumably they know what does and does not work.

• With the proper approach, trainer expert teams can determine quickly the essential issues to be covered in the proposed training.

• Other than by conducting expensive studies, you are unlikely to find better information than you can obtain from expert opinion.

• Subject-matter experts know tricks of the trade; they know what job elements are the toughest, what you can skimp on and what you can ignore altogether. These are the very things that will let you design an exceptional program.

When dealing with experts, however, remember:

• Sensitivities of team members will differ: The ego drives of a jet pilot or a salesperson with a six-figure salary tend to be different from those of an administrator or computer programmer.

• Respect the years of experience standing behind your chosen experts.

• There's a natural tendency for some "old pros" to look down on novices. But if you penetrate the crust, you'll generally find that they want to share their wealth of knowledge and skills.

2 Identify roles. When members know their roles and are willing to perform them, the "team" becomes an extremely effective unit for getting things done. Identify everyone's role before doing any work. Each member of the team will have strong and weak points. If you can discover these, you'll be able to fill in gaps.

One way to do this is through exploratory, fairly informal meetings in which members will begin to show where their individual abilities and interests lie.

Role identification probably should be your first order of business. For example, in one program whose objective was to identify every task required to operate and maintain a particular computer system, the new team promptly determined that a group of programmers and engineers would be responsible for technical documentation. The trainer's role was to provide a standard, easy-to-use format for documenting the task and skills analysis, and to do the editing and production work necessary to come up with a finished program. This clear division of labor yielded tasks easily translated into learning objectives and training materials for several courses.

3 Complement one another. It is vital that you accept responsibility for the role of manager. This role begins when you start planning for the task of working with experts. Even with willing, able partners and well-defined roles, adjustments will be needed. Your responsibility — like any manager's — is to see that the work gets done.

One of your first jobs is to define the expert's level of training awareness and skills. Ask respectful questions. Find out what he or she has done in the way of analysis, instructing and testing.

If nothing else, your experts probably have attended courses and workshops. Relate elements of their experience to training functions. Based on this, begin a process of training them to be trainers. This may or may not involve formal training. In any case, give them as many down-to-earth examples as possible. There's a threshold beyond which the expert neither needs nor wants to know about esoteric theories or principles or techniques. You must know when to stop the process.

If the training ability of your experts needs shoring up and you can't send all of them through a formal training pipeline, don't despair. In-house training can be done informally. You can try discussion groups, do-it-yourself courses and assignments from among the treasure trove of reading materials in the training field. But avoid highly technical expositions, especially those that are full of jargon.

On the other hand, you should try to learn all you can about your experts' field. The idea is to create an environment in which knowledge and skills are shared freely.

It helps if you and your team can speak a common language. You may have to give a lot here, so try to pick up on the buzzwords. Language peculiar to the subject may be critical. If you're training Navy people, for instance, and you keep referring to the right-hand side of the boat, little round windows and floors, you'll be a joke, not an effective trainer.

Confronting Problems

You can expect to hit snags now and then. An expert may, for instance, insist on teaching a certain work procedure as part of a course, even though you know it isn't feasible or shouldn't be done (e.g., the procedure violates company policy). What do you do in a case like this? If it is a vital point, you may have to press hard. Use win/win negotiating techniques. Compromise if necessary.

Suppose your expert insists that role-playing is the only way to present a vital segment in a sales-training course, while experience has convinced you that classroom discussion mediated by an experienced salesperson is a faster and more effective way to go. The solution may be to do it both ways.

When it comes down to it, however, you have to run the team and that means giving direction to your experts. Since you're unlikely to have line authority in the situation, you can only do this in an atmosphere of mutual trust and respect. It is up to you to build this trust early to avoid confrontations.

The right subject matter, in the right amount, is what training is all about. If your delivery methods are also effective, then you have all the ingredients for a top-quality product. Maybe it's time for you to mine a new lode of expertise.

Notes:

How to Select Good Technical Instructors

OK, so the best performer won't necessarily make the best trainer. That doesn't mean you can't find good trainers among your organization's technical experts.

BY RUTH C. CLARK
AND PHYLLIS KYKER

Even in sports it's a cliché. The best athletes often make lousy coaches. In the training business, it's axiomatic that people with the best technical skills, be they mechanics, power-line troubleshooters or computer programmers, do not necessarily make the best instructors. Technical skills don't guarantee communication skills, and communication is the essence of training.

In fact, ample evidence suggests that those with the highest levels of expertise often make poor instructors. Their wealth of experience makes it difficult to appreciate the learning needs of novices. The depth of background knowledge that for experts has become automatic or self-evident tends to lure them into several traps: They leave gaping holes in the information they present; they fail to sequence topics from simple to complex; they become impatient with trainees, who, in turn, feel intimidated and fail to ask questions.

All of which is why trainers have been telling managers for years that "You can't just pick out the best technicians and tell them they're now classroom instructors."

That said, if a company is seeking technical trainers, a good place to start looking is among the ranks of the company's own technicians. The fact that subject-matter expertise is

---

FIGURE 1
TECHNICAL INSTRUCTOR SELECTION SKILLS AND PROCEDURES

1. **Job-Related Technical Competence**
   - Has reached top promotional level
   - Supervisory recommendation
   - Performance appraisals
   - Screening of technical behaviors/products

2. **Written Communication Skills**
   - Simulation: Develop written lesson
   - Evaluation of prior writing samples

3. **Individual and Group Verbal Communication Skills**
   - Simulation: Present lesson developed to panel
   - Role Play: One-on-one communication skills
   - Interview: Evaluation of presentation style and content

4. **Ability to Relate to Supervision, Peers and Students**
   - Supervisor recommendation
   - Interview: Look for evidence of teamwork and cooperation

5. **Ability to Work With Minimal Supervision**
   - Supervisory recommendation
   - Interview: Look for willingness to make decisions, set priorities

---

FIGURE 2
INSTRUCTIONAL SIMULATION RATING CRITERIA: WRITTEN LESSON

Candidate's Name _____   Date _____

Company Division _____   Instructional Topic _____

CRITERIA	POINTS	
1. Contains no more than one grammatical/punctuation error	Essential	_____
2. Sentences are complete	Essential	_____
3. Information sequenced from simple to complex	2	_____
4. Information chunked into short sections	2	_____
5. Mager-style behavioral objectives included	1	_____
6. Content effectively communicated using definitions, examples, procedure tables	1	_____
7. Information mapping formatting techniques used appropriately	1	_____
8. Practice exercise included that matches objective(s)	2	_____
9. Evaluation items included to measure acquisition of objective	1	_____

FIGURE 3
INSTRUCTIONAL SIMULATION RATING CRITERIA:
LESSON DELIVERY

Candidate's Name _____   Date _____

Company Division _____   Instructional Topic _____

Start Time _____   Finish Time _____

CRITERIA	POINTS	
1. Speaks in clear, understandable English	Essential	_____
2. Presents information conversationally rather than reading it	1	_____
3. Presents and clarifies lesson objectives	½	_____
4. Moves around room, varies voice modulation, uses natural and animated hand gestures, maintains eye contact	½	_____
5. Uses written materials, board, flip chart, lecture and discussion to present information	½	_____
6. Gives a demonstration of procedures	1	_____
7. Includes practice exercise directly related to objective(s)	1	_____
8. Gives clear directions for practice exercise(s)	½	_____
9. Monitors practice by checking individual student responses	½	_____
10. Gives feedback on practice at conclusion of exercise(s)	1	_____
11. Asks students questions to check understanding	½	_____
12. Evaluates learner acquisition of skill objective(s)	1	_____
13. Gives learners positive reinforcement for questions/responses	1	_____
14. Learners are actively involved for at least 50% of lesson	½	_____
15. Completes lesson in time allowed with appropriate allocation of time to all major portions	½	_____

Other Comments:

_____

not sufficient doesn't mean it isn't necessary. Yes, you can hire professional trainers and teach them the subject matter, but you also can teach technicians to be trainers. And technical experts have an advantage in that they gain automatic credibility with trainees by virtue of their expertise. The experts themselves may benefit from the experience as well. In Southern California Edison's customer service division, for example, the instructor position serves as a grooming opportunity for potential supervisors.

Many skilled technicians can become perfectly good classroom instructors — provided they have the prerequisite abilities to benefit from the train-the-trainer help you can provide. The challenge is to identify those prerequisites and then come up with a valid and reliable way to select technicians who have them. Here is a step-by-step approach based on a process we have found useful at Southern California Edison.

Getting Started

The first step is to define the entry-level skills you're looking for. These have to be determined on the basis of your instructors' job requirements. Some skills, such as "effective verbal communication," are likely to be on everyone's list, but others will depend on the specific job. For example, if instructors are responsible for developing written materials — manuals, job aids, etc. — you'll have to screen for writing skills. If they aren't, you won't — and for legal reasons, you probably shouldn't.

Begin by examining the job's major responsibilities. If they haven't already been defined, spelling them out will not only improve your selection process but will help you set performance standards and appraisal guidelines. Books, articles and published research are helpful in outlining the skills instructors need in order to meet various responsibilities, but don't rely on them alone. "Validate" your list by going to your current and past instructors, former students and supervisors of those students. Ask them to identify behaviors or describe incidents that characterize effective or ineffective instruction in your organization.

Once your list is complete, you'll have to decide which skills you can feasibly develop in new instructors by training and which ones need to

FIGURE 4
INTERVIEW QUESTIONS: FOCUS ON DIMENSIONS

1. Ability to Relate to Supervision, Peers, Students
2. Ability to Work With Minimal Supervision

1. What if you had your greatest idea ever but your fellow trainers were not very receptive? You really want to implement your idea. How would you handle the situation?
(Look for strategies to involve others and persuade without being overbearing.)

2. Describe a situation that required many things to be done at the same time. How did you handle the situation?
(Look for setting of priorities, time management strategies, planning.)

3. If you were an instructor, what would be some situations where you feel you should consult your boss before taking action?
(Look for situations involving personnel implications, areas of uncertainty, etc.)

4. What kinds of decisions do you think you would be making if you were an instructor? How would you make those decisions?
(Look for appropriate decision-making strategies depending on the situation.)

5. How would you determine whether you were getting your point across as an instructor?
(Ask questions, monitor practice, give quizzes, chat with students.)

FIGURE 5
CUSTOMER SERVICE REPRESENTATIVE TRAINER INTERVIEW SUMMARY

Key to scoring: Weight score has been previously determined. For each section of the assessment, use 10 points as the highest, i.e., exhibiting all behaviors in outstanding manner, and score downward to one point.

	10 to 1		
1. Written Lesson Simulation	10x _____	=	_____
2. Lesson Presentation	10x _____	=	_____
3. Related Education/Experience B.A. or beyond or	4x _____	=	_____
A.A.	2x _____	=	_____
Training Experience	2x _____	=	_____
4. Company Experience 2–3 years or	2x _____	=	_____
3+ years	4x _____	=	_____
5. Interview: Role Play (Communication)	4x _____	=	_____
Questions: A.	1x _____	=	_____
B.	1x _____	=	_____
C.	1x _____	=	_____
D.	1x _____	=	_____
E.	1x _____	=	_____
F.	1x _____	=	_____
G.	1x _____	=	_____
Communication Style	2x _____	=	_____

Total _____ _____

Total Possible _____ 430

Candidate's Name _____   Interview Panel _____

be entry level. Your selection process will be designed to identify these entry skills.

But your process also has to be reliable. That is, you want a procedure in which different people or panels screen a given candidate and arrive at similar ratings. Reliability is best achieved by evaluating each candidate according to very specific behaviors. It isn't enough to say, for example, that you want instructors who "show enthusiasm." You need a checklist that allows screeners to rate that trait in specific behavioral terms, e.g., "moves around the room during presentation; varies voice modulation and pace; uses verbal and visual clues to emphasize important points." All of your desired entry-level skills will have to be broken down into such checklists.

Designing the Selection Process

Obviously, there are a lot of ways to set up a procedure that helps you evaluate each candidate's skills against your selection criteria. At Southern California Edison, we rely on a combination of technical qualification, simulation and interviews. Figure 1 summarizes our list of skills and selection procedures.

Technical competence. We draw candidates from a pool of employees who have reached top promotional status via a combination of seniority, promotional tests and supervisory recommendations. Any employee who reaches the top level is eligible to apply for an instructor's job.

In-house evaluation of performance over a period of time provides an effective screening device for technical capabilities. If you were to hire trainers from outside your organization, you'd need a process to rate both their instructional skills and the entry-level *technical* competence you decide they would need.

Simulation. Because our instructors write training materials, they are evaluated for basic writing skills as well as oral presentation ability. We have found simulations very useful in evaluating both types of skills.

Each candidate is given one hour to write a lesson on a familiar non-technical topic such as "How to Write a Check" or "How to Use a Pocket Calculator." Figure 2 illustrates the weighted checklist used by our training specialists to score the lessons. Note that the checklist includes both basic and advanced skills. Because we initially appoint instructors on a six-month trial basis (a "temporary upgrade"), we generally interview both inexperienced and upgraded candidates for permanent positions. Typically, candidates who have been serving as instructors on an upgraded basis fill the permanent job openings. The temporary upgrade positions are then filled by lower-ranked, inexperienced candidates.

Following the written simulation, each candidate is given 15 minutes to present his or her lesson to a panel consisting of an instructional specialist and two training supervisors. The panel uses the checklist shown in Figure 3 as a guide to rate each presentation. Again, the list includes both basic and advanced skills.

To increase reliability, the panel watches a videotaped presentation by an experienced instructor and uses the video as a model for rating each candidate. In other words, candidates are evaluated against the model video performance, not against one another.

Interviews. Following the simulation, each candidate is interviewed by the panel, which uses questions with "correct answer" guidelines, such as the ones in Figure 4. The questions emphasize job dimensions not captured by the simulations, such as the candidate's time-management strategies and teamwork experiences. Candidates are rated both on what they say and how well they say it.

Choosing Instructors

The entire process takes about two hours of the candidate's time (an hour to develop the written lesson and an hour for the presentation simulation and interview) and one hour of the panel's time. Summary scores for each candidate are entered on the weighted worksheet shown in Figure 5. The criteria and associated weights shown were developed during a number of validation trials. The worksheet reflects the major criteria we have found related to job success. If several candidates wind up with high, closely grouped scores, the training supervisor does the final rankings.

Following Up

No selection process is foolproof, which is why we initially select candidates only for a six-month trial period. During those six months, "upgraded" instructors receive formal training on teaching skills and are closely evaluated on the job. Supervisors sit in on their classes to rate their skills using the same checklists as in the selection process, interview their students and evaluate student performance. Instructors on temporary assignment who have not performed satisfactorily are returned to their former jobs after six months.

We have found that employees whose technical skills are good, rather than expert, often *do* make better instructors. But that doesn't mean that the experts can't be useful in training. It's not unusual for the top technical expert in some area to wind up serving as a consultant to the instructor.

Notes:

A Three-Part Plan for Making Your Training Staff More Effective

Cross-training, constant sharing of 'lessons learned' are the keys.

BY DAVE ZIELINSKI

Keeping your training staff's skills and operations knowledge up-to-date is more important than ever these days with so many functions shifting from classroom-based training to performance consulting and greater use of alternate delivery methods. And with organizational structures and strategies constantly in flux, trainers have to work harder to stay in tune with boardroom decisions.

Kelly Miller and her staff at Sallie Mae have worked hard and often at developing new skills and content expertise. Their effort won the team a 1995 Training Directors' Forum Award in the category of developing the training staff.

In 1993 Sallie Mae's technical training staff was reorganized under Miller, manager of training and development. Group cohesion was the first challenge: Many trainers in the newly reconfigured group had never met each other, and had no sense of feeling a part of a team. The other pressing issue was a reporting structure: Miller had 20 trainers reporting to her, far too many to manage effectively given her workload. To distribute some of that management responsibility, she created three "coordinator" positions, technical trainers who were given supervisory responsibility for four to five other trainers in the group, which includes doing performance reviews. "A lot of mentoring goes on in those relationships," Miller says.

Also, all job descriptions were rewritten and new career paths developed. All trainer positions are now exempt — replaced by new positions emphasizing performance consulting and facilitation.

Miller works to build a mindset of independent contractors in her staff. "I tell them just because we are internal rather than external consultants doesn't mean we can't be cut loose at any time," she says. "We have to approach our jobs as if we are under contract, and if we aren't adding value, why should the company renew our contracts?"

She also teaches her people to continually market training. "We have to self-promote, and let the line folks know that just because the lights are off in the training room, that doesn't mean trainers aren't doing important work somewhere."

3-Part Training Staff Development Plan

Miller's development plan for the new-look department had three phases:

1 Hone basic training skills. Miller's first move was to conduct a basic, five-day train-the-trainer session to teach her technical experts — many of whom had little stand-up experience — basic platform delivery and facilitation skills. Included were skills like handling problem trainees, fielding difficult questions, maximizing participation, making and using visuals, writing learning objectives, and making job aids. The course was designed by a vendor, but delivered entirely by Miller. "I wanted to build my credibility early with this group, and in delivering the training I was also trying to set an expectation of how training should be presented," she says.

2 Develop internal consulting skills. The most difficult skill for most to master in this area is assertiveness, Miller says. "Typically our people are consulting with those at higher levels than they are — and often they are trainers' former bosses, which can be intimidating," she says. Miller's coaching focuses on the fact that trainers are paid for their expertise and can't be afraid to use it. "That includes saying no to any frivolous training requests," she says.

Miller stresses that when line managers come to trainers convinced that training can solve a specific problem, and the trainer knows training isn't the solution but goes ahead with it anyway, that decision does double damage. "We not only waste valuable training resources with those unnecessary programs, the perception is the training is faulty" because it doesn't solve the performance problems."

Once a week the whole staff takes time out "to talk about assertiveness and do some role-playing around that, to talk about the customer partnering process, and what keeps us from performing that role well," Miller says.

The staff typically feels they can't afford to be away from clients that long, but after the sessions everyone feels it was a great use of time, says Miller. "It's hard to be a coach when you're always in the game."

The staff holds similar refresher sessions on the "information mapping" trainers are taught for creating training procedures and documents. Miller says one in-house trainer was certified to deliver the mapping training. Another regular team-building session is called Straight Talk and Generous Listening. This, Miller says, is about "learning to be honest with each other, and to take time to really listen to each other."

3 Cross-train to increase experience. All staffers get rotated for short periods into areas where they have little experience. "The more they are cross-trained, the more they can move to where the work is," Miller says. "I hate to say to a customer with a real training need, 'Gee, all of my design or delivery resources are tied up right now. You're going to have to wait.' " One professional development employee used to handle all new-employee orientation training, for example, all staffers now take turns at delivering that training.

HRD Degrees: Who Needs Them?

More and more trainers are earning advanced degrees. But the value of these credentials is not universally acknowledged.

BY MARGARET KAETER

Lt. Cmdr. Terry Bickham knew there were tactics that would help him do his job better. He just didn't know what those tactics were. As commanding officer of the Pacific Area Training Team for the U.S. Coast Guard, Bickham's job is to ensure that all Coast Guard units in the Pacific Ocean know how to perform the technical aspects of their jobs, such as towing boats and aiding sinking ships. "I saw we were doing things the hard way," he says. "Sometimes people didn't have enough training to do the job, while in some areas they had too much training. I knew there had to be a better way."

With a 1982 bachelor's degree in political science and government, and a decade-long career with the Coast Guard that was more attuned to law enforcement than training, Bickham turned to San Diego State University for help. He received a master's degree in performance technology in 1993.

The result, he says, is not just better training but also more enthusiastic participants. "A couple of years ago our training programs were something to be endured," he says. "Now people say they look forward to them. I couldn't have turned this [training team] around without the academic work." He insists that he "could never have gotten the same combination of information and experience" from the seminars and workshops available to trainers at professional conferences or via private providers of "train the trainer" courses.

Bickham has plenty of company. Many training professionals have decided they need some formal academic training to complement their on-

the-job experience. The number of universities awarding postgraduate degrees in subjects related to human resources development (HRD) has increased more than 100 percent in the last decade, although some of that gain is illusory: It has been possible for decades to cobble together some courses in vocational/technical education, say, with courses in psychology or business to create a customized master's or doctoral degree. Now some colleges have formalized such combinations into "HRD-degree pro-

> ## "I couldn't have turned this [training team] around without the academic work."

grams," but without actually creating any new courses.

Still, there's no doubt that trainers are clamoring for advanced degrees. The American Society for Training and Development (ASTD) has identified 180 university graduate-level programs in the United States that prepare people to work in HRD. ASTD's enrollment figures for these programs suggest that there are, conservatively, more than 18,000 people working toward advanced degrees in the field.

But why do we need these degrees? After all, trainers got along without them for many decades. Granted, there is a big difference between a training careerist and a person serving an 18-month stint in the HRD department as a steppingstone to a headquarters job in marketing. But even

among genuine, longtime training professionals, only a small fraction have degrees in HRD or instructional technology. Why the sudden rush for another piece of paper to hang on your cubicle wall?

Some of the reasons are obvious. "I've been promoted three times because I have a master's degree in this field," says Kathi Tunheim, director of leadership development at American Express Financial Advisors in Minneapolis. Tunheim got her master's in communication with a training and development emphasis from the University of Wisconsin in 1984 and is pursuing a Ph.D. in HRD from the University of Minnesota. "The academic information is great," she says. "It prepares you for a classical approach of assessing, designing, developing, implementing and evaluating a training program."

On the other hand, adds Tunheim, "I have two people on my staff who are smart trainers and I'm not telling them to go to graduate school. They don't need it because they're great at what they do. They've intuitively picked up the skills they need. Graduate school isn't necessary to be successful in this field."

What's a training professional to do? When even a firm believer in an advanced degree can't unequivocally recommend the path a professional should pursue, how do you know what's right for you?

The question is as old as the first Greek who couldn't decide between being a student of Socrates and taking an apprenticeship with a tradesman. And the answer may be much the same: It depends largely on what you want to do with your life and what forms of learning you personally enjoy.

The Case Against

Many training professionals are thoroughly unimpressed by advanced degrees in HRD. "Postbaccalaureate degrees are helpful to companies only when the individuals are able to apply their learning in practical [situations]. Without this, the theory they've learned cannot provide much value in a human resources role," says Rich Hable, senior human resources generalist with Zytec Corp. of Eden Prairie, MN, a high-tech manufacturing firm with about 1,000 employees.

Indeed, the biggest argument against these degrees is that they're just too theory-based. "All the researchers live in a theory world," says Maria Hruby, an Ohio State University doctoral candidate in human resource development. "But in the business world, time is an important element. Plus, people are unpredictable; you can't control them....You can't put those two elements into an academic setting. Theory is predictable and can take all the time it needs."

"In the academic world they take a model and follow it step-by-step," adds Ari Galper, training and project manager with United Parcel Service's corporate sales training group in Atlanta and a 1982 graduate of the San Diego State University program. "In the real world, if you need the program tomorrow, you have to skip the analysis. I had to learn a whole set of skills that they didn't teach me in graduate school: how to be flexible and change at the last minute because the project's scope changes, how to deal with different personalities, how to deal with the politics and approval processes when developing programs, and how to develop a training program under intense deadline pressures."

Not all students make the transition well. "Many people are ineffective because they're so schooled they lose sight of what they're trying to do," says Gerald Jones, general manager of the DuPont/Forum Partnership in Wilmington, DE, the training function for chemical giant DuPont. "I'm careful when I hire people with graduate degrees in training and development because I want to ensure they've made the connection between the information they've gotten in school and the business world they'll be using it in. I've hired people with Ph.D.s and little experience who've failed because they couldn't make that link."

Some question even the academic value of many training-related degree programs, suggesting that the theoretical knowledge base itself often constitutes pretty thin gruel. Says Zytec's Hable: "I don't need a Ph.D. to know that some people learn better with pictures and some with hands-on experience, that some people are verbally stimulated and some are visually stimulated."

Another argument is that these degrees focus too much on one small part of the business world, perhaps creating capable specialists but leaving the professional unprepared for the multidisciplinary role of today's training department. "I think the smart training professional would pick up an MBA with a minor in human resource development," says David Brinkerhoff, president of Abbott Smith Associates Inc. in Millbrook, NY, an executive recruiting firm specializing in human resources professionals. "A few years ago I might have said the master's in HRD was good, but I'm finding that many of my clients want people who understand business, who can point to training's effect on the bottom line. You can pick up the training information you need at a conference. If you want to rise to a higher level in the HRD field, you need the business information."

The Case For

Not so, say the directors of many of the country's top HRD programs. They argue that training and development has become such an important component of many business strategies that it can no longer be overlooked by academicians. Long seen as an academic extension of adult education, HRD is now viewed by many businesses as a competitive edge, a force driving important changes that are remaking the business world. It's an activity that demands a distinct field of study.

"Today we're seeing a more systemic view of human resources is," says Ron Jacobs, an associate professor with Ohio State University's human resources development program. "It's a broad view of organizational development, structured change and group

WHICH COMES FIRST: THE PROFESSIONALS OR THE PROFESSION?

Corporate training directors complain that academic programs in subjects related to human resources development often fail to equip graduates with precisely the skills they need to be successful in the real business world.

Hold on, the professors respond. The problem is that it's almost impossible to define what a graduate should know when training departments can't even decide what it is they are trying to do.

"This is a field trying to find itself," says Gary McLean, professor and coordinator for the HRD and adult education programs at the University of Minnesota in St. Paul. "We first have to define what human resources development means."

More precisely, the need may be to define what HRD doesn't mean. The American Society for Training and Development, for example, includes a number of human resource management areas in its formal descriptions of the field, such as compensation management and benefits management. "But many of us think it should be limited only to individual or organizational development," says McLean. "Until we sort this out, how can we guarantee what our graduates will know?"

Despite this fundamental confusion, the academics insist that their programs at least provide some level of certainty that the graduate knows something about training and development. "The tug-of-war all of us think about is how to professionalize this field," says Karen Watkins, an associate professor of adult education at the University of Georgia in Athens. "There's a concern in this industry that there are too many unethical charlatans, that the industry is vulnerable to the fad of the week. People want to be certified to show they know what they're doing. Programs like ours attempt to take a stand that our graduates will behave in a competent, ethical manner."

That call for professionalism is echoed by Allison Rossett, a professor in San Diego State University's department of educational technology. "I'd like to see a field of people who've read more, who see more options and have more exposure to the literature," she says. "This is crucial if we are going to have a true impact on business. After all, where would medicine be as a field if everyone was not formally trained? We're dealing with lives in this field, too."

— M.K.

ENGINEERING A DEGREE PROGRAM

How broad a variety of skills and specialties are we talking about when we refer to advanced degrees in "HRD-related subjects"? Consider the example of Reg Parker.

You would expect that whatever the focus of a particular program, the intended purpose of obtaining an HRD degree would be to work in a training and development department or as a consultant. Parker, a manufacturing engineer, is manager of manufacturing and human resources for Joslyn Sterilizer Corp. in Farmington, NY. He pursued his 1992 master's degree in instructional design from Syracuse University because he wanted to ensure that engineers understand one another when they're trying to design new products.

"I was with General Electric Corp. as manager of advanced manufacturing engineering during the 1980s," Parker explains, "and I saw a number of [new-product development] programs fail because we didn't address the human side of things. The typical human resources people didn't know the technical problems, and the engineering people didn't know or understand how people learn and think."

At Syracuse University, Parker concentrated his studies on the diffusion of information to technical workers. "I figured that if I could combine my engineering knowledge with instructional design, I could solve the problems," he says. "The best part of the program was the fact that the instructors let me maintain that emphasis through all my work."

His coursework showed him how to help engineers gain a common understanding of the issues that needed to be addressed in concurrent engineering programs, says Parker. In concurrent engineering, various design groups work on a project simultaneously as opposed to one step at a time. "It's a great idea if everyone will communicate, but that's just not realistic," Parker says. "The guy in chemical engineering might not understand the basic electrical engineering concepts that are making his ideas infeasible."

The result often is a stalemate. At General Electric, he says, "we'd be in meetings with the heads of the various engineering departments and they'd be fighting for their own turf instead of looking at the best interests of the project. They'd say something had to be done this way or that, and it would conflict with the way another department head said something had to be done."

Today, Parker says, the knowledge he picked up at Syracuse often points him to unique solutions. "Often, I'll identify a technical area that an engineer needs to know more about. I'll put together a basic review, then sit down with him or her and say, 'Let me show you what the other guys are doing and why that's important to you.' I found ways to address these high-level, highly egotistical engineering types so they could understand how another area affects their area. The result is a much more effective work force."

— M.K.

---

dynamics. Train-ing is no longer just a process. The field has evolved from straight training and development to a philosophical view of human resources development. You have to understand both the hard and soft issues of any project."

Adds Bill Rothwell, associate professor with the instructional systems program at Penn State University in University Park, PA: "Philosophically, human resource development is headed in a number of directions: performance technology, performance improvement, learning management, organizational development, total quality, reengineering, customer service, teams.... It's all happening at once, and suddenly you're looking at learning all this as part of the whole work environment. People are looking for performance problem-solvers. They're not just interested in education and training, but information support systems, electronic performance support, documentation, performance environments, etc."

Given this expansion of concerns, many trainers see a definite need for advanced degrees. "The degree opens up a lot of avenues of approach that wouldn't be there otherwise," says Ray Frankowski, human resources director for Westinghouse Electric Corp.'s government and environmental services group in Monroeville, PA. "You can think in broader perspectives. Ten to 15 years ago we had zero people with these advanced degrees, and we still just cranked out training programs. But this is a different environment. It's changing so fast that the degree has become more important."

One reason it's important is that at least some of the programs may help to forge the very link between business savvy and HRD expertise that Brinkerhoff, for one, finds so vital. "When I hire people for my department, I want them to understand how organizations operate in addition to the basics of developing sound training programs," says Lucien Rouze, director of training and development for Bell Helicopter Textron in Fort Worth, TX, and a graduate of the University of Texas' weekend program in adult education and human resource development leadership. "With an HRD-related graduate degree, they are familiar with organizational development or program

design as well as business operations. If they have just a general business degree, we have to bring them in at a lower level."

Other training directors look for specialists, much as the finance department might be headed by a finance generalist but employ specialized accountants for various activities. For instance, Motorola's Brenda Sumberg, director of Motorola University for the Americas in Schaumburg, IL, seeks out people with advanced degrees in instructional systems design. "This is a systematic approach to designing and developing training," she explains. "If trainers don't have this background, they tend to develop a course from a content perspective, laying out everything they know about a subject. But instructional design involves doing an analysis of the need, then creating performance objectives and developing the training around them, then evaluating the training to make sure it's working. It's analogous to engineering design. It requires very specific skills. And if our trainers don't have them, we find that their learning curve is much longer."

Building Bridges

Most academics in the HRD field agree that their efforts to create the best training professionals are far from perfect. The arguments against advanced-degree programs are all valid to some extent, admit many of the professors and program directors. But in many cases, they complain, their programs are being unjustly criticized based on experiences more than a decade old. They insist that over the past 10 years they have developed tactics to overcome the skeptics' concerns.

For example, many programs today offer the option of taking a number of traditional MBA courses. "Most of the programs have a cross-disciplinary flavor that may draw from adult education, traditional business, organizational psychology and even labor relations," says Karen Watkins, associate professor of adult education at the University of Georgia in Athens and president of the Academy of Human Resource Development, headquartered in Austin, TX.

In other cases, the academics charge that the critical professionals are simply blind to the pragmatic value of the information provided by degree programs. As the saying goes, there's nothing so practical as a good theory.

Everyone who's worked in the real world before attending college knows how frustrating academic theory can be, the professors concede. In that area, HRD programs are no exception. But the academics argue that it's crucial to provide a solid foundation in theory, especially in a field that hasn't given much credence to academic research.

Theory can help drive professionalism, says Gary McLean, professor and coordinator for HRD and adult education programs at the University of Minnesota in St. Paul. "The HRD field tends to be driven by fads and vendors, resulting in a lot of things that we find are inappropriate for true human resources development," he says. "If you don't have a strong theory and research foundation, you can easily get caught up in that.... If we want our training and development professionals to be good consumers, they need that grounding in theory to make the right choices."

Most programs use theory as an introduction to reality, say the professors. "We try to balance the theory and the practical," says Ohio State's Jacobs. "We introduce the theoretical framework then discuss how you can use it practically in real-life settings."

One reason for this increasing emphasis on reality is that the students simply won't stand for less. Virtually every HRD-oriented graduate program in the country requires students to have at least a few years' experience in the business world. Many programs are offered in evening sessions or on weekends, attracting people currently working in the field. And even the few undergraduate programs and certificates generally require previous business experience.

"One of the best parts of the [University of Texas] program is that we had experienced and mature people in it," says Bell Textron's Rouze. "We knew the trends and needs. We knew how to design programs and we knew what wasn't realistic because we worked with it every day.

"We also had a wide variety of per-

"I don't need a Ph.D. to know that some people learn better with pictures and some with hands-on experience."

---

spectives," Rouze continues. "We had people from the DOT, the IRS, Texas Instruments, and a number of other companies. It gave a much broader perspective to the issues."

Today's faculty likely wouldn't stand for an all-theoretical approach either. Some have risen through the academic ranks, specializing in HRD through interests in business, psychology or education, but many of the newer professors have entered academia after decades in the corporate training world. Rothwell, for example, was a practitioner for 20 years before turning academic. And both groups of professors tend to spend much of their time as consultants to outside organizations.

"A lot of our instructors have extensive backgrounds in the field, actually trying to solve real business problems," says McLean, echoing the words of his peers across the country. "Many of them serve as consultants to businesses. This helps us make sure we're grounded in reality."

As for seeing that the students get some real-life experience, the vast majority of today's graduate programs require at least one internship. UPS's Gelper points out that the internship requirement isn't a cure-all ("I interned for Anderson Consulting and all I did was the grunt work no one else wanted to do"), but it at least provides some opportunity to get out of the classroom.

Even when the students aren't in internships, professors use real-life projects to guide the learning. At Indiana University in Bloomington, master's students find that all of their first-year courses are centered on problems or projects. "We'll go through items such as a classic curriculum design, a needs analysis, a task and learner analysis, etc.," says Tom Schwen, department chair of the university's instructional systems technology program. "They have to deal with the issues of how they are going to convince people to change and how they will implement the training. Then they will develop the products — the videos, tool books, etc."

At Ohio State University, all of the core courses are project-based, says Jacobs. "For example, teams of students develop training programs for companies that want structured on-the-job training. They will work with a live organization, analyzing the best approach, making presentations to the management, and possibly even developing the program."

Putting It Together

When the student is motivated and works to relate his or her educational and internship experiences to the job back home, the results can be extremely rewarding. Witness Bickham's experience:

His group's annual training visits to the Pacific Coast Guard offices were a prime example of the problem he saw with his whole operation. "It used to be we did training for training's sake," he says. A group of instructors would spend one week per year at each station delivering training. Training in what? Training for what? Nobody seemed to give those questions much thought. "It was the same old thing every year. It didn't matter if it was Hawaii or Alaska. It didn't matter if they never used the skill or if they used it every day."

His coursework at San Diego State covered a variety of topics, including how to conduct a training needs analysis, how to design effective train-

RESOURCES FOR DEGREE PROGRAMS

If you're planning to work full time while attending graduate school, you may find more options than you thought. Chances are a local university offers an evening or weekend program in human resources development.

The problem is you'll be limited to the approach and emphasis presented at that school. "Because of the diversity in faculty, there are quite pronounced differences in philosophies in the various programs," says Ron Jacobs, associate professor with Ohio State University's HRD program. "Most every program seems to be experiencing good acceptance by employers and students, but there's no guarantee that any one program will meet any one student's needs."

Many programs seem general, offering a wide range of choices under the HRD umbrella: human resources, psychology of learning, vocational education, industrial psychology — even subjects such as organizational communication and intercultural relations. Others provide a narrow focus. For example, San Diego State University's program focuses on creating experts in instruction, information and technology, says professor Allison Rossett. "Our students focus on being the analysts. Then they reach out to the other HRD people. They are educational information-technology experts but recognize that solutions come from systems that involve other HRD people, as well."

If you're looking for a degree program, a place to begin might be with the American Society for Training and Development's *Academic Directory: Programs in Human Resource Development*, 1995. It lists programs by state and addresses the degrees offered, the number of students in the program, the length of the program, class schedule options, financial aid opportunities and internship opportunities. ASTD can be reached at 1640 King St., Box 1443, Alexandria, VA 22313, (703) 683-8100.

— M.K.

---

ing programs, how to document success, and how to use the latest technology such as computer-based training and distance-learning programs. "I graduated with a toolbox for building good instruction," Bickham says. "But I also learned to recognize when training isn't the best answer."

He says his internships and class projects were especially enlightening. In one class, he worked with the San Diego Police Department to assess the need for volunteer training and to write the necessary materials. For his internship, he wrote a correspondence course on maritime law enforcement for the Coast Guard. For his final project, he conducted a formal evaluation of the San Diego Police Academy's diversity training program. "This absolutely prepared me for the real world," he says. "There were no surprises. When I was done, I was able to offer a lot more than the job asked for."

Today, Bickham says, he has revitalized his group's training efforts. "Now, before each visit, we do an assessment to find their weaknesses, then tailor the training to the needs of the people there. If they have towed a lot of disabled boats with no mishaps, we don't need to spend a long time on that. In Alaska, we'd concentrate on towing fishing boats; in Hawaii, we'd concentrate on sailboats."

But What Do You Learn?

Let's grant that many or most of these degree programs offer some value that couldn't be gained either from seminars or from the school of hard knocks. From the perspective of a potential employer, however, the eclectic nature of the various programs creates a little problem: Neither headhunters nor department heads nor human resource directors have the foggiest idea what any one degree means.

"If it's an MBA, you have a good idea what the person knows," says headhunter Brinkerhoff. "But when I present people with these HRD degrees to a client company, I have to substantiate what they've actually done."

The problem isn't just that different degree programs cover a wide range of material, Brinkerhoff adds. Some programs are so vaporous that their graduates can't be assumed to have studied or accomplished much of anything at all. "There are a lot of degrees that aren't degrees," he says.

The very fact that HRD is still in its infancy as a distinct field of study has created a large amount of confusion in the academic world. The American Society for Training and Development has identified 11 subject areas, all of which, the association maintains, help prepare a person for a career in training. Those areas:

- Administrative/educational leadership.
- Adult education.
- Career development.
- Human resources development.
- Human resource management with an emphasis in human resources development.
- Industrial psychology.
- Instructional design and development.
- Instructional technology.
- Organization communications.
- Organization development.
- Vocational/technical education.

And don't let the titles deceive you. While vocational education or instructional design may sound concrete and highly specialized, the department heads may simply not have gotten around to changing their names to reflect a broader training and development emphasis.

"Part of my frustration is that the students aren't guaranteed they'll come out of a program with any specific knowledge," says doctoral candidate Hruby. "Every program is different and every student's experience is different. It becomes the student's job to guide their education."

And that is the lesson for the day. "This field is very different from other business fields such as accounting," says Penn State's Rothwell. "In accounting, the degree is virtually the same at all the schools and the employees all have defined career ladders. In training and development, the student has to know what he or she wants to get out of it."

Toning Down Young Trainers — Without Turning Them Off

Troubles with novice trainers can complicate your work as training director and confuse trainees, too. Here's how to be firm with new blood without stifling creativity.

BY FRANK T. WYDRA
AND KATHLEEN WHITESIDE

Novice trainers can be the bane of the training director. They do not know, thus fail to follow, the rules of the trade. Consequently, they often cause problems for the unsuspecting training director.

Novice trainers are usually drawn from the ranks of the technical experts, the upwardly mobile or the newly graduated. Regardless of where they come from, they view their stay in the training department as no more than a way station on the track to their career objective.

Experts expect to move to other opportunities that will provide an even greater depth of knowledge. High-potential, upwardly mobile line managers expect to be awarded their own lines. New grads, brimful of theory, expect to find fame, and occasionally fortune, as consultants. None expect to stay in the training department. They are movers. Because they are transients, their actions, as they enter the training department, are predictable; they will try to change things.

Novice trainers want to change what is taught, how it is taught or both. They are invariably impatient with things as they are. Inexplicably, they are usually given the chance to make change. Accommodating their quest for change may be a part of our cultural heritage. Training departments have traditionally been peopled by corporate nomads, or those who, given the opportunity, migrate from position to position. In this environment the novice trainer is unwittingly given license.

Ergo, the novice trainer who is an expert will be permitted to demonstrate expertise and show the posses-sion of "new" knowledge. The high-potential person will try to bring the "real world" into the Ivory Tower and, incidentally, to make a visible mark in that tower. Newly graduated novices will try to implement laboriously learned theory, often without regard to its utility in the situation. It is what they know; it is what they were hired to demonstrate. For all of them, and for the unsuspecting training director, the code word is *innovation*.

The Altar of Innovation

To innovate is to create. To innovate is to make the world a better place in which to live. To innovate is to make that mark, to garner that reputation. But, in the end, to innovate is to initiate change.

In a discipline that prides itself on innovation it is sometimes difficult to insist on caution. Indeed, that change may be counterproductive. Innovation has such charm that training professionals sometimes make it an end in itself. Never mind that the change is not needed; that it has been tried before and has demonstrated a failure to meet objectives. Never mind that it conflicts with, or ignores, what is known about the technology of learning. Never mind that it is less effective, more expensive or less efficient than other approaches. And, never mind that it is irrelevant to the task at hand. For it is innovative. And so, when trainers stand before the altar of innovation, they ignore its faults.

Aside from the fact that novice trainers are often encouraged to inno-vate, it usually is to their advantage to do so. The personal agenda must be met; the track record must be established; the expertise must be displayed. These are significant incentives for novices who seek change.

And, being rational, they respond to the incentive.

These circumstances make it difficult for training directors who on one hand want to encourage innovation but who, on the other hand, are responsible for generating effective, efficient, validated instructional programs. How can you manage this built-in conflict? How are you to mediate between the bright, aggressive, articulate, on-the-way-to-the-top course developer and the naive, vulnerable learner?

Accomplished training directors will use their entire repertoire of skills to manage the novice trainer and protect the learner. They will clearly specify outcomes, deliver assignments in manageable chunks, provide timely and appropriate feedback and reinforce the novice as mastery is successively approximated. But these are broad-sweep strategies. On a scale less grand, the training director can set down some rules for the novice trainer to follow.

Rules of the Road

Unfortunately, rules are anathematic to the training professional. In a permissive society, particularly one that values creativity, rules are often avoided. The rule makers are reluctant to develop them and the rule followers ignore them. But without rules progress is, at best, erratic.

The energy spent on activity is greater than the result produced. And it is this shortfall that so often frustrates the training director charged with the responsibility for accomplishment. If we are to have a training discipline, we must have people following rules. The rules must benefit those who make them and those who follow them. The investment in rule making and the cost of aborted creativity must produce outcomes that clearly justify the expenditures.

Like honest people, good rules are hard to find. There are three, though, that can be suggested to help you manage novice trainers, for it is they who most often violate them.

Rule 1: *Follow established training procedures until you have mastered them; introduce change only when you can show, from your own experience, that the standard methods will not work.*

This rule insists on rigid adherence to a model, any model. It matters not what model is used. Instead, it is important to follow a predefined course. For if the route is known, it is always possible to determine where the traveler strayed from the path. In the design of programs, and in their execution, there are often steps that do not make sense to novices.

To the neophyte designer, developing unambiguous objectives or validating tasks may seem like academic exercises. The creativity of writing a program is far more exciting than the routines of specification and evaluation. So they are skipped, or at best, glossed over. But when the program fails or is judged to be irrelevant, the culprit is usually found to be innovation without experience, change in the name of creativity. The novice, under the guise of innovation, has abandoned the model.

When it appears that a process does not work, often it is the trainer and not the process that is deficient. Before jumping to conclusions about fault, both the training director and the novice trainer need to assure themselves that all steps of the program or process have been faithfully executed. Then, if the results are still unsatisfactory, the validity of the program (rather than the quality of its execution) can be legitimately questioned.

From time to time, though, the training program or process is in fact faulty. It doesn't work. It is then, having won their stripes through experience, that the novice trainer can rightfully take command of creation. They can revise with authority.

Rule 2: *Remember that your program is not as important as the response of the learner.*

The second rule requires novices to put the needs of the learner first. It shifts the focus from the process of training to its product, the learned person. Trainers become emotionally involved with programs they design or present. Programs seem to take on a life of their own.

This relationship is akin to that of parent and child. The trainer conceives the program, breathes life into it, shapes its character and takes pride as it develops to maturity. The presenter, through tryout after tryout, develops a style that could be mistaken for the personality of the program. Even in the naming of a program the deliberation is reminiscent of the naming of a newborn.

Given this emotional and intellectual investment, it is understandable why a trainer might resist changes that would be made solely to benefit an emotionally distant, impersonal learn-

er. But, in reality, a program is not a person. It has no personality. There is no life, no death. It is the learner who has life and the need for the trainer's attention. It is the learner who needs to be nurtured, developed, strengthened and brought to maturity. If a learner suffers in an overzealous drive to keep a program or a presentation intact, then true harm has been done.

Rule 2 reminds the novice trainer that the object of training is the learner's response. If the learner fails to make the expected response, the program is faulty and must be changed. The long-forgotten motto of merchandising can be paraphrased to read "The learner is always right." The learner is never at fault, only programs are.

The only direct control a trainer has is control over the program. Consequently, if the trainer is to change anything, it has to be the program. This second rule will keep the priorities of the novice trainer in proper perspective. In the process, the needs of both the training director and the learner will be served.

Rule 3: *Measure your program by whether it does what you said it would do and not by what it actually does.*

Obviously, to apply this rule, you must state performance expectations and measure performance outcomes. At issue is the standard used to gauge accomplishment.

Our technology is based on predictability. Although it is possible for great training programs to be created accidentally, it is not probable. Competent trainers are technicians more than they are artists. To move from artist to technician, the novice trainer needs to embrace the rigorous discipline of prediction, application, measurement and comparison.

In the act of comparison, you establish standards. If the standard is rigorous, you'll find a precise comparison of outcome to prediction. Lax standards, however, make for hazy comparisons. A dishonest standard yields a forced or fabricated comparison. The novice trainer who has not learned the differences between lax, rigorous and dishonest comparisons can easily employ a practice that would measure a program by what it does and not by what the trainer said it would do.

Standards vary from company to company. They come in all flavors; some are lax; others are rigorous; most fall in between. You can achieve lax

standards without effort or discipline. Although they are not very challenging, lax standards are basically honest. But it is both sloppy and dishonest to establish standards after you know the results of training.

And yet frequently, in testing a program, the objectives are gerrymandered to conform to the responses of the learner. Worse yet, sometimes the objectives of a program are developed after the program has been written and tested. These "standards" are phony, although they allow the trainer to state accurately that the outcome "matches" the objective. People who don't know better assume the objective was specified before the outcome was known. This sleight of hand surely defeats the purpose of validation.

On the surface, the transgression seems minor. After all, the outcome being claimed for the program actually happened. It was an outcome demonstrated by a learner. But the comparison is not set up to test the response of the learner; it is the program and its predictability that is being validated.

If you can't predict the outcome of a program, it is poorly designed. Unpredictable results are unfair both to the learner and to the organization that requires the program. Both invested something in the product of the trainer: one, time; the other, money. Neither deserves to take a risk that could have been avoided. Neither deserves less than a predictable result.

By insisting that novice trainers follow the third rule, the training director will bring discipline to the training process and challenge rather than inhibit precision. In the process the novice trainer will learn that training is not an exercise in unbridled innovation, but rather a discipline for the effective and efficient transfer of skills and knowledge.

The novice trainer need not be the bane of the training director. Regardless of their background, experts, line managers and academically trained specialists can learn to become effective trainers. Converting the novice to the master trainer is the responsibility of the training director. The task is made easier if, in the process of conversion, the training director uses the rules of following process, regard for the learner and predictive validation. Once mastered, the time for creativity will have arrived.

Instructive Moments: Every Trainer Has One of Those Days

Every trainer has had one of those days. This session is exploding like a stink bomb. Why? And what can we learn from it all?

BY MARC HEQUET

Susan McClive was just about to lose it — her composure, maybe her mind, probably this job.

How could this be happening? She had set it all up perfectly, by the book, no loose ends.

Her assignment: Help two warring departments — client service and accounting — work together to provide better customer service for a single large external client.

New York communications consultant McClive had interviewed people in both departments to find out what the contentious issues were. Managers in both departments checked off on her findings: Yep, those were the issues, all right. The managers had agreed with her 100 percent that their departments were withholding information from one another and calling each other names. They had a lousy working relationship.

The managers agreed to get their people to a session where they could all hash things out and find ways to work better together. On the appointed day, 10 people from one department and eight from the other gathered. The company's training director sat in to observe.

McClive laid out the issues they had agreed to discuss and launched into her facilitator mode.

Then came the stunner. They stiff-armed her. Complete stonewall.

The flow of information between the departments was consistent and forthcoming, they told her. Workers got along fine across department lines. "You misunderstood when you met with us," someone told her.

"These are nonissues."

Nonissues. The observing training director's mouth dropped open. And there was McClive, turning a radiant crimson, transfixed in the middle of the worst non-situation of what, just then, seemed dangerously close to being her noncareer.

Heart of Darkness

Exquisite, is it not? Let's call this "Memorable Classroom Moments You Wish You Never Had But from Which You Learned and Profited Anyway."

At its heart, this is about the dark side of the journey taken by all who train for a living. People in the class just aren't getting it. How come? They're disruptive and uncooperative. How come? They don't like me. How come? This is just not working. How come?

Maybe there are no real answers in some cases. But good trainers take a stab at figuring out what's wrong, make some changes, and then plunge in again and see if it works — or at least if it's no longer a disaster.

Aside from unresponsive, uncooperative or outright hostile learners, we are also talking about the day the equipment didn't work during your authoritative presentation on How to Present with Cutting Edge Audio-visual Support. We're talking about the unanticipated power failure. The loose cannon. The high school band in the next room. The Blank Look. The dozers. And any number of other adventures to which the trainer is heir.

It is no dishonor to have been down this trail. Indeed, to have endured such an ordeal is an emblem of achievement. The adventure confers what no institution of higher learning could offer, no train-the-trainer course could match. It is the defining experience for the professional trainer. Survive such a day, and you're among the hardened, proven initiates to the order of high trainerhood.

"The steel needs to be forged in the fire," intones Lilly Walters, executive director of Walters International Speakers Bureau and author of *What to Say When You're Dyin' on the Platform!* (McGraw Hill, 1995). "Until you've gone through the really stupid mistakes a couple of times, the good advice really doesn't mean as much."

Adds poor McClive: "I think it happens to every trainer. What you planned for the group isn't what's transpiring. It's a turning point for discovering your abilities as a trainer."

And what else is it? "Terrifying."

Go to Your Rooms

Let's not leave our friend McClive hanging. What happened? "They were afraid to open up with each other," she says now. So McClive gave the group a safe place to start. She sent the departments to separate rooms to make a "wish list" of 10 changes, no more, that they thought would contribute to better customer service.

When the groups came back with what turned out to be near-identical lists, McClive breathed a sigh of relief. The session was on track again. After reviewing the lists with the whole group, she called for another breakout session; this time it was mix and match, with both departments represented in both groups.

Each group took five of the 10 items from the first list and brainstormed what they would do if they had free rein to bring about those changes.

That was a year ago. At last report, says McClive, who declines to identify the client, the departments were behaving themselves and doing useful work together. Interdepartmental committees now monitor key issues, and the departments are even cooperating on customer service surveys — a key sticking point pre-McClive.

McClive gained, too, learning an important trainer skill. She learned how to punt. "The most important thing you need to be able to do," she says now, "is to be ready to deviate from the setup."

Experienced trainers know they

can call a time-out — hold everything — and conduct an impromptu heart-to-heart with the group to figure out what's not working.

"Stop the locomotive," says Irv Schenkler, associate professor of management communication at New York University's Stern School of Business. "Don't assume that the day is lock-step. You have the opportunity to step aside, roll up your sleeves and say, 'Let's talk a little bit about what you're not getting.'"

Schenkler, who instructs corporate clients as well as college students, thinks it's important to *signal* that you're making some changes. He means literally roll up your sleeves or take off your jacket or something.

Be Quiet

And when you ask the group's opinion of what's going wrong and how to change things, don't fear a prolonged hush. "American trainers are very uncomfortable with silence," says Schenkler. "They usually don't give people enough time to think. If something is going wrong, do the time-out, ask a question, and don't say anything. You be quiet. Somebody will say something."

Sometimes, of course, it's only too obvious what's wrong. Dottie Walters — Lilly Walters' mother and likewise a speaker and author — says she once tried to give a speech in a hotel ballroom in which a cross-wired public address system treated her listeners to audio from a presentation by another person in a different ballroom. No one seemed to be able to fix the glitch. So Walters led her group into the only available area — the lobby — and finished there.

Adjusting on the fly is the hallmark of a polished presenter. What if your listeners are tired? What if they're emotionally spent?

Another story from the Walters clan: The younger Walters, Lilly, knew it was going to be a tough gig as soon as she peered into the meeting room of the New York hotel at which she was to speak that evening.

She had been asked to do an upbeat presentation on the secrets of successful speaking. She took a look at the room, where the afternoon's last session was just winding down.

The people who would be her audience were in there, and they were bawling like they were at a four-alarm funeral. They had been talking about down-deep childhood issues, and the

---

---

facilitator evidently was very good at bringing up sad feelings from long ago. The most lighthearted moments came, Walters learned, when somebody would say, "Hand me the crying towel," and they would laugh at that running gag and then start weeping again.

She stared in disbelief. "I'm going in to teach presentation skills," she thought, "and they're still trying to get over the fact that their father raped the cat, or something. They're emotionally drained."

Organizers approached her and apologized for the scheduling oversight, saying they wouldn't do it this way again, that she should understand if participants just didn't have it in them to stay through an evening session. "They've been through a lot," someone blubbered through his tears.

When the time came, Walters plunged ahead with her talk. Her instinct was to look for relief in humor. She probed for an early opportunity to make a joke related to the previous session.

The opportunity came soon enough: During the give-and-take she encourages, a participant commented on one of her books — but mistakenly attributed authorship to her mother, Dottie Walters.

Daughter Lilly jumped on that one, stagily hinting at an anguished struggle to establish her own identity in her mother's shadow. "I wrote that book," the younger Walters whined to the crowd. "It's a book that I took two years to write. And you think my mother wrote it! Never mind. I can deal with it." Pause. "Where's the crying towel?"

With that, she had them. The gag resurfaced several times during the

session, blowing off any leftover languor. She claims nobody left early and she got a standing ovation.

When emotions are running high, a good presenter can plug in. "It really doesn't matter if it's anger or love or hate or frustration," Lilly Walters says. "Whatever it is, you can use it."

Charming a Disrupter

Not every tough spot can dissolve in humor, though. Rebecca Ray couldn't help but notice the man who came in tardy. Ray, at the time an independent trainer, was leading a session for a major client a few years ago on effective presentations. The latecomer made his way up the long executive conference room and noisily prepared a cup of coffee — *behind* her, where it was most distracting. Then he nonchalantly found a seat, leaned back, and put his feet on the table.

Ray read the signals. "I wouldn't say confrontive," she assessed, "but he's very clearly telling everyone he doesn't want to be here."

As she continued the presentation, it quickly dawned on Ray that the disrupter was the only 50-something participant. The others were in their 20s and 30s. She guessed that the disrupter felt this kind of training was beneath him.

At break she greeted him. "I'm so excited you're in this workshop," she said. "It's important to have someone more senior in the room to model the behaviors we're talking about."

Bull's-eye. His countenance softened, and when the session resumed his behavior improved. "I've gotten better over the years at doing the quick read on somebody," says Ray, who now is management resources and development vice president with

---

Merrill Lynch & Co. Inc. at its Princeton, NJ, corporate training center. "But I could have guessed very wrong on that one. It could have blown up. That incident helped me realize how important it is to find out in advance who's going to be sitting in those seats."

Likewise, it's important to let the people in the seats be right sometimes. Brad Theado learned that the hard way. "I started at a business school training displaced factory workers," the Staunton, VA, trainer says via e-mail. "I was teaching a class on WordPerfect 6.0. The subject was using sort features. The students were to create a list of numbers and sort them in ascending order.

"The computer returned with numbers like 45 being smaller than numbers like 8 or 9. I kept telling my students that they were doing something wrong. Heaven knows that I couldn't be making the error.

"The students got angry and I foolishly held my position. After class I realized that there are two types of sorts, alphabetic and numeric. I felt very foolish the next day when I had to explain my error. The students loved it."

In short, don't insist that your way is the only way. "When things start to come unraveled, more frequently than not it's when you're sticking to your agenda," says Chip Bell, Dallas-based senior partner with the consulting firm Performance Research Associates Inc.

Bell was sticking to his agenda — to what had worked in other settings — when one of his warm-up lines fell flat at a presentation before a West Coast hospital group in 1991.

To loosen up his crowds, Bell likes to pose a series of questions like "Why do we drive on a parkway and park in a driveway?"

The crowd cooled at, "Why is it a pair of pants, but it's only one bra?" Moreover, Bell got a scolding later from some participants. That muddled him. The line had worked elsewhere. Later, he surmised that this mostly female group was averse to sex-tinged humor just then because of the sexual-harassment allegations during the recent confirmation hearings for Supreme Court Justice Clarence Thomas.

The message: Timing is everything. But so is geography. Here is a Bell gag that bombed in San Fran-cisco: The little boy peeks in and sees his older sister looking in the mirror saying, "I need a man!" Sure enough, she gets a date. So the kid looks in the mirror and says, "I need a bicycle!"

Now, why would that work elsewhere but not in San Francisco? Bell learned later that his Bay Area audience was largely lesbian, which he didn't suspect at the time.

Learning to Love the Bomb

While we're on the subject of jokes bombing, here's one that fell flat but worked on the rebound: Two caterpillars see a butterfly float past. One says, "You'll never get me up in one of those things."

That got blank looks from English-speaking Chinese managers in Hong Kong, says Scott Simmerman. Simmerman, a Greenville, SC, consultant who gives cartoon-based presentations to business audiences around the world, recovered by asking participants to discuss at their tables what they thought the story meant.

"What I got back was absolutely amazing," he e-mails. "I thought the joke was about resistance to change. What the audience gave me was diverse thinking and a richness of response. They had nearly 40 explanations when I only thought there was one."

Is there any salvation when the equipment crashes and the presentation is entirely based on the equipment? Cyndi Gaudet, assistant professor at the University of Southwestern Louisiana in Lafayette, was teaching a class on how to use the Internet with a single big monitor screen on the wall. It froze. Worse, she couldn't even bring up the Internet sample screens she had brought with her on an external hard drive. "All my toys that I needed were just not there,"

Gaudet sighs. "I had to drop back, regroup and adjust: That screen's frozen. What is teachable from that screen?"

Indeed, some things were teachable from the locked-up interface. She did a tour of the icons, explaining what each meant and where it led. That was useful to the Internet newcomers in the class, but not to those who had already been cybersurfing. You win some, you lose some.

What did Gaudet learn from that experience last year? "I needed to have something else prepared for that worst-case scenario," she says. "Maybe getting people into groups to share what they do with computers." And, she adds, hard-copy screen examples.

Crash Training

Brad Wheeler, assistant professor of information systems at the University of Maryland's Business School in College Park, had his class store collaborative course work on a server. It crashed without backup, and a contrite Wheeler had to tell his graduate students the bad news.

He framed it as a lesson in what happens out there in the real business world. "We got caught. I could have avoided it," Wheeler told them.

Now, he adds: "Don't try to hide the problem. An object lesson is always a very powerful way to convey information."

The irony is this: When you screw up, you may be giving your trainees the best lesson they ever receive.

Allen Weiner, president of Communication Development Associates Inc. of Woodland Hills, CA, will never forget April Fools' Day 1992. He and a colleague were leading a session for top executives with a major client on improving presentation skills.

THE LAWYER AND THE COCKROACH

The worst thing that happened was that a lawyer got pissed off because he couldn't learn the computer and threw a pen at me. It stuck in the wall right behind me," a computer trainer named Patti e-mailed us in response to a posting about this story we placed in CompuServe's DP-TRAIN discussion group.

"A close second was the presentation I fussed over for weeks, worried sick I was going to screw up. Five minutes into the seminar a huge cockroach ran across the room heading straight for me. My reaction was to jump up on the table, knocking over the monitor, which hit the floor, pulling the computer right after it.

"My presentation was over, my credibility was ruined. My only salvage was that I bought beers for everyone in the room as soon as I recovered my composure."

— M.H.

The four men and four women had each received a packet with a videotape. They took turns giving a short practice presentation, for which Weiner slipped each person's videotape into a camcorder and taped them as they spoke. After he had videotaped several practice presentations, Weiner began the standard group critiques. He popped a tape into the video player.

As the group watched the first presenter, Weiner stood at the front of the room with the monitor behind. Alternately, he observed the speaker's technique on the tape and turned to the group to comment.

Weiner happened to be looking at the group as the short taped presentation ended, and he saw the transfiguration in their expressions as they gaped over his shoulder.

Weiner turned to look as well, and in that split second his outlook was dire indeed. *Lawsuit*, Weiner remembers thinking. *I'm going to be the subject of a lawsuit for emotional distress caused to high-ranking employees of a major client.*

His high-ranking trainees were watching a six-way orgy on the videotape he had provided.

Weiner's hand found the video console. He snapped off the monitor. "Let's take a five-minute break," he said.

As the room emptied, his worst dread came into focus: that this tape, the one he had chosen to play first, would be the only one with the naughty pictures. That, Weiner feared, would make him look like some kind of pervert with a business death wish.

It was with strange relief, then, that Weiner checked the other videos and found the same porn film on each. He sent a colleague out for new tapes.

Collecting himself with a will of iron, he called the group back. He calmly explained that instead of blank tapes the wholesaler evidently had shipped his company 300 copies of a film called "Heat Wave," and noted that someone would be back soon with blank tapes.

Weiner apologized — but not profusely, not repeatedly. Then he went on with the session.

He was at that moment living the training that his company gives its presenters. He didn't fidget or pace. He didn't let his hands go to his face, almost always a gesture of nervous dismay.

The blank tapes arrived and the session continued. Client relations remained unchanged — except for some occasional good-natured ribbing.

Was that the best lesson in presentation skills those executives ever got? Maybe so, Weiner acknowledges. "Take five and go to Plan B," he summarizes. "It's the same lesson in tennis: You do not let the other player take you out of your game."

So when things go wrong, stay cool. Go to Plan B. Stay in your game. It could be the opportunity of a lifetime for your learners — *if* you can keep from losing it up there.

Notes:

Performance Reviews: Practicing What We Preach

Your sure-fire appraisal methods won't fly well with managers if you exempt yourself from using the same techniques.

BY STEPHEN P. BECKER

Training managers don't always practice what they preach. Most trainers have conducted programs for other managers and supervisors on MBO and performance appraisal. These concepts have met with wide interest in the world of professional training. That is, the trainers have been interested in getting all the other departments to adopt a managerial style based on performance objectives. In many cases we, as training managers, have not clearly thought through the implications of MBO and reviewing performance for our own departments.

Before setting up a performance review session with a subordinate, you should take some time to consider your own responsibility as a manager of other people. In this regard you have the same responsibility as any other manager. Simply put, your responsibility is to cause the performance of the people under your direction to improve.

Let's look at what this statement really means. First, it means that you, as a manager, have an obligation to help all people who report directly to you do a better job. You shouldn't consider only those who you feel aren't living up to your expectations. Even the good performers can get better, and it's your job to develop them, too.

Realistically, most of your staff will be somewhat below or above what you might consider to be average in terms of training knowledge, skill, and contribution. As is true with any population, only a small percentage of trainers are truly excellent performers. By the same token, only a small percentage are poor performers. The great majority lie somewhere in the middle or average range. Your great task, then, is to get the performance of your individual department members moving in the direction of excellence.

One point to keep in mind is that any trainer may be good at some things and not as good at other things. For instance, a trainer may be especially good as a classroom instructor and as a one-on-one coach. This trainer's great strength is in implementing a course that's already developed. If you think about all the trainers you know, chances are that you will find relatively few "general practitioners." In your performance appraisal planning for your staff, you will need to decide what your own philosophy is on this issue. Do you want generalists or do you want specialists?

The answer is important, because if you want generalists, you must be prepared to make a long-term investment in your individual staff members. Assuming that the people involved also want to be less specialized, you will have to be responsible for lengthy training of the trainers in the areas where there are needs for additional competencies. The specialist can apply his/her competencies immediately and even learn to be more specialized in a much shorter time than it takes to develop entirely new skills. New abilities may take months or years to develop and take much of your own time in the process.

Even if you're not training the trainer yourself, you will have to be highly involved in the planning, resource selection, measurement and application of the training. All this takes time. That doesn't mean that it shouldn't be done. You should carefully think about your staff and the pressure of your organization before you reach a conclusion about how specialized or unspecialized you want your staff.

Now that you've thought about your own responsibility as a manager (to cause individual performance improvement) and about your philosophy regarding specialization, you are ready to consider the performance of individual staff members. You should begin by sitting down and making some personal notes about results that have been achieved by the staff member over the past six months. As you think about the results, try to identify what the payoff has been for the organization, the training department and the staff member.

The idea is to be able to describe results to the subordinate in tangible terms as follows:

1. You developed and taught a sales training program on how to get more sales leads. Within two months, leads increased by 20 percent.

2. You completed the development of two audiovisual programs that are being used daily to teach new employees how to operate the widget machine. As a result training time has been cut by 50 percent and is being done by the immediate supervisor on the shift rather than the area training assistant.

Once you determine the positive achievements, you should attempt to list the performance weaknesses of the individual. These might include things like:

1. The sales training program cost 25 percent more than was projected because of poor control over expenses.

2. The AV programs were two months late in development because of inefficient use of time.

After you have done a lot of thinking fairly and objectively about performance results in terms of strengths and weaknesses, you are prepared to conduct the actual interview. During the session, you should allow the staff member to do most of the talking. Your methodology should be to ask good questions so that the staff member has a chance to be heard by his or her "boss." You want to get the staff member to describe results in order to see if his or her perspective about performance achievement is the same as yours.

Your should not voluntarily tell the interviewee what you wrote down about his or her performance. Rather, look for places where you can agree or disagree about what the staff member believes has been achieved.

Where you agree, expand the point and recognize the value of the contribution. Where you agree, let the discussion revolve around problems that came up and how effectively they were handled.

Where problems arise, you should attempt to get the staff member to identify the cause(s) of the problem. Remember that a problem can have more than one cause and that there may be a variety of solutions that could be applied to each cause. The staff member should be encouraged to create the solution(s) to whatever causes the problem.

The reason for this lies in the concept of dependency. If you, as the manager, identify causes of problems and the appropriate solutions, then the staff member could become dependent on you to deal with the same kinds of problems (or all problems) in the future. What you want is for your staff members to become more independent of you, more self-sufficient. The only way you can make people more independent of you is to allow or force them to take as much responsibility for solving their problems as they can handle. They then can check out the quality of those solutions with you, their manager.

In essence, what you are doing is helping your staff members stay in touch with themselves. You are causing them to be confronted with their own behavior and performance in terms of the results they achieved. You are, in effect, holding up a mirror of their lives at work. While you are in the process of getting staff members to look at themselves, you are functioning like a manager.

Don't be naive about the kind of impact this type of session can have on people. It is quite possible that they will be overly critical of their performance in a negative sense. Most people are very critical of themselves.

You, as manager, must be aware of this tendency and help keep the balance in the discussion. It is important that a person be proud of strengths. What you want is for a person to feel successful and at the same time be cognizant of areas where performance needs improvement.

As staff members become more conscious of competencies, successes and area for improvement, they will be more able to propose performance objectives. The word propose is appropriate here, because you still need to agree to these objectives. You may have knowledge about organizational needs that can influence the objectives as well as the methods of achieving them.

Receiving information about the development and needs of your organization is one of the benefits your staff members should get out of a performance review. It is always necessary for individual objectives to be congruent with organizational objectives.

Many managers think that every time they talk to a department member about work or progress toward objectives, they are conducting a performance review. This is not the case. A performance review should be formal, take about two hours and be done at least twice a year. When it's over, you and your staff member should better know where you've been and where you're going.

After the interview, you should write some notes to yourself about what took place — that is, what was discussed, what performance objectives were set and what things you (the manager) agreed to do before the next interview. The reason for the notes is that without them you probably won't remember all the points you should refer to in the follow-up session.

It's important that performance

interviews be linked to each other. What you want to look at are patterns of performance. You want to see consistent and continuing development. It's not as valuable to your department or to the trainer involved to think of each interview as isolated. In a sense, you both should be able to graph performance improvement over a period of years. This type of mental graph can be done when objectives, and achievement against those objectives are used as the basis of measurement.

One acid test of a performance review is to ask yourself if your relationship with your staff member is more productive as a consequence of the interview. If, after the interview has ended, the staff member feels that you were unfair, abusive, unwilling to listen or unwilling to help him or her be more successful as a trainer, then you have failed the test.

This is not to say that you can't be honest or give negative feedback about performance. In fact, you must be able to say what you feel and believe in order for the interviewee to value your comments. It is necessary for you to be sincere in order to have an effective interview. One key outcome of all such interviews should be that the working relationship between you and your staff person has been enhanced. At the very least it shouldn't slip backward.

Like any other department head, we training managers usually recognize the need for formally reviewing the performance of department members. Our intentions are good, but somehow we forget to put this kind of activity on our schedule. If we work hard to teach others that this is the professional's way to manager, then it may be time for some of us to appraise our own performance.

The Power of Positive Feedback

Formal performance evaluation meetings can intimidate managers and employees. But suppose these tete-a-tetes were redesigned along less ambitious lines...

BY DONALD V. SCHUSTER

In most organizations, performance evaluation creates quite a quandary. Most managers don't know exactly how to carry it off and, consequently, their employees don't have a clue as to what to expect. While all parties generally agree that employers have a *right* to require some kind of performance review, managers are often hesitant — even timid — about conducting the necessary evaluations.

There are a number of performance evaluation systems to choose from, although in reality nearly all of them are minor variations on the same theme. When a company does select an approach, it normally embraces its choice with a notable lack of enthusiasm — nevertheless, the new system becomes "the only game in town."

Employees, too, are left with a sense of ambiguity. They genuinely want to know how they are doing, but their uncertainty about how the meeting will be handled often overwhelms any desire for feedback. As a result, they go into a performance evaluation interview with feelings ranging from mild apprehension to outright dread.

Are such feelings on the part of managers and employees alike simply inherent in the performance evaluation process? Those who say "yes" proceed as if they are as concerned with minimizing "losses" as they are with achieving objectives. And this ambiguity, of course, does not go unnoticed.

Although some management theorists disagree that this type of internal inconsistency is in the nature of the beast and offer useful analysis and insight, they have provided little in the way of workable change models.

The whole subject of performance appraisal is on the front burner today, as a quick look at training, industrial relations and personnel literature will demonstrate.

Reevaluating the System

All performance evaluation systems (with the possible exception of MBO, which has some unique vulnerabilities to accompany its strengths) have certain difficulties in common. These include rater biases, the fact that evaluation criteria may not be perceived as job-related, and management's failure to follow through or support the stated objectives of the performance evaluation.

Proponents of any evaluation system are quick to insist that the most important element is how it is handled by the immediate supervisor. They also stress thorough training in advance, especially when "minimizing losses" is a major consideration. They recognize that a poorly handled evaluation interview may not only fail to deliver the expected benefits, it may work against the company.

If employee sensitivity is a major obstacle to the truly worthwhile objectives of a performance evaluation, then shouldn't you try to eliminate it, rather than just reduce it? Simply improving supervisors' interviewing techniques and sharpening their human relations skills won't do the trick. Why ask a supervisor to compensate for the system's known deficiencies? Why not reevaluate the system itself?

To reevaluate your company's performance appraisal system, the key question to ask is, "What are we really trying to accomplish?" It's unlikely that your organization has reached a consensus on its objectives. It's even

more doubtful you have seriously considered whether your system actually meets those objectives.

Let's take a look at some of the most common goals for performance evaluation:

- *Provide a record of performance.*
- *Provide a basis for wage increases.*
- *Identify employees' potential for advancement.*
- *Determine training and development needs.*
- *Let employees know "where they stand."*
- *Motivate employees.*
- *Provide an avenue of communication.*

To reach these objectives, organizations generally use one or more of these standard performance evaluation systems:

- Graphic Rating Scale.
- Rank Order Method.
- Forced Distribution Method.
- Critical Incident Method.
- Forced Choice Method.
- Goal-setting Method.

Most performance evaluation systems "fail" because they try to accomplish *too much* — they ask too much of one document (an evaluation form) and one event (a performance interview). Even a glance at the objectives stated above will convince you that the challenge is formidable.

If you accept the "too much" criticism as valid, your options become fairly simple. You must either abandon some of the objectives (which few of us would accept) or consider alternate routes for meeting some of them.

Sacred Cows

Let me goad a "sacred cow" here by questioning the validity of one of the traditional objectives of the formal performance evaluation — letting employees know where they stand. Most people consider that objective one of the most important goals of performance evaluation. In practical terms, It means giving employees an unbiased assessment of the good and bad elements of their performance and behavior. Logical enough. Yet it is the single aspect of the performance evaluation interview that most exacerbates sensitivities and is often either unproductive or counterproductive.

Most of us will agree that employees need to know how they are doing on the job. But is the formal interview the best place to deal with the negative points of performance? It's an article of faith among trainers that there is no substitute for ongoing performance evaluation, which is communicated implicitly as well as explicitly. You know employees are getting the message — positive or negative — by the way they respond on the job.

To try to use the formal interview as a net to catch all the cases in which the supervisor failed to give feedback along the way suggests a lack of supervisory skills. If supervisors have not kept their employees informed of performance deficiencies, the delay, from the company's standpoint, is inexcusable.

It's hard to see how formalizing a criticism which the employee already knows about — or at least should know about — can serve a useful purpose, unless terminating the employee is the objective. Behavioral psychologists generally agree that constructive criticism is far more acceptable to the employee and more likely to produce results when it is handled informally, rather than in an episodic, highly judgmental fashion. Positive and complimentary remarks, on the other hand, do have a place in the formal performance interview.

Recognition, Not Evaluation

An interview that fails to give a "balanced" picture of the employee (negatives as well as positives) has little relevance to performance evaluation as we now know it. Instead of *performance evaluation* then, the process I have in mind might better be called *performance recognition*.

In addition to omitting negative evaluations, performance recognition also would exclude most of the other objectives of a typical evaluation and concentrate on just two: *motivation* and *communication*. Splitting off the other objectives doesn't mean abandoning them. They meet real needs, which I'll refer to later.

The totally positive PRO (Performance Recognition Opportunity) approach is designed to motivate employees with meaningful personal recognition and, at the same time, open up an avenue of communication between supervisor and subordinate. I presume that these objectives meet a need in the organization, or at least offer a chance for improvement.

PRO is based upon some ideas that not everyone goes along with. The first is that virtually all (nonpathological) employees would prefer to do good work rather than poor work. We must, of course, add the

usual qualifier, "all other things being equal," which they often are not. Trying to eliminate that qualifier as much as possible is one of the practical focuses of PRO.

Another assumption is that employees genuinely value nonmaterial forms of recognition, *if* they are meaningful and fairly administered, and that the opportunity to communicate one-to-one with a superior, in an atmosphere of respect and relaxation, is also highly regarded.

A third assumption is that employees don't perceive any contradictions between the company's and their supervisors' attitudes, policies and procedures and the first two assumptions.

PRO requires a certain type of job description for each employee, like the type we have produced at World Color Press. Clarity and adequate detail are the first two considerations. Almost *anyone* should be able to read the job description and get a good idea of what the person actually does. Generalizations are not tolerated. Each duty or activity in the job description contains (wherever possible) some statement of the level of competence expected for each duty. Job descriptions written in these terms have several additional uses for a company:

- Taken altogether, the job descriptions present an intelligible view of the interrelatedness and various functions of the different departments within the organization.
- They provide an excellent definition of position requirements to aid both interviewer and candidate when new positions open up.
- They are basic training documents for new employees. They also aid the trainer in conducting cross-training between departments.

PRO in Action

PRO, which we've defined essentially as a motivation and communication tool (although some of the other evaluation objectives are met indirectly), works like this.

At least once a year, the immediate supervisor invites selected employees to attend a one-to-one PRO meeting. Only those employees whose performance has been deemed minimally acceptable or better are invited for "recognition." Being invited, therefore, constitutes a basic level of recognition, and employees are advised well in advance.

Conversely, the 5% or so of employees who are not invited will interpret this exclusion as a strong comment that their performance level (as they should *already* know) is not acceptable. It's important not to deny an employee this recognition interview without the agreement of the supervisor's manager and the approval of the personnel director. When in doubt — recognize.

The totally positive approach of the program has been communicated in advance, so the meeting begins on an upbeat note. Using the employee's job description as a guide, the supervisor discusses the *job itself*, not the employee. The supervisor must listen carefully to the employee's interpretation of how work is progressing and what help the employee may need to improve performance. Sometimes there are roadblocks to "professional" performance that the supervisor may be able to remove.

The supervisor takes every opportunity to comment favorably on some aspect of the employee's work that is going especially well. The supervisor avoids bringing up any aspect of the employee's performance that is *not* satisfactory. Should the employee voluntarily initiate discussion on a problem or deficiency, the supervisor is free to discuss it. But the supervisor should remain as positive as possible and, in any case, offer to help. If this approach seems a bit subtle, remember that the situation is no more demanding than conventional performance appraisals.

Discriminatory?

Is it discriminatory *not* to interview an unsatisfactory employee? So long as the approach remains completely positive, and the objectives are clearly perceived as performance recognition and improved communications, any union objection should be without merit. Unions, themselves, have long been on record as proponents of recognition for their members.

In any case, there is no known *requirement* for a company to recognize any employee's performance. If the union pressed the issue, however, it wouldn't violate the integrity of PRO to give a candid evaluation of the poor performers, one that includes full disclosure of performance and attitude deficiencies.

As we mentioned before, not recognizing the 5% doesn't mean abandoning or ignoring them. It is important to take pains behind the scenes to find out *why* they don't measure up and then to take appropriate action. If your informed judgment is that the reason is simply lack of concentration or effort, the personnel department should pursue the usual disciplines.

When the employee is unsuited to his job, lacks training or has personal problems, these conditions also should be handled appropriately.

Can the union successfully use the fact that an employee has received PRO recognition as a barrier to subsequent discipline and/or termination? Probably not, as long as you stick to the twin objectives of recognition and communication instead of evaluation. But it is a complex question, one better fielded by legal experts.

Clear Objectives

The interplay between supervisor and subordinate during the recognition interview will vary as all normal communication varies in tone and style between different people and at different times. Friendliness and informality, to some degree, are necessary to accomplish the objectives. The only imperative is to remain constantly aware of the basic intent of the program.

Employees should perceive that supervisors (and therefore the company) are eager to recognize whatever they are doing right. More importantly, they should understand that the company is validating this goodwill by helping each employee reach pro-fessional performance levels and achieve personal self-development goals.

PRO, then, is a way to provide formal recognition as an incentive to superior performance. If PRO succeeds as an incentive, employees become more professional in their work. An added bonus: After a number of "recognition interviews," supervisors get an excellent picture of their employees' attitudes, capabilities and needs.

Further Possibilities

Most companies have individuals in each department who are clearly outstanding, an opinion shared by fellow workers and management alike. They generally perform to self-imposed standards and are exemplars of professionalism in their jobs. They aren't perfect, but few managers would hesitate to hire a clone if one could be found. It's not uncommon for fellow workers to complain that these people don't receive their "dues."

One goal of the PRO process might be to single out these people for some sort of special recognition or rewards.

On the other hand, however, the PRO approach should not turn into a competition. Employees, in order to be motivated, need to see that the company wants to recognize *all* good performance. The worth of PRO will be validated to the extent that a significant number of employees value the opportunity for recognition enough to perform accordingly.

Just how well the PRO concept would meet the motivational and communications needs of a given company depends on the unique needs of each organization. Models already exist for the type of job description that is essential to the program. Several years ago, the basic model for the formal performance recognition event (based on the standard of professionalism) was successfully implemented by the space systems division of General Electric Co.

How do you meet the *other* objectives of the conventional performance evaluation interviews? I don't have a final answer to that one. Some of the conventional performance evaluation forms might be useful here, as long as only the job description is used in the performance interview and the interview is kept totally positive. These other forms might be kept on file in the department and/or personnel office, so that employees could have access to them. Is this keeping two sets of books? Not really. They are not (or at least shouldn't be) contradictory.

They simply meet different needs in different ways.

The PRO approach is more than a program. Company "programs" are traditionally perceived as extraneous activities that come and go with predictable regularity. PRO should reflect a company's fundamental people-management philosophy and become an integral part of it.

Notes:

Zeroing in on Your Staff's Performance

Trainer appraisals deserve more care and attention than they often receive.

BY DAVE ZIELINSKI

Effective evaluation of trainer performance is a frontier of management that badly needs further exploration. At least that's the feeling of several training directors interviewed by the *Training Directors' Forum Newsletter*.

The paperwork, hassle, routine inevitability, and ambiguity of performance appraisals are frustrating, yet there seems to be a consensus that performance appraisals are becoming a more critical part of managing the training process. While there may have been a tendency to overlook or downplay them in the past, such sentiments are no longer realistic.

Conrad Haas echoes the feeling of many training executives. "I'm just not satisfied with the job I'm doing," says Haas, director of training and development for Blue Cross/Blue Shield of North Carolina. "Do we have the appropriate measures? Are we zeroing in on the specific results needed by the corporation?"

At Blue Cross, performance appraisals for trainers establish goals for each trainer in terms of contact hours, a fairly straightforward measure of activity; but also in less easily measured terms such as outcomes, including standards for participant reaction, knowledge gains, behavior change and job results. While reaction and knowledge gained are under the control of the trainer in the classroom, behavior change and job results can only be tracked with the support of line management. ("We couldn't do it without them," Haas says.) Behavior change and job results can be especially difficult to track because of the time required for evaluation and the difficulty of getting data from operations.

"One of the things we ought to be looking at is measuring desired behavior or outcomes in terms of analyzing training needs, planning training needs, conducting training and evaluating training," Haas says. "Most performance appraisals do a good job of tracking the training process but not the results of training. We need to move up another notch and become more skillful at measuring the results that trainers produce." The elusive key is setting specific or measurable goals in advance.

Creative Approaches

For Rita Cloutier, manager of field employee training for Aetna Life & Casualty, the problems with performance appraisals are the lack of time and the abundance of paperwork. That seems to be especially true when performance appraisals must be completed during a short time period and are required to conform with corporate-wide performance appraisal forms. "It's a subject close to my heart since I teach a seminar on it, and it's unfortunately true that people have a tendency to feel, 'Oh no, it's that time of year again.'"

When the corporate process doesn't fit the unique requirements of trainer evaluation, Cloutier and others speak of trying to balance the paperwork with what Cloutier calls creative definitions of standardized performance factors. If a corporate-wide performance appraisal form must be followed, modify it like Cloutier does to reflect the unique requirements of training. Or, if you're Jim Krattenmaker, manager of training for Honeywell's corporate headquarters, don't pay much attention to it at all.

"Like everyone else, once a year you fill out an appraisal," Krattenmaker says. "But I view that as conforming to the system; it means nothing. The kind of feedback I give is very much spontaneous stuff. It's on the spot, at the moment, ongoing. The key thing is talk to them while things are happening, constantly as you observe, as you see the need. To me, that's part of the appraisal process; it's real time. You see how responsive the trainers are, how willing they are to listen to where their groups are at and adjust — or whether they follow their agenda religiously to a room that is emptying out."

Even so, Krattenmaker acknowledges that you can't be "totally subjective" and that the formal corporate performance appraisal has its place. At Honeywell, Krattenmaker can use one of four formats. He says he really doesn't use any of them. Instead, he has employees evaluate their own performance and then compare that evaluation with his. "All we really do is compare differences," Krattenmaker says, "and because we know our goals and there's been a lot of feedback, there usually aren't many." Later, Krattenmaker transfers the results to Honeywell's official appraisal form and sends it off to administration. Student evaluation sheets play a part in the process, too, although their usefulness is limited to pointing out serious problems rather than evaluating the true quality of a trainer's performance.

When it comes to the corporate appraisal form, Krattenmaker can rate employees "not competent," "competent," "commendable," or "outstanding." Like many managers, he feels that the top-of-the-scale designation is designed for employees who don't exist — the perfect human being who does everything in an exceptional fashion. "The compensation people put the system together and made it impossible to be outstanding," Krattenmaker says. "You've got to be able to walk on water. I've been fighting that for the past year-and-a-half." As a result of what Krattenmaker believes is unrealistic corporate performance objectives, "all I do is evaluate between competent and commendable. But my people truly accept that the system is nuts when it comes to being outstanding."

That's one more reason why Krattenmaker keeps the official performance appraisal in perspective. The whole idea is to let employees know where they stand, Krattenmaker says. "If I fill out a form once a year and they still don't know where they stand, then I've complied with the system but I haven't really done any appraisal at all."

More Variations

The reality for professionals who supervise technical training programs may be a little different. David Reilly is director of education at Sorbus Inc., a national computer maintenance and repair company. Reilly calls the Sorbus method of evaluating trainer performance "the classical appraisal process," but it contains a number of unusual variations. For one thing, Reilly evaluates his trainers on their yearly employment anniversaries, so performance appraisals are staggered throughout the year. Reilly is also a firm believer in the power of data to reveal individual and department-wide strengths and failings, and Sorbus's appraisal process generates plenty of data.

Sorbus's performance appraisal form for trainers is divided into three areas that cover position activities, functional skills, and a joint agreement worked out between trainer and manager that maps out the trainer's development plan for the coming year. When the appraisal is routed into the corporate system, a salary action recommendation goes along with it. Some companies separate the two for numerous reasons, not the least being that employees may argue over performance ratings if they feel their paychecks are dependent on them.

Sorbus, however, makes no attempt to decouple performance appraisals from compensation reviews. "That's one of the things that drives the appraisal process here," Reilly says. "No matter what people tell you, performance appraisals are an important part of salary action. People have been trying for 20 years to unlink these things. Companies want to tell people that their salary increases aren't related to their performance appraisals. But there's no way behaviorally and intellectually that that doesn't happen. I've even worked for companies that stagger performance appraisals and salary reviews; your performance appraisal may be in April, your salary review in September. But everyone knows darn well that the better your appraisal in April, the more money you're going to get in September."

Even so, it's not so much the performance appraisal process that sets Sorbus's evaluations of its trainers apart as it is what happens before and after, Reilly says. Training managers informally review each training course with instructors soon after training courses are completed. The review is based on critiques — the smile sheets from students — and on interviews managers conduct with students. Since courses last from five to 20 days, trainers at Sorbus may receive personal feedback as frequently as four times a month.

A month after students have returned to the field, a brief questionnaire about the training is sent to their managers. But the heart of the evaluation system lies in the extensive Quality of Education survey that students receive 60 to 90 days after they've completed a course — a period that gives them plenty of time to reflect on how that course improved their abilities to do their jobs. They are asked to rate 13 areas with a five-item scale. Areas covered include the quality of the technical documentation used in the course; the overall usefulness of the course; the distribution of time spent on lecture, lab exercises, discussions and exercises; the availability and working conditions of equipment used in the course; and the overall classroom learning environment. Students are also asked to rate the instructor's knowledge of the product, the quality of the lectures, and his or her ability to assist and coach students through hands-on exercises.

Finally, students are asked, "Are you confident in your ability to repair the equipment covered in this course?" Students are also encouraged to make comments in a space provided.

Says Reilly: "This says to each individual instructor, 'OK, your customers have consumed your product and have been out using it. Now here's what they think.'"

Reilly receives a statistical analysis of all returns for each quarter. The information helps him determine strengths and failings for both individual trainers and the department as a whole. Later, the Quality of Education information is rolled into Sorbus's formal performance appraisal process. But while the data is useful, Reilly says his department never loses sight of the bottom line, which is reflected in that final question on the survey. Reilly estimates that 98 percent of their trainees are saying "Yes, I am confi-dent in my ability to repair the equipment covered in this training course."

Setting Performance Standards

Ray Gill, group supervisor for electrical and electronic training at Philip Morris, USA, takes an approach similar to Reilly's. For one thing, the sheer size of the company's work force (14,000 in the Richmond area alone) and the unionized, blue-collar nature of the employees Gill's department trains require a standardized, highly efficient training program (one that is cognizant of delicate union relations), and equally standardized and efficient ways to measure its impact.

PM's size, in fact, recently forced the company to rethink its performance appraisal process. "We have about 50 instructors divided up among five supervisors, and each group tended to have a different set of trainer objectives based on what specialties those particular trainers had to perform," Gill says. "We began to lose sight of individuals. So last year we implemented a performance standards committee made up of a group of trainers who decided what the performance standards would be for all trainers, regardless of their specialties."

The committee devised a five-part appraisal form that rated trainers with a three-part scale. In addition, trainers are weighted according to what their duties actually involved over the past year. (For example, a trainer who spends the majority of time developing course materials can't be expected to be as inspiring a classroom performer as a full-time stand-up instructor.) In addition, Gill and his managers conduct less extensive quarterly appraisals with trainers. This frequent feedback helps ensure that neither managers nor trainers are in for big surprises when the annual appraisal is done.

"We take performance appraisals fairly seriously," Gill says. Not only does the new program set objective, measurable standards, it also helps make the case for training with corporate managers.

"It gives you some measurement of your success when you report through to the tiers of management," Aetna's Cloutier agrees. "It allows us to say this is what were doing and this is how our attendees react to what we've done."

But there's still all that paperwork to be compiled. Nothing may ever solve that problem, but Cloutier says that this year she plans to automate, updating an informal file of observations and comments she makes on her trainers with the help of a new personal computer. As notes are made during the year, she'll enter them into an appropriate data file. When the annual performance appraisal process rolls around, comments on trainers will have been collected and stored under appropriate headings. In addition to a check-off-the-box appraisal form, Cloutier will have a year's worth of observations at her fingertips. That may help make this arduous process less of a paperwork nightmare and more like the constructive process it is meant to be.

Notes:

Taking Care of Troubles

Prevention is the best way to manage performance problems on your training staff.

BY BRIAN MCDERMOTT

The best thing to do with a lousy trainer is to never hire one. But mistakes happen; it's not always obvious up-front if someone is unsuited to be a trainer, and at times good people go through periods of poor performance. Training directors interviewed by the *Training Directors' Forum Newsletter* agree that under circumstances where training is failing because of an instructor, it's time for the department manager to lend some aid.

The first step, suggests Keith Hoyt, is to determine if the failing trainer has skills that can be improved. While he was corporate director of training for Harry M. Stevens Co., Hoyt gauged the success of their training programs by looking at five aspects of each course: the measurable objectives; the design and development of the tools needed to reach that objective; the implementation; the follow-up with trainees and managers to see if the training stuck; and the evaluation to determine if the objectives were met.

"Based on that, we could say whether the trainer performed properly. We could look at each specific area and pinpoint where any problems occurred and determine which of the trainer's skills needed help."

To prevent faulty performance by his line-manager trainers, Hoyt says his department developed detailed guidelines for delivering each particular course. Each trainer was put through a two- or three-day train-the-trainer session to "get them to understand what happens during the actual training; to show them how to use the reference guide; to give them a chance to perform on actual parts of the course; and to be evaluated by their peers." Once in an actual classroom, the new instructors worked with experienced trainers until they were gradually able to work alone.

On occasion, Hoyt says, he has used — and recommends — trainer workshops from the American Management Association for people who have strong technical skills but weak training competencies.

In the rarer situations when a trainer has to be let go, the most important thing is that the trainer not be degraded in the process, Hoyt says. "I think when you work with somebody over a period of time it becomes obvious for everyone if it isn't going to happen, if it's not going to work; no one will probably be surprised. So, it's not that

---

There are lousy trainers who want to be part of your staff; it's up to you to weed them out or help make them better at what they do.

---

you just get rid of someone; you look for other areas of the company where the skills that person was able to demonstrate can be used. You look for how else those abilities can be applied."

Stephen Ashlock, director of training for ADP-Dealer Services, says, "We try to do the fair thing for the employee when trainers have performance problems. It may just be that a person got into a job he or she isn't fit for; if so, we try to find them another home."

If an employee does seem to fit in training but has some problems, Ashlock says he develops a performance plan, looking for specific areas of improvement. He uses student critiques and information from man-agers, as well as first-hand observations from the classroom, to evaluate teaching techniques and technical skills and knowledge.

If trainers lack product knowledge, Ashlock recommends they attend another trainer's course on the same subject, or suggests they go back into the field for a while. Trainers lacking teaching skills can return to ADP's train-the-trainer program, offered three or four times a year by their own certified instructor. Ashlock also recommends books or outside seminars that might be useful in developing the needed skills.

Ashlock, too, believes prevention is the best cure for trainers who perform inadequately. To that end, ADP has initiated a new certification process for use in hiring regional trainers. "We're trying to work out the problems up-front. In the past, we assumed people were good employees and we would let them sink or swim on their own. Now we're trying to get them up to speed beforehand."

Current job descriptions, Ashlock believes, are also a critical element in hiring or promoting trainers. Out-of-date descriptions may lead employees to assume things that are not true.

Ashlock, who manages 30 curriculum developers, says, "Probably all training directors have encountered problem employees. I think the most important thing is that we give very specific feedback about what the problem is. We tend to beat around the bush. We've got to say, 'In this class on this day, you did this.' Often, people just aren't aware of their actions and their effects."

One-on-Ones

Trainers from outside the company who perform poorly are easy to deal with, according to Paul Reeve, corporate director of training and development for the Providence Journal Co., because there is the option to not use them in the future. With full-time employees the situation is more delicate and calls upon the most basic of management skills.

Most important in dealing with performance problems, Reeve says, "is close and immediate follow-up discussions after a training session." When there are problems Reeve coaches one-on-one, reviews and rehearses programs to be delivered, and reiterates the keys to reading and encouraging interest and participation in the classroom. He often will observe the troubled trainer at work, or to lessen the anxiety of being watched, have another trainer observe and provide feedback.

"I take a subtle, low-key approach to coaching. I let people see where their weaknesses are. If they don't recognize them, I might back them off from training and give them time to think about what they want; give them time to get feedback from others. I find sometimes that if you back someone off from the chance to train because they view it as a perk — they finally see a need to get some help."

Temporary Problems

So far, says **Dave Podeszwa**, manager of the Johnson Controls Institute at Johnson Controls Inc., his selection process has protected him from having to deal with any "outrageous cases" where a trainer is totally mismatched to a job and detrimental to his department. It has not prevented the occasional case, however, when the performance of individuals suffers because of personal problems such as divorce, child-settlement cases, or drug and alcohol abuse.

Classroom instructors play a critical role in customer satisfaction, Podeszwa says. "Standing up in front of a class is a difficult job. If I have personal problems, I could probably come to work and enter data on a computer all day. But as an instructor I have to convey information in a positive manner. Students travel far and devote a lot of time to participate in training, so I can't afford any downtime."

When it comes to personal problems, managers and even co-workers can be almost blind to what is happening. Once a problem is identified, Podeszwa suggests it's often best to turn it over to the company's employee assistance program. Also, he says, "Rather than throwing these people out the door, it's possible to readjust their assignments so that they are less stressed. It's a good way to take advantage of their strengths and it can also spread goodwill."

Podeszwa also believes that identifying — and avoiding hiring — potentially poor performers is the best way to manage performance problems. With the help of Johnson Control's human resources department, which does the initial review of job candidates and "refers the cream of the crop," Podeszwa conducts an extensive screening process. "We look at their backgrounds, their histories, their successes in the last five years, for instance. We never hire anyone on the first round of interviews. We bring them back a second time to get a better idea of who they are and to give them a chance to meet some of the staff."

At times, Podeszwa says, even that is not enough to confirm or deny a gut feeling about a job candidate, so some are invited back to do sample presentations.

"I guess it all boils down to, 'Would I want to go camping with this person?' If not, I don't care how talented you are, you probably won't fit. When there are problems on staff, we tackle individual faults with individual solutions." Podeszwa uses counseling and outside programs, such as the Technical Instructor Institute at the University of Wisconsin at Eau Claire.

One factor in never having had to let a poor performer go, Podeszwa believes, is many trainers tend to burn out and want to move on in about three years. "I have had some people for 12 years, though, and keeping the stars of the organization going can also be tough. Typically, the stars are promoted and put in charge of one of the five functions within the institute. Some of the stars are recognized outside the institute, too, and are drafted for starring roles in other departments. I never hold up anyone's advancement. It hurts when they leave because we have to pick up the pieces and keep up our standards. But personal advancement is important, and I'm glad to see people being able to take advantage of those opportunities."

In addition to problem performers, Podeszwa says, "You have to keep paying attention to the good folks; pay attention to their success and keep them challenged.

"Chances are none of us have really hired lousy instructors. There probably are reasons for whatever is going wrong. If you can eliminate the reasons, chances are you'll probably have a good instructor again.

HOW TO DECIDE WHEN TO FIRE A PROBLEM STAFFER

What factors should determine whether to get rid of a trainer who is not performing up to standard?

In Managing People at Work Desk Guide, (Executive Enterprises Publications, New York) Thomas L. Quick suggests, "You are probably justified in terminating the substandard performer if you answer no to all three of the following questions:

"Can she do it? Does she have the ability — or at least the potential? If she is not exercising her potential, turning it into actual ability to do the work, then she needs help in training, coaching or guidance.

"Is she willing to do it? Does she have the motivation to commit herself. If she seems to have good intentions and to act in good faith, then you might conclude that her motivation is there. So strengthen it. Give her feedback, especially recognition, when she does things well. Reward the behavior that you want, which is adequate performance.

"Is she capable of understanding her job duties? Don't assume that she should understand them just because she was told once. It may be time to review what you expect of her. You may have to find different ways of explaining her duties. For example, you may have to break her duties down into small tasks. Perhaps she has been unable to grasp the whole."

Quick suggests there are several arguments that favor rehabilitating poor performers. They are:

- Known quantities.
- Know your operation.
- Probably are loyal.

Also, it's normally cheaper to retrain or rehabilitate than to recruit a replacement. And ethically, Quick says, a manager should consider whether everything possible has been done to help a poor performer.

Quick also suggests, "In every case of employee failure, two people are involved: boss and subordinate. This is not to say that the boss is always to blame or even bears the blame in most cases. But the boss always has to be concerned with the possibility that there has been a managerial contribution of sorts to the failure."

Building Trust

Sharing your values gives your staffers a foundation of expectations on which to build their performance standards.

BY STEPHEN P. BECKER

An effective training department manager knows the importance of establishing, developing, and protecting trust with subordinates. If there is a high degree of trust in your relationships, you will find that the members of the training department will set high performance expectations for themselves, ask for your help in solving problems, bring you information, challenge and add to your thinking, follow your lead, have a high degree of commitment to you and the department, accept more responsibility, and cope with special pressure like working late for two months to meet a deadline.

The other side of the coin is that low trust will mean poor collaboration, little performance improvement and a minimal amount of enthusiasm. High or low trust will be reflected in the programs and products of your department. This means that both the quantity and the quality of training output will be directly affected by the degree of trust between you and your subordinates.

The more you trust each other, the more productive you can be as a team. You, as the team manager, must assume the most responsibility for initiating trust. To do this you'll have to manage yourself in ways that allow trust to grow and flourish.

The first thing you need to do is provide a foundation for a relationship. You do this by setting ground rules. The reason for ground rules is that a trusting relationship between people is based upon knowledge about the values and beliefs of the people involved.

Since you are the manager, you should take the initiative in letting your subordinates know what you value and believe. You shouldn't sit down and ramble for hours about your philosophy of life (you do have one, you know). What you should do is state as clearly as possible what is important to you as a manager of training. Tell how you want the department to operate, what you expect, what you won't tolerate, etc.

Examples of ground rules might include statements like:

• "I expect you to do whatever is necessary to get this program going by (such-and-such a date)."

• "The programs we produce must be of extremely high quality. There will be no exceptions to this policy."

• "You can buy all the materials you need up to a limit of $1,000. Beyond that amount, you need my signature."

• "We will have a staff meeting once per month. At that meeting everybody will give a status report on all the projects for which they are accountable."

Your subordinates will begin to understand you as they become familiar with the ground rules you specify for the training department. The ground rules will set the working atmosphere of your department and provide a framework that governs on-the-job behavior and the way you will relate to each other. As their understanding of you grows, your subordinates will be able to predict how you will respond in various situations or what decision you would probably make under certain conditions. They will understand "how your head works."

As you work with your staff, they will learn more about your preferences, style and personal needs. For instance, if you have a high preference for work being delivered on time, they will be able to trust you to get upset or frustrated when work is not completed on schedule. You may also be the kind of manager who can be trusted to ask the opinions of department members before making important plans.

The point here is that trust is not inherently good or bad. It is simply a description of what a person normally can be counted on to do in a given a set of conditions. It is a person's typical pattern of behavior. Some people can be trusted to be indecisive, to be overly cautious, to be impulsive, not to listen, to talk too much, to dominate, to avoid confrontation, always to say the wrong thing, to be timid, to make a good presentation, to stand up for what's right, to act thoughtfully and intelligently, to knuckle under, to take too long, to follow through on a commitment, etc. To begin a trusting relationship, it is necessary for you to "show and tell" people what you want, like and will do. They will begin to know and understand you.

Since trust is a two-way street, it is as important that you trust your staff as it is for them to trust you. Here you just reverse the situation. In addition to deliberately letting them get to know you, you must conscientiously become familiar with what they can be trusted to do. Again, because you are the manager, you should take the initiative.

The first of two steps is to initiate frequent discussions with each individual. These discussions should not be about what the person can do, but rather why he or she does things. Try to get at the motivations. Try to keep the discussion on a fairly personal level. What you are trying to discover is what this particular person believes and feels is important, what he or she values.

The second step is to come to some conclusions about what a particular trainer thinks is important by observing his or her performance. You should seek to answer questions such as whether this trainer organizes work well, performs assigned tasks, generates good ideas, manages time effectively, prepares objectives, measures results, takes interpersonal risks if they are appropriate, and so on.

You want to know what this trainer can be counted on (trusted) to do. The rub is that this kind of performance-observing takes a long time. You generally can't form your conclusions from one or two performance samples. That's why people don't instantly trust each other.

The cornerstone of trust is honesty. It is the key ingredient that can cause relationships to improve. It means more than being truthful. The critical part of honesty for training professionals is not to withhold feedback, opinions, ideas and feelings. In a sense, to establish trust trainers must let it all hang out.

If you can encourage an honest atmosphere in your department where trainers feel an obligation to help each other improve their training skills, develop more interpersonal competency, and give and receive performance feedback constructively, then you will find that all members of your department will develop more "intimate" knowledge about each other. As they learn more about each other, you will be able to plan, stimulate and observe emotional growth in your staff members.

One indicator of emotional growth is that your staff will take more interpersonal risks by giving more direct and on-target performance feedback to each other. In addition, they will be able to accept "hard-to-take stuff" with less defensiveness and embarrassment. They will be better able to use feedback for their own personal and professional growth. They will also have more insight into, and be more willing to talk about, their own performance and professional training inadequacies.

In turn, they will develop the "giving" skills. That is, they will be better able to tell just how much feedback others can take and they will develop the skill of delivering that feedback at the critical moment and in a manner that is acceptable to the recipient. As trainers learn to develop trust through honesty, they can become superb partners in a helping relationship either as giver, takers or catalysts. Isn't that what a big part of training is really about, anyway? In essence, trainers help people to help themselves. There is no chance for

this to happen without trust, and there is no chance for trust without honesty.

Once you have fostered a trusting environment in your department, you had better not assume it will just keep going. You have to protect it. You have to fan the fire. You maintain trust with and between your staff by creating opportunities and conditions for talking with each other. There needs to be "get togethers" in pairs, small groups, or as a total department. If everybody is constantly isolated because of various projects or geographics, it is not possible to increase your knowledge of each other. Phone calls are not enough. You need to schedule extended periods of time when your staff can really achieve some depth in their conversations.

Many department heads attempt to manage by objectives only. They don't believe it's necessary to confront feelings. They think that only results count. What they fail to grasp is that trust is a feeling and that behavior is connected to feelings. Without trust, relationships are shallow, superficial and sterile. When people have that kind of poor relationship with their boss, then they will perform only well enough to meet the stated objectives. Personal motivation dies.

Because your training department is so visible — in the sense that many people see, hear about or experience what you do — you cannot tolerate only satisfactory performance by staff members. If this happens, you and your entire department will not have the reputation for quality work that you might otherwise enjoy. As the training manager, you are supposed to be proficient in the art of management. All good managers know how to help their staff members release their own potential for self-development. You must constantly strive to build trust relationships that stimulate personal growth. This kind of dynamic process in your department

will be the foundation and the heart of creative training that can permeate the entire organization.

Let's conclude with a word of caution and some straight-out advice: You may encounter people with whom you cannot change. No matter what you do, you either can't trust them (can't let them know you) or they can't trust you (can't let you know them). You may also find some who do not have the capacity to mature or contribute to a relationship. If you have people like this in your department — get them out.

They could hurt the efforts of everybody else because most of the time (investment) spent with them will be frustrating.

While others are achieving growth through their relationships, the gap between the winners and the losers becomes greater. When this happens, any time spent with those you cannot change becomes an even greater waste. Part of the excitement about having the kinds of relationships that we are referring to is that they can be used as springboards to help those involved become better people and better trainers. It's not wrong to be used, or to use somebody else in this way. Relationships should be profitable.

What you must actively be working toward is a department where your trainers are training each other as well as themselves. You want a working atmosphere characterized by inquiry, experimentation, honesty, aggressiveness and personal growth. To achieve this kind of professional climate, you must take the lead in building trusting relationships. If you are good at that, it will show in your department's performance. If you're not skillful in creating trust, you're still OK. All that means is that you need to learn how. Remember, charity begins at home.

CHAPTER 3

USING OUTSIDE RESOURCES:

Suppliers, Consultants and Contractors

Calamitous Consulting —
A Cautionary Tale of
Using Outside Help

The story is fictitious. The advice in the margins is real.
It comes from veteran training directors who know exactly
where this rookie went wrong in managing a consultant.

BY BEVERLY GEBER

Rory Patterson was feeling the strain. The first eight tumultuous months he had just spent as the new training director for Amalgamated Acme Corp. were nothing compared with the pressure he began to feel during the meeting yesterday with Amalgamated CEO Sylvia Popham. She had called the meeting to discuss what the company ought to be doing in the way of human resources development (HRD).

Amalgamated, a Cleveland company with 850 employees, had spent much of its 62-year history concentrating solely on making feather pillows. ("We stuff 'em. You fluff 'em.") The business was a staid one that enjoyed gentle domestic competition and reliable profit margins — until recently.

About three years ago, inexpensive imported pillows began flooding into the United States, deflating Amalgamated's market share and profits. Sylvia responded on two fronts. As she tried to plump up the pillow business, she also diversified. She bought a small mattress company, partly because it was a related business and partly because its factory was just 15 miles away from Amalgamated's plant — close enough to supervise. She investigated new market niches for pillows. As she met with Rory yesterday, company designers were trying to create a hypoallergenic pillow, as well as products designed especially for hospitals and the hotel industry.

Yet these actions, plus the severe cost-cutting Sylvia imposed on the pillow and mattress companies, had failed so far to make Amalgamated thrive.

Sylvia was unsure what to do next. She was not what you'd call a professional manager, much less a turnaround artist. She had come up through the traditional, male ranks at Amalgamated, fighting for every assignment and promotion she got. In the old days, Sylvia was called a tough broad; now, they just called her tough.

Throughout her career, she had resisted every attempt to shunt her into staff positions such as personnel or communications. She knew little about such corporate support services, but from the business magazines she had been reading lately, she had grown convinced that the human resources function might hold a key to a company turnaround.

That's why she had called in Rory. She'd been reading about companies that sped up their processes, instituted quality improvement plans, empowered workers and grouped them into teams. As far as she could tell, all of these issues were lumped under the rubric "culture change," a concept that received approving treatment from almost all the business magazines she read. She wanted to turn Amalgamated from a plodding, blindered, reactive underachiever into a nimble, entrepreneurial, inventive, wildly profitable superstar. Rory, who was in charge of human resources, could help.

Rory, 38, had been with Amalgamated for 12 years, less than a year of that in HRD. Amalgamated believed strongly in promoting from within. So when the previous training director left abruptly, it was not an unusual move for the com-

Bravo! Here's a fresh breeze.

Uh-oh. She's a victim of Harvard Business Review *overload. You can see it all coming, can't you?*

Blood pressure or no, here's where Rory needs to explain that small, focused steps toward a goal succeed much better from a flailing attempt to do everything at once.

pany to promote Rory from his position as lead supervisor on the pillow-stitching line and appoint him to head the two-person training department. He knew he was green but he had always prided himself on being a quick study. Ever since the promotion, he had been reading voraciously — everything from Warren Bennis to Geary Rummler, with Robert Mager in between.

Rory had absorbed enough from the experts to know that he would need to spend a great deal of time on needs assessment before he could figure out what type of interventions the company needed for this latest dream of Sylvia's. No go. Sylvia turned grim and pounded her desk for emphasis. "Our problems require a bias for action and it's imperative — Imperative! — that we begin this change as quickly as possible. The future of the company is at stake," she exclaimed, her blood pressure rising.

Rory felt stuck. He was in the latter stages of a project right now, one that Sylvia had deemed imperative six months ago. It was an orientation program with a long-term goal of meshing the pillow company and the mattress company a bit better. Even after the acquisition, the mattress folks insisted on doing things their own way and keeping their distance from Amalgamated.

This is the wrong first step. How does he know what to search for if he doesn't know any specifics about what he needs?

The only way to do everything Sylvia wanted was to hire a consultant. Rory went to the phone and called another training director who had taken Rory under his wing at a recent conference. Rory trusted Harvey Yeutter, who had been a trainer for three years.

"Harvey," Rory said, "my CEO wants a culture-change program, and she wants it yesterday. I've never done anything this complicated before. Know anybody who can help me?"

"Sure," Harvey said. "We've had a consultant helping us design performance appraisals lately. She's real sharp."

That's it? One networking phone call and the consultant is all but hired? Sure, Rory's busy, but this is not a task to be rushed.

Rory got the consultant, Emily Cortez, on the phone. He explained that he was looking for someone to help his company with a culture-change project. Its

SOME TIPS FOR WORKING WITH CONSULTANTS

You've probably already spotted most of the ways Rory Patterson went wrong in his first attempt to hire and manage the work of an outside consultant. But just in case you missed a couple of the pitfalls, we've compiled the advice gleaned from more than a dozen experienced training directors. Use this information. You'll find that your dealings with consultants will run more smoothly — and the consultants will thank you for it. They can do their jobs much better when their clients are as specific as possible about what they want.

DO YOUR OWN FRONT-END ANALYSIS. Since you know — or should know — the company better than any consultant could, it will usually save time and produce better results if you investigate training needs yourself. You will feel more certain that the recommendations for solving performance deficiencies are the right ones if you do the analysis.

On the other hand, some experienced training directors occasionally use consultants for such work. But they are careful to limit the scope of the assignment. For instance, a training director might ask a consultant to assess how well the performance appraisal system is working in the organization. But the director would ask only for an assessment of the existing system, not recommendations for changes. And he would specify exactly how the consultant should conduct the assessment — for instance, a companywide survey with pre-approved questions and three focus groups with carefully chosen participants.

CHOOSE CONSULTANTS CAREFULLY. You may have had a happy experience working with a particular consultant in the past, but that doesn't mean she's the best one for a new project on an unrelated subject. Besides, it's useful to work with a stable of consultants so you can take advantage of the different perspectives and knowledge they possess.

When looking for a consultant, get recommendations from several knowledgeable sources, not just one. Go to training conferences and attend sessions given by consultants to size them up. Do a telephone interview with a consultant to "prequalify" him for a particular project. Then ask for references and check them. One training director asks for three-year-old references; she wants to see if an intervention succeeded and is still showing results today. Another training director — who goes to great lengths to check out consultants before she hires them — sometimes asks for a sample outline if she's looking for a consultant to deliver a course. If she's hiring a consultant to deliver an off-the-shelf course, she also insists on sitting in on the entire course as the consultant delivers it to another client. It's usually no problem to find a client company that doesn't compete with her own company, and although it's very time-consuming for her, she considers it a good investment. She's never had a bad experience with a consultant since she began this system.

This same training director also conducts a "pre-briefing" to go over all materials a consultant may plan to present to trainees. The training director may spot information or techniques that wouldn't work in her company.

One more thing: Don't assume that one consultant should complete the entire project. Break it down into discrete parts, and assign them to consultants according to their expertise. For instance, if you're trying to teach peo-

He's implicitly asking her to take over the project. If he'd done his homework first, he could have told her what he wanted. After all doesn't he know the organization best?

If Rory had figured out the parameters of the project, he could have broken it into parts, assigned one or more of those parts to a consultant and offered a set fee for the job.

You can't expect consultants to produce what you want unless you guide them toward the goal you have in mind. Rory is shirking his duty to oversee Emily.

dimensions were as yet unknown. He told her he was sorry he couldn't be more specific but that he expected the consultant would be heavily involved in helping to define the project. Would she be interested?

The next day, Emily came to see Rory. He recounted his recent conversation with Sylvia, explained that he'd been in charge of training for less than a year, and asked how she would suggest such a project might be approached.

"Well," Emily said, "of course, the first thing to do is a front-end analysis. It would involve talking at length to your CEO to find out exactly what she has in mind for this organizational change effort. We'd also have to take the pulse of the organization to find out where it is now. Once we know those two things, we'll be better able to decide what needs to be done."

Rory thought that sounded reasonable. He asked Emily about her usual fees for a project of this sort. "For something this complicated and open-ended, I usually charge an hourly rate plus expenses," she said.

They shook hands, and Rory took Emily to meet Sylvia. Then he issued a memo to line managers telling them to expect visits from Emily. He felt as if a weight had been lifted from his shoulders.

Rory originally asked Emily to check in with him at two-week intervals to report on the project, but several things got in the way. The first time Emily called to schedule an appointment, Rory was spending 12 hours a day at breakneck pace trying to finish his orientation course so it could be pilot-tested on schedule. He asked to meet with Emily the following week, but she already had a full schedule of interviews planned with company employees. They agreed to skip the first meeting and catch up with each other at the next meeting.

Some weeks later he got a phone call from the manager in charge of the pillow-stitching line, his former supervisor. "Rory," Keith said, "I just wanted to let you know that consultant you sent over here has been a great help. She pointed out to me that I wouldn't have as much trouble supervising these guys

Rory has dangled an open-ended contract before her. At least he could have qualified her by asking about her experience with culture-change consulting, her knowledge about the topic, and whether she's worked in a soft-goods manufacturing firm before.

He should be feeling terrified. He's just turned Emily loose with an extremely vague mandate. No contract. No deliverables. No deadlines. No way this is anything but trouble.

---

ple to use a new computer system as you're teaching them to work in teams, you might want one consultant in charge of the technical training and another in charge of the soft skills development. Be sure the consultants know they must work in tandem, and watch to be sure they do.

GET ALL THE DETAILS IN WRITING. The contract — and the discussions leading up to it — is the most crucial part of the project. You should have a very clear idea of what the consultant should do and how she should go about it. All that information should find its way into a contract. Some training directors use a boilerplate contract they've created for outside consulting projects, but they attach addendums that contain details pertaining to each assignment.

Each contract should spell out very specifically such things as the goal of the project, what the consultant is expected to do to achieve the goal, a timetable for achieving it, the date the project will be finished, the nature of the physical product (10 four-hour train-the-trainer sessions co-facilitated with the training director, let's say), the number of checkpoints along the way, how communications will be handled (a biweekly progress report meeting, for instance, supplemented by weekly phone calls), the payment amount and terms of payment.

If you have a relatively open-ended project, it's especially important to have a clear timetable with specific goals to be met along the way. Some training directors also advise that if you are hiring a particular individual based on his reputation and expertise, you should specify in the contract that he is not allowed to have a colleague substitute for him unless you agree.

KEEP TRACK OF THE PROJECT. Don't assume that because you've done such a good job of drawing up the contract, things will proceed smoothly. Two people often interpret seemingly specific instructions in different ways. It's imperative to keep checking on the project's progress to make sure the consultant isn't going awry.

This is especially important in situations in which you have hired a consultant to work directly with line managers. You must continue to keep an eye on those projects to make sure the consultant is doing only what she's supposed to be doing. It's inappropriate for consultants to market their services to others in the organization without your blessing. If something goes wrong, it's your credibility at stake, not the consultant's.

Tracking the consultant's progress also means you should be cognizant of any contacts he makes with anyone in the organization. You should ask for a weekly itinerary that details whom the consultant plans to contact. As director of this project, you should also be privy to all the raw data gleaned from surveys, focus groups and conversations. Some training directors take this one step further: They help write any report on the project that goes to top management.

STICK TO THE ORIGINAL PLAN. Consultants will often stumble across other problems as they try to solve a problem in your company. It's their duty to bring it to your attention. But you, as the training director, must decide how that problem fits into your list of training priorities. If some unforeseen issue must be addressed in order to make the current project succeed, redo the contract. Don't give the consultant a verbal go-ahead to tackle the new problem. Misunderstandings are bound to arise.

on a daily basis if I had a better plan for doing performance appraisals on them."

"You're already doing that, aren't you?"

"Yeah, but she has some ideas for doing it better and she's going to give me and the other managers some training in how to do it."

This is a sure sign Rory has lost control of Emily. A consultant should never be allowed to market new services to line managers without the training director's permission.

Rory hung up and called Emily, whom he had seen just twice since he handed her the project. "She's at Amalgamated today," her secretary said.

An hour later, Rory found Emily in the office of the vice president of operations, Leroy Stippe. She was mapping out to him a flowchart of the project she was planning.

Here's another bad sign. Rory shouldn't have to hunt down Emily. He should know in advance about all her contacts with company employees.

Back in his office with Emily, Rory asked why she hadn't yet shown him that flowchart. "As you know, Rory," she said, "it's absolutely necessary to find champions and get some initial buy-in before you attempt such a significant change. That's all part of the assessment stage. I was able to identify Leroy as a possible champion and I was just trying to bring him aboard with a very sketchy idea of what we had in mind. Once I had his buy-in, I intended to come to you to talk about what we need to do next."

Notice how Emily's assuming the lead position here? It's Rory's responsibility to decide how to proceed after Emily gives him her assessment. And she's out of line trying to recruit champions on her own.

"OK," said Rory, who had forgotten all about performance appraisals. "Let's see the flowchart." Over the next hour, Emily explained that changing Amalgamated into a nimble, quality-driven organization was going to require massive amounts of training. First, every employee should go through a four-day course to raise awareness of what changes were needed. Then, a long stretch of skill-building courses, including interpersonal relations, team-building, conflict resolution and project management. Finally, there would be another rather long period of individual coaching to make sure the changes "took."

These are not "deliverables." These are vague intentions.

Rory noticed that Emily's flowchart had no time line. "How long will this take?" Rory asked. "And how much will it cost?"

"It's impossible right now to answer either question accurately," Emily said. "The time line depends entirely on how receptive people are to these ideas and how willing management is to let people go through training. And as for the cost, I'm going to lower my hourly rate to make it more affordable for you. Keep in mind that this project is an absolutely top priority of your CEO, so you aren't likely to face any budgetary problems."

Famous last words.

"OK," Rory said. "But I'd like you to check back with me every couple of weeks or so. I just want to be aware of how the project is going."

"No problem."

Rory needn't grovel. It's not only his right to demand regular meetings and reports, it's his responsibility.

Several months later, with considerable hoopla, balloons and banners, Amalgamated kicked off its "Nimble Nineties" program. Up on the stage with Sylvia was Emily. As Sylvia explained the effort, she introduced Emily as the consultant who would be carrying out the program. "Consultant?" whispered a manager into Rory's ear. "I thought she was one of your staffers. I figured you were doing some empire-building over there."

Already she's ingrained in the company, people think she's an employee. Emily may never leave.

Time went by. Rory tried to keep a distracted eye on Emily, who was doing a terrific job, judging by the comments he kept hearing from trainees. That's not to say that Emily delivered all the training; her associates did much of it. Still, Rory understood that she couldn't do it all, and he had no spare time himself.

Some consultants sell their services based on their personal reputations and abilities, then use associates to do much of the actual work. Nothing wrong with that, as long as you know who's doing what, for what fee.

About six months into the "Nimble Nineties" project, Sylvia called Rory into her office. "I'd like to know what the results have been on our Nimble Nineties program," she said.

"Results?"

"Results. It's been up and running for six months, and when I look at the operating figures, I don't see any evidence that we're doing any better than we did before. If our people are nimble, I'd like you to prove it to me," Sylvia said.

"Well, the last time I talked with Emily, she told me she's finding it necessary to do much less coaching than she thought she might have to do. People seem to have caught onto these new ways of doing things."

"I have no quarrel with Emily. But, frankly, I don't think you've managed her very well. We've spent a massive amount of money on her fees, but it doesn't seem to me that she's been allowed to achieve the goals you and I set in this office a year ago when we had our initial discussion.

"I'm afraid, Rory, you're going to have to fall on your sword."

A year later, Rory was still looking for a job. This time, Harvey had been no help. Through the grapevine, Rory heard that Amalgamated had launched a new organizational change campaign. It was called "The New Us." It was directed by the company's new vice president of organizational quality and change, Emily Cortez.

The Who, When & Why of Hiring Consultants

Recommendations about how to work effectively when seeking help outside your company.

BY BRIAN MCDERMOTT

Consultants can be annoying, cluttering your mailbox with unwanted pamphlets or pumping your hand and weighing your corporate purse looking for business. Quite often, however, there are critically important programs to deliver or training problems to solve and no staff or in-house expertise to do things right. The common solution is to use a reliable outsider to help. The question is, How?

The following suggestions are based on panel discussions by training executives and consultants at three Cost-Effective Training conferences sponsored by Lakewood Conferences, and a review of a variety of published materials.

What's a Consultant?

Clarity is perhaps the most critical element in successfully using consultants; in plain English, in terms that everyone involved is agreed upon: What is the problem and what is the proposed solution?

The first nebulous term requiring clarification, however, is consultant.

Ask each self-proclaimed expert/specialist what it is he or she has to offer; is it contract training by an external trainer who freelances established delivery skills or a specific training program? Is your consultant a vendor who fits every problem to a single solution? Is your consultant a skilled problem-solver who analyzes a situation, recommends solutions, plans the implementation, then oversees, follows up and measures what your staff delivers? Or, is your consultant "an unemployed executive with a briefcase?," which too often is the unfortunate reality, according to *Small Business Report* magazine.

Four Major Steps

In addition to always clearly stating needs and expectations, there are four major steps for efficiently working with consultants: Establish the need; find the consultant; negotiate a plan and a contract; measure the results.

Consider these points when establishing the need for using a consultant to solve a training problem:

• There are two reasons to use consultants, according to Penny Levine, project manager at the Arthur Andersen & Co. Center for Professional Education in St. Charles, IL: Because your company lacks the in-house expertise to develop or deliver the training needed, or because of insufficient staffing.

• Most companies use consultants on nonrecurring problems, according to *Small Business Report*. The magazine recommends that before a consultant is called in, a detailed and unbiased study is conducted to determine if a need really exists. Too often, the magazine advises, managers simply have consultants make routine visits. Carefully consider your situation and whether a consultant can save you time, get you closer to reaching your goals or improve the effectiveness of the people you train, and can that consultant do it cost-effectively.

• If you bring in a consultant to perform a needs analysis before implementing a major training effort, know what kind of "expert" you have hired. A vendor has a lot to lose by telling you that someone else's product is the solution to your problem or that his or her product can't help you; an ex-trainer with a limited number of training solutions might misdiagnose your difficulties.

• Before deciding to bring in an outsider, suggests Kenneth Silber, supervisor of course development for AT&T Communications, Chicago, determine if there is time to develop in-house expertise to meet your company's need. In the long run you may be better off.

Finding a Consultant

Consider these points when looking for a consultant to solve a training problem:

• Develop a list of potential consultants. Talk to other trainers. Read trade journals and note the consultants who contribute in areas of interest to you. Attend conferences to see consultants in action.

• It can be beneficial to encourage competitive bidding for specific projects, but the process can't work if there is no clear plan for what is needed. If you don't have a clear plan to present to bidders for a major project — and no time to prepare one — consider using a consultant to prepare the plan, which will be a comparatively minor job, and then open bidding.

• Proposals prepared by consultants are a good way to weed out those who are incompetent, but won't help much to distinguish between those who are competent.

• Check references, preferably with people you know personally who have worked with the consultant. If you must use a consultant's list of references, determine if all his or her clients are included or if it is a hand-picked group.

• Ask the references all the questions you want, including did the consultant have the necessary skills? Did he or she fit the company's environment well? Were time lines met? Were budget estimates accurate? Was the individual flexible and willing to consider alternative plans? How well did the individual interact with managers? Was there trust and confidence? How well did the consultant communicate? Most importantly, would you hire the person again?

• From consultants, find out how long they have been in business, their educational background and reasons for being in consulting.

• Some training directors say they choose consultants based upon what consultants ask about their companies, not upon the consultant's sales pitch. Make sure your consultant is listening to what you say, Silber suggests. Be certain any outsider you hire will understand, not ignore, your company's quirks.

• Determine if your consultant is willing to teach you something so that the solution offered is ongoing, not a one-shot deal.

• A consultant's ability to appraise the facts and opinions of your company's managers and then suggest creative solutions may be more important than actual experience in your company's industry.

• Most vendors are willing to customize training packages; for some, however, that means merely filling in the blanks.

• *Don't* use a consultant to reinforce an idea that is already established in your company.

• *Don't* use a consultant to hatchet someone else's idea.

• *Don't* use a consultant just because some top executive in your company is fascinated with using consultants.

Negotiating

Consider these points when negotiating plans and contracts with consultants:

• A consultant should be willing to give you a few hours or even a full day — at no charge — to talk about your problem.

• If a consultant is not willing to spend a day with you for free, don't use that person; he or she is probably more concerned with your money than your problems.

• Ask your top three or four candidates to perform for a small group of your managers. Don't hire someone unless you can see the individual in action first.

• Include in your written agreements minimum and maximum cost limits. Administrative expenses often amount to about 15 percent of a total estimate.

• A job proposal should include an estimate for the cost of completing a project.

• A job contract should include detailed steps for the project, time estimates, milestones and roles of all those involved.

• Don't measure what you pay in consultant fees only against your staff salaries. Many consultants measure a client's fees as one-third of their expenses and rates.

Measurement

• Ask for 100 percent guarantees. If a consultant defers responsibility to your company for the final outcome, rewrite your agreement because the consultant has agreed to something he or she can not accomplish.

• Oral reports by a consultant on the progress or final results of a project may be sufficient for your needs, and certainly should be cheaper. Specify in your contract how the results should be reported.

• Be certain that your project objectives are written in terms of the desired final outcome.

Notes:

Use of Contract Trainers, Designers Now Strategic Tool for Training Leaders

Wise use of contractors helps control labor, and frees up your staff for more strategic activities.

BY DAVE ZIELINSKI

Once, using freelance or "contract" trainers to design or deliver portions of training was something of a stop-gap move for training managers, done to plug temporary staff shortages or to match periods of surging training demand. Now, however, more of you use contractors as a centerpiece of your training strategies. It's a way to better control labor costs — you pay only for services you use — and to free up your staff members for more-strategic performance-consulting work.

Given the improving quality of this freelance pool — compliments of downsizing and more entrepreneurial trainers hanging out their own shingles — you're also finding contract trainers deliver quality at, or even above, levels formerly delivered only by staff instructors.

Using 'Brokers'

Patricia Romines, manager of organization development for Phillips Petroleum Co. in Bartlesville, OK, regularly uses a pool of 11 contract trainers to deliver behavioral-skills training and computer training.

The impetus for using contractors came when the performance consulting unit Romines headed up was merged with a traditional training function. Some trainers were converted to consultants, which created a need for additional delivery help, she says.

Not wanting to hire additional full-time staff — whose delivery services would be needed only sporadically — Romines turned to a nearby vocational school for help. She had already hired trainers from the school to do some PC-skills training, which proved the school could probably do more, "although there was concern — unfounded in the end — that employees would look down their noses at getting training tied into a vo-tech," she says.

She hires the contract trainers using the vo-tech as a broker. Romines pays a small amount of overhead to the school for that service, but the school pays benefits to trainers, and handles much of the training record-keeping. (She does use commercial vendor reps to deliver other training, but says their labor costs are often double what she pays for her vo-tech trainers, whom she pays by the class.)

Most of the contract instructors have corporate training backgrounds, but Romines makes exceptions for the right candidates. A former music teacher, for instance, had such exemplary stand-up and facilitation skills that she overcame initial reservations about lacking corporate experience.

The vo-tech reviews résumés and checks credentials of candidates, using Romines' criteria. Then, after this first cut, she requires mock presentations or videos so she can see trainers in action.

> **The quality of the freelance pool has improved steadily in the aftermath of downsizing, and with more trainers striking out on their own.**

These contractors even travel for the company; they go to remote sites where it is often difficult to find quality instructors locally.

Use of contractors at Phillips makes sense for another reason, Romines says: The company no longer relies as much on subject-matter experts (SMEs) to deliver training and buys more training content from the outside. Phillips recently bought rights to 60 modules from Zenger Miller, for instance, as part of a move to a more competency-based curriculum.

"With the quality of these materials, all you need is a good, credible facilitator," she says. "We knew we needed materials that were superior in terms of instructional design if they were going to be delivered by contractors."

Contractors deliver the training in Phillips' new facility, which makes their freelance status even more difficult to discern. "When we use the same trainers often enough, they start to feel like part of the Phillips' staff."

Romines makes a conscientious effort to educate contractors on Phillips' unique culture and idiosyncrasies. She has offered several full- and partial-day workshops for contractors about Phillips and about the people attending classes.

An additional challenge for contractors: Many Phillips employees arrived in classrooms skeptical as a result of a corporate downsizing. Employees initially didn't feel "outsiders" could identify with their unique challenges and travails. That seems to have abated some with time, and through adjustments made by the trainers, Romines says.

The biggest drawback with using contractors, she says, is their tendency to get hired away to full-time jobs.

Increase Focus on Consulting

At Phoenix-based Circle K Corp., the largest operator of convenience stores in the U.S., director of training and development Tom Roney has also outsourced most of his delivery work to contract trainers. Roney got his own start at Circle K as a contractor, doing freelance development and delivery, and he wanted to perpetuate that structure.

By using contract instructors only on an as-needed basis, he says, "You don't have the downtime; you only pay for what you use. I ran internal training centers for many years, and I could never, in spite of my best efforts, get more than 123 delivery days out of one trainer in a given year — that was my high. The consistent demand for training wasn't there. That's a lot of delivery downtime."

Roney uses six regular contract trainers to train employees in 2,500 Circle K stores. They deliver two classroom-based programs for Circle K, one for store managers and one for first-level supervisors. They deliver the standard courseware and materials created by Roney's training staff.

He also uses program designers on contract to collaborate on technology-delivered instruction. Circle K now uses CD-ROM to train 34,000 new-hires a year, which pushed Roney to find new sources for instructional development. His team chose an authoring package — IconAuthor and CBT Express from AimTech — then hired ex-AimTech employees who had formed their own company to assist with design.

Roney has also outsourced delivery to vendor Executrain for three large technical-training projects. Executrain delivered computer-systems training to Circle K store managers and first-level supervisors in 26 states. When Circle K first automated some stores, Executrain taught 5,000 people in some 60 days, Roney says.

"Executrain's trainers fly into Phoenix, we do some train-the-trainer to teach them what they need to teach, and off they go, using classrooms and computers near our locations that they set up."

Indeed, Roney says his bigger challenge now is how to get employees to training — the logistics of coordinating training for a widely distributed work force — rather than how to deliver training to them once they're in a classroom.

New Titles and Roles

Last year Roney reorganized his six-person training staff to reflect its changed roles and increased use of teamwork and project management.

One staffer carried the title of "manager of instructional delivery," for instance, and since the staff no longer does delivery, the title no longer made sense. Ditto for the "manager of instructional design."

So Roney's five direct reports now all share the same title — "performance consultant" — and have similar job duties.

Ensuring quality from contract workers: On the delivery side, Roney's quality control of contractors consists of "sitting in on them from time to time, giving the normal feedback you would give a staff instructor," he says. "Their delivery styles might vary a bit more widely, but our chief concern is to make sure they meet our program objectives."

On the development side — with CBT design, for instance — Roney's payment structure helps create incentive for producing quality work.

"We typically pay contractors one-third up front, another third when they give us a beta version we can experiment with, and pay the final third when we get a final working product. That's our quality control."

Notes:

Inventive Outsourcing Helps Some Trainers Thrive Even as Staff Sizes Dwindle

But be sure you choose your outside partners wisely.

BY DAVE ZIELINSKI

Outsourcing continues to be the training watchword for the '90s. As more training functions seek to save time, dollars, or boost quality, they're increasingly looking outside the organization to make it happen. In many cases, the growing use of contractors is a direct result of mandates from top management to freeze hiring or limit new investments in equipment for technology-based learning.

Training managers, however, continue to show their resourcefulness in the face of this challenging environment. They're tapping expertise from nearby community colleges and state universities — in the case of one company, loaning pieces of machinery to a college in exchange for the free services of an instructor — striking unique arrangements with vendors, using contract trainers like recently laid-off public school teachers, and jobbing out time-eating but less strategic duties such as registration.

Most say the key to making such relationships work is the front-end work put into developing clear expectations and contracts that leave little room for interpretation by either side. Without those detail-laden agreements, they say, outsourcing can end up adding more work for the training staff rather than subtracting it.

Technical training in particular continues to be outsourced at a fast pace. To wit: A recent study by the American Society of Training and Development of more than 100 *Fortune* 500 HRD executives found that 97% outsource or contract out some portion of their technical training. About 44% contract out "some-times," 32% "seldom," 18% "often," and only 3% of the organizations surveyed "never" contract out technical or skills training.

Of those organizations in the study that do contract out for training, 43% contract for training delivery, 35% for design, 11% for needs assessment, and only 4% for evaluation.

Staying Viable Amidst a Hiring Freeze

At USF&G Insurance in Baltimore, training manager Carolyn Williams says a trend toward outsourcing training is driven largely by a hiring freeze. "It wasn't a downsize, but a requirement that there be no increase in existing staff," she says. "We were told we could have more funds to train, but not more people on staff."

Williams oversees all corporate technology training at the insurance company, including mainframe and PC systems training for both home office and field staff. She also is responsible for technical training for the information services department.

One way she deals with restrictions on adding staff as training needs continue apace is to outsource PC training for all employees in the headquarters office. She contracted with vendor Comskill, which specializes in interactive video training, to create and manage a "learning center" within USF&G's home office. Within that captive center is also a self-study computer lab run by another outside vendor based on the East Coast, Hammond & Associates. The arrangement has a couple of big advantages for USF&G, Williams believes. "Because of the vendors' arrangement with equipment distributors, they brought to us the equipment and courses that enabled us to leap quickly into interactive multimedia training without making any big commitments to capital equipment — equipment that might change again in a few years."

The vendor conducts needs assessments, designs and delivers training, handles course registration, payment, and other administrative duties that can be time-eaters for the training staff. In turn, USF&G pays a contracted fee that covers, in the case of Comskill, the services of two employees, one executive who manages the center and another instructional designer/trainer. "The alternative would've been for a training staffer to fill both of those roles, and we would have lost a lot in expertise because the vendor employees are specialists." Staff trainers do periodically teach in the learning center, she says.

Williams is delivering most of the company's basic computer skills training — such as use of Microsoft's Office Suite, Lotus 1-2-3, and Lotus Notes — through the learning center. Trainees have the option of following up the interactive video training with workshops featuring facilitators who review procedures and specific work samples. "It's a safety net that provides a comfort level trainees may not have gotten through multimedia," she says. "We had to make a big cultural shift to get people to accept training that is not led by instructors. But now it is a big hit."

Training in the learning center has another advantage of being "near just-in-time," says Williams. "When an employee identifies she has a training need, particularly if it's a basic-level need, she can call the center, walk down, have her needs assessed, have a training plan put together and start training that afternoon or the next day," she says. "The center is not schedule-driven — we don't even publish a schedule of courses. People call the center when they think they have a need, so they don't have to wait two weeks for a course to start."

The biggest stumbling block in the partnership with vendors, she says, was not having clearly defined expectations from the start. "Roles and responsibilities weren't as clearly defined as we would have liked, and since we had two different vendors operating out of the same site, they saw themselves as competing, and we had to end that."

Williams wanted the vendors' employees to look and act as much like USF&G employees as possible. "We had to indoctrinate them into our culture, the unwritten rules and management styles, while at the same time they had to hit the ground running at the center, because they didn't have much time," she says. "But now unless I tell them, most trainees in the company don't realize it's an outsourced function."

Training content that requires a big dose of customization and is more strategic in nature is still handled internally, but Williams says the learning centers have become so integrated into the company that "they are every bit as effective now as our internal staff at customizing computer and software training."

At Van Dorn Demag Corp., the criteria for outsourcing boils down to something like this, says HRD manager Janet Jankura. "If we look at our training needs and determine that they are fairly complex and very much related to our company's culture — and if we think it would take an external supplier a long time to get up to speed in delivery — then we will develop or deliver internally."

Lack of time to take on new training initiatives also plays a big role in the decision — often more so than a desire to cut costs or boost training quality.

Jankura regularly taps area community colleges, vocational institutions, and state universities for a variety of what she calls "inexpensive, effective" training which often includes basic skills and theory. For one course on basic electrical practice, for instance, she pays $3,000 for delivery on-site and another $1,000 for materials. Employees go through the course in groups of 30.

In another example, a community college instructor comes to Van Dorn to teach a module from Development Dimensions International on coaching skills for $100 per hour, which Jankura considers "a steal."

Jankura and her staff have created some unique arrangements within these partnerships. In one case, Van Dorn donated a couple of its plastic injection-molding machines to a community college for use in classes in exchange for an instructor teaching some classes free at Van Dorn.

Jobbing Out Administrative Duties

In keeping with the trend toward outsourcing "low-impact" skills training or routine tasks and keeping the

strategic training in-house, more training functions are outsourcing administrative duties. At Pittsburgh-based Bayer Corp., training supervisor Diana Kamyk says the department has launched a pilot to experiment with outsourcing some of its administrative functions. "The idea is to free up our training department to not only work on what we consider higher-value customer projects, but to improve the quality of the administration process."

For the past five years the department has outsourced the bulk of its PC and Macintosh-related training to vendor Executrain and to the University of Pittsburgh Computer Learning Center, setting a successful precedent for using training contractors.

The idea to outsource registration was hatched when the department began thinking of outsourcing some of the prework for its courses. They took it a step further by creating a pilot test to outsource course schedules, materials distribution, class rosters, and correspondence from trainees confirming registration, including e-mail, phone, and fax. The test is being done in conjunction with Bayer's Akron site. "We wanted rapid turnaround from whatever vendor we selected, and we wanted to maintain a certain control and some of the registration duties," she says. "We wanted all evaluations to continue to come to us for summary and analysis. We wanted to maintain control of the marketing of courses, creating training reports for divisions, and processing invoices.

"We also needed it to be seamless for trainees. There is a four-digit number they can call at the outsourcing company staffed by a live voice, not voice mail, just as if they're calling our training department." The vendor is now busy tying its computer systems into Bayer's registration system, so they'll be able to do things like dial into Bayer's system via modem and update class rosters, allowing the training staff to continue to chart progress. "There was a lot of upfront work with the vendor, and you need to be very, very clear in situations like this about who is responsible for what, deadlines, and how things will work," Kamyk says.

Outsourcing Run Amok?

Wendie Morris, director of network and information systems training at Pacific Bell, counts herself among those concerned that the outsourcing trend may be getting out of hand.

Specifically, she believes there's not always thoughtful analysis and concern for maintaining training quality contained in recommendations from consultants that significant portions of training be outsourced.

At some of her fellow "Baby Bell" companies like Bell South and Bell Atlantic, for example, she has heard reports of consultants recommending that all training services be outsourced, bar none. "I get concerned when I see no data to substantiate those recommendations that all training can be done more efficiently when outsourced," Morris says. "In telecommunications there are many pieces of knowledge and skill that can be considered strategic, competitive advantages. And in my mind, training for them should only be developed and delivered internally, by people with an intimate knowledge of the business. But these consultants are recommending that training be looked at as only a production shop. I don't think they feel these vendors really need an integral knowledge of the business.

"I believe those things that differentiate the quality of service we give our external customers are things we should continue to nurture internally."

Morris says Pacific Bell does outsource a significant chunk of its management development training, which she largely endorses because it exposes leaders to fresh, outside thinking and resources. She estimates that about 20% of her training "work force" consists of full-time contractors. "I tend to use vendors in the areas of computer hardware or software training, or high-end skills that can change very rapidly, like programming."

It's now common for vendors to build training services into contracts Pac Bell signs for new computer systems and other hardware. Says Morris: "Our procurement and engineering departments have discovered that training is a very viable partner in that negotiating process. We've helped construct the wording that is part of those contracts and how we intend to measure training quality. I am the policeman of that; I review the quality of materials, and how well the vendors' instructors perform in the classroom. If they don't cut it, we ask that they be replaced."

These vendors get a quarterly report card from Pac Bell based on their performance, and Morris says training quality is a big part of that grade.

Community Colleges
Go Corporate

Lean and hungry and long overlooked, community colleges claim to be the hottest new player in the workforce-development game.

BY DAVID STAMPS

Herb East's dilemma was not so different from that facing a lot of managers at small manufacturing firms these days. His people needed to upgrade their math, chemistry and computer skills, but he had neither the budget to hire an outside training consultant nor the resources to do the training in-house.

On a chance, the operations manager at Cytec Engineered Materials Inc. in Havre de Grace, MD, decided to give the folks at the local community college a try. While turning to community colleges as a last-resort training source is not unheard of, the happy results of East's experience may come as a startling surprise to those who haven't ventured down that road lately.

Harford Community College in nearby Bell Air, MD, had been beseeching local firms with marketing brochures that seemed to address both of Cytec's most pressing needs. At $100 per class hour, they were cheap. East was able to purchase 15 hours of instruction for an entire roomful of employees for $1,500. "I couldn't touch an outside consultant for what they charge," he says. The college also touted itself as having a staff familiar with teaching adults. "That's something we don't have," says East. "We have good technical people, but they aren't teachers."

But what ultimately impressed East was Harford's flexibility. After the basic classes proved popular, East began looking for ways to tailor the instruction to Cytec's business as a manufacturer of specialty chemicals. Could the instructors incorporate proprietary mixes and formulas into the math and chemistry classes? No prob-

lem. The instructors visited the plant and spent several hours familiarizing themselves with Cytec's formulas. "They put in as much time learning our processes as they spent teaching," says East.

Chalk up another happy supporter of a newly aggressive player in the work force-development game — community colleges.

Giants and Dwarfs

Community colleges aren't exactly newcomers to the corporate-training

---

While money is the main draw, it's not the only reason community colleges are piling onto the corporate training scene.

---

marketplace. A handful of schools have provided contract training to local businesses for over a dozen years. A few college programs have become renowned for ambitious training partnerships with large companies. In 1989, when Motorola launched its famed Training and Education Center (now called Motorola University), it tapped Maricopa Community College in Phoenix to help. The college pulled together a team of 75 instructors — including part-time college instructors, private contractors and retired Motorola employees — to teach subjects ranging from accounting to statistical process control. Today the college continues to provide an array of training offerings, includ-

ing a special curriculum that supports Motorola's semiconductor-manufacturing processes.

Delta Community College in Saginaw, MI, became one of the early pioneers in this arena in 1983 when it had the temerity to suggest to General Motors Corp. that it could provide technical auto-maintenance training. Today Delta's College of Corporate Services manages technical-training centers for Saturn Corp. in Spring Hill, TN, and at GM's proving ground in Milford, MI, and trains most of GM's "Mr. Goodwrenches" across the country. It also operates Dow Chemical Co.'s corporate-learning center in Midland, MI. Last year Delta's contract-training arm enrolled 25,000 workers in 23 states and 19 foreign countries, and raked in $6.7 million in fees.

But programs at Delta, Maricopa and a dozen other community colleges stand out as giants among dwarfs. And until recently, there weren't all that many dwarfs. Five years ago, perhaps half the nation's 1,200 community colleges offered some sort of contract training to local businesses. Today, the American Association of Community Colleges in Washington, DC, estimates that 90 percent of its member colleges are, to a greater or lesser extent, in the business of training workers for specific companies, rather than just teaching generic subjects or trades.

And make no mistake about it, contract training is a business. Money is the prime reason community colleges are scrambling to form partnerships with local companies and touting themselves as experts in everything from English as a second language to ISO 9000. "It's less speculative than the sort of continuing education we used to do," says Scott Epstein, director of the corporate-training department at Harford Community College. In the old days, says Epstein, colleges would dream up a class they thought people in the community might be interested in, print a brochure, and wait to see who showed up. "Today, when I negotiate a fee for a training course, I can be sure we'll break even," he says.

While money is the main draw, it's not the only reason community colleges are piling onto the corporate-training scene. Many see it as a natural extension of their mission to serve the local community. And community colleges insist they are ideally

SOLUTIONS 101

College has changed. It's no longer a simple matter of picking a class from a catalog and putting butts on chairs in a classroom. When a company calls a community college these days, it's likely to be seeking a new training solution where traditional approaches haven't worked.

To Marsha Swanson, production training supervisor for Oregon Freeze-Dry Foods in Albany, OR, it was painfully apparent that many workers lacked basic reading and math skills. But when Swanson offered to pay book and tuition costs to send workers to school, fewer than 5 percent accepted the offer. "It was a sensitive subject," says Swanson. "No one wanted to admit they couldn't read."

Training sessions held at the plant carried less of a stigma than being sent back to school, but that alternative posed problems of its own. With three around-the-clock shifts, scheduling classes that worked for everybody was next to impossible. "Where are you going to find an instructor who's willing to teach a midnight class on fractions?" asks Swanson.

The ideal solution appeared to be a computer-based training program that workers could use on their own. But that was beyond budget. Swanson turned to Linn-Benton Community College, a local institution that had conducted some train-the-trainer and project management classes for Oregon Freeze-Dry's supervisory staff. "This was a different challenge," she says, "but I thought they might have some resources we didn't."

Community colleges are hardly known for their boundless resources, but they are resourceful. Carol Schaarfsma, a project coordinator in Linn-Benton's contract-training department, wrote a grant application and obtained funds to purchase the needed training software. She then worked with Swanson to develop a program in which all production staff at the plant, including managers, were required to take a computerized math- and reading-skills assessment. Following the assessment, it was left to each worker to decide if he needed help. Of

140 production workers, 125 took the training. The college even helped find instructors willing to tutor workers at scheduled times each week, including one who took the dreaded 10 p.m.-to-midnight shift.

At St. Louis Community College in Missouri, the specialty is instructional design. "We approach every contract from a performance-improvement perspective," says Rebecca Admire, director of the college's Center for Business, Industry and Labor. "We ask, 'What can workers not do now that they need to be able to do? What's needed to get them performing?' Our clients often have technical knowledge, but don't know how to do up-front analysis or how to design instruction in a way that will deliver needed skills."

St. Louis Community College is not alone in taking this approach. A survey of community college contract-training programs in Minnesota found that two-thirds of the schools routinely do needs assessments when working with clients. "I'd be surprised if that many private training consultants do needs assessments up-front," says Doug Parr, a consultant in Minneapolis who helped conduct the survey.

Of course, doing needs assessments sometimes means having to tell the client that the training he thinks he needs isn't what he needs at all. One company came to St. Louis College asking it to train forklift drivers not to crash their upraised lifts into an overhead door frame. The college persuaded the company to install job-aid reminders on the forklifts instead.

In another case, a telemarketing firm requested operator training to correct a sudden, mysterious drop-off in call-handling efficiency. The college agreed to do the training, but only after warning the client that it might not address the "attitude problem" among workers. "The real problem," says Admire, "was that they had increased everybody's workload three hours a week with no increase in pay."

—D.S.

---

suited to serve local business interests in ways their stodgy brethren, four-year colleges and universities, are not.

Universities are big, bureaucratic, and more interested in doing research than in solving the training needs of local employers — or so claim small-college marketing spiels. Moreover, four-year schools, with their fat endowments and ties to state legislatures, have never had to scramble for funds the way two-year colleges have. Accustomed to running lean operations, the small guys know how to do things on the cheap. And they are hungry. Call a community college near you for training when you want it, where you want it, how you want it, and at a price you can afford.

That's the pitch at a whole slew

of two-year schools these days. And while not all the players measure up to the hype, a fair number of them appear to be delivering on their promises. Some even back their claims with a guarantee: They'll repeat the training free for any worker who fails to perform to an employer's expectations.

Harford College's corporate-training operation is a good example of the new style of small but nimble college team that is prowling the corporate-training field. It relies on a core of just 24 instructors, many of them outside consultants, to teach everything from computer design to Spanish-language safety classes to chemistry to total quality management. And though it took in just $400,000 last year from 60

local employers, it hustled no fewer than 420 contracts through its offices to bring in that modest sum, earning a profit of about $15,000. "We do a lot of short programs and half-day workshops because that's what industry wants," says Epstein.

Not exactly big business. And yet contract training has blossomed on two-year campuses to the point that it's now a recognized specialty. It even has its own trade show. Next month corporate-training practitioners from community colleges across the nation will gather in Orlando, FL, at an annual get-together called Workforce 2000. The meeting, sponsored by the League for Innovation in the Community College, based in Mission Viejo, CA, provides an opportunity to share success stories and to swap tips on how to win the confidence — and training contracts — of American business. For despite their successes to date, establishing credibility with business remains an urgent discussion topic among college trainers.

Bold Talk

The Workforce 2000 confab will likely be the venue for some lofty rhetoric, too, about how community colleges are positioned to become a major provider of work force training. "Contract training will become the biggest piece of the community college system," predicts Larry Warford, vice president of instructional services at Lane Community College in Eugene, OR. There are more incumbent workers than emerging workers, notes Warford. If changes in technology continue to escalate, so will the need for training. "Someone has to provide that continuous education," Warford says. "Why not community colleges?"

In Warford's case, the bold talk may be justified. His contract-training department recently signed a $250,000 agreement with Sony Corp. and Symantec Corp. to provide pre-employment training for 200 prospective workers at the two companies this year. The instructional services group, which has grossed over $1 million in fees the past two years, is aggressively pursuing deals with several other firms moving into the expanding high-tech corridor between Eugene and Portland.

But community colleges overall have yet to emerge as a major force in the corporate-training arena, and a glance at the numbers suggests just how far they have to go. *TRAINING Magazine's Industry Report* estimates that U.S. businesses with 100 or more employees spent $10.3 billion on products and external service providers to train workers in 1995. No one knows exactly how much of that goes to community colleges, but the best estimates suggest their share is minuscule.

In California, one of the few states that tracks contract-training fees paid to community colleges, the state's 107 schools last year collected $51 million in training fees (including one $21 million contract with the U.S. Navy). "In the overall scheme of things, we have no market share to speak of," says Catherine Ayers, director of economic development for the California Community College Educational Development Network (EdNet). That is not to say community colleges haven't made a significant impact in a few areas, Ayers points out, notably in Silicon Valley, where a handful of schools run aggressively entrepreneurial training programs.

Terry O'Banion, executive director at the League for Innovation, estimates the top 50 contract-training programs in the country average about $1 million a year in fees — the break point, he says, that differentiates start-ups from established programs. But O'Banion optimistically predicts that

---

> ## "This is the new model for contract training. If we aren't working in concert with business and industry, we might miss the target."

---

half of the country's 1,200 community colleges will have grown their programs to that $1 million threshold within the next couple of years.

One person who dearly hopes that prediction proves true is Phyllis Eisen, senior policy director for the National Manufacturers' Association in Washington, DC. "The cost of training workers has gotten so high, few small manufacturers can afford it anymore," says Eisen. "Community colleges hold the best hope for low-cost training to smaller companies." But Eisen, who talks to a lot of community colleges and companies that use them, believes that most colleges still have some catching up to do. "We consider maybe 300 as really viable, as really doing something in the work force-development game," she says.

And the gap between the viable programs and the wannabes is not just one of money or critical mass. In many cases, it's a performance gap. While community colleges portray themselves as lean and entrepreneurial and service-oriented, the experiences of companies that have done business with them — or tried to — suggests that some schools don't entirely measure up.

Business Unusual

Consider the experience of Collagen Corp. in Palo Alto, at the heart of California's alleged pocket of entrepreneurial community college programs. Two years ago training director Carolyn Balling contacted a local community college to ask if it could provide technical training to some of Collagen's workers. "A woman in the contract-training office seemed incredibly eager to work with us," recalls Balling. "Then she asked when could I come for a visit. I thought that was a little odd, that I was the one to visit them. That's not the way things normally work when you deal with a contract trainer." The woman at the college promised to mail Balling a parking voucher allowing her to park on campus, but the voucher arrived late. "There were just a lot of little things like that which made it seem like it really wasn't business as usual," says Balling.

Balling did eventually meet with people at the college. The woman in the contract-training office was still thrilled at the idea of collaborating. "She asked me to sit on an advisory board," recalls Balling. But when the faculty members who were to do the actual instruction got involved, discussion ground to a halt. "We talked, but we spoke different languages," says Balling. "They said they had to stick to their academic schedule and that just didn't fit our timing." Collagen eventually hired a private contractor to provide the training.

Collagen's experience serves as a warning to any company looking to outsource training to a community college: Be aware that not all schools have made the transition to a customer service frame of mind.

Harford College and the institution that Collagen attempted to work with represent opposite ends of the spectrum. One has established a separate, independent organization that runs contract training like a small business. The other tries, less successfully, to operate a contract-training department within the confines of a traditional community college structure. "To turn from a campus orientation is a huge leap for most schools," says Jack Jonker, executive director of Delta College's corporate-services operation.

The good news is that much talk and energy these days is focused on making college-training programs more responsive to business needs. The not-so-good news is that progress toward that goal is sporadic. "There is no one model that is followed from state to state or even college to college," says Jonker. Or, as a former director of California's EdNet put it: "We have 107 community colleges in California, which translates into 107 different ways of running a contract-training business."

Your Place or Mine?

While no single model for these programs exists, successful programs have some traits in common. One key indicator is whether a community college will bring its instruction to the client, or whether it insists that workers come to its campus. Where training takes place matters for a couple of reasons. For starters, it can make the difference between training that's cost-effective and training that's not.

Vince Liotta, a training supervisor for Chevron Information Technology Co. in San Ramon, CA, looked into using a local community college to teach PC software classes two years ago when he learned the college charged just $6 per person for a class. Chevron's training department charges $200 a day for six hours of classroom instruction for up to 12 Chevron employees. But the college only offered the class at its campus and required students to attend two separate sessions. "When we figured in time away from the job, it was cheaper to do the training in-house," says Liotta.

The question of who comes to whom carries broader implications, as well. A willingness to take its instruction to the client indicates a philosophical shift away from an academic mentality to a customer service mentality. "If you have the mind-set that I'm a college professor, that you have to come to me and let me teach you, the opportunities will pass you by and you won't even know you missed them," says Kenneth Allen, president of North Metro Technical Institute in Acworth, GA. "[Most community colleges] don't spend nearly enough time in business's environment," says Allen. "We have to get onto their turf."

Goodbye Mr. Chips

Another indicator of a college's customer service quotient is whether it contracts with outside consultants or part-time instructors to provide training, or whether it insists on using its own faculty. The more innovative programs rely largely on private trainers. Harford College, for instance, prefers to make deals with local training con-sultants in which it uses a handful of consultants for all its training; in return, the consultants are asked to urge their local clients to use the college. "We have some very good faculty instructors, but we like the practitioner slant for our contract training," says Epstein.

Union contracts at some schools, however, require that faculty handle all instruction. In other cases, it may simply be the policy of the college. Whatever the reason behind them, such policies can lead to the sort of scheduling conflicts that scuttled talks between Collagen Corp. and its local community college. "Once a business gets around to deciding that its workers need training, it wants that training right now," says Allen. "If you can't provide it when they want it, they'll go somewhere else."

Scheduling conflicts aren't the only problem that can arise when a college insists on using its own faculty. The fact is, some college professors aren't as current in their discipline as they might be. Others simply don't think about training the same way businesses do. "A college professor walks into a classroom with the idea that he is going to lose a certain percentage of students," says EdNet's Ayers. "You can't have that mind-set in the business world. You have to go into a session thinking, 'How can I get all these people up to the performance level their employer expects?' "

Shadow Colleges

Another trait of successful contract-training programs, say observers, is that they are separate from the rest of the college. "You need leadership that lays down a sharp line of division between the traditional kind of education and corporate-contract training," says Delta's Jonker.

Programs that operate, say, out of a "continuing education" office are less successful. "For some reason it seems to work best when these programs are actually physically separated from the rest of the campus," notes O'Banion. "We call them 'shadow colleges.' "

Operating apart from the rest of the college can help sidestep the troublesome questions that arise, for instance, when a company asks a local college to provide training to employees in another state. It's a situation that comes up more frequently as larger firms turn to community colleges for worker training. Hewlett-Packard Co., for example, has contracted with San Mateo Community College to train workers in both its Palo Alto, CA, facility and at its plant in Idaho.

Contract-training departments are generally eager to lunge at such opportunities, but to some these arrangements violate the community college's mission of serving the local community. And the issue grows thornier if a college's contract-training activity is subsidized by state funds. Programs that wish to be able to operate outside the local community typically set up a self-supporting program that uses no state or general college funds (though state economic-development funds may be available directly to companies for worker training).

While "shadow colleges" must be free to do their own thing, they can't be seen as a maverick operation; they need the backing and support of the college, the president and board. Otherwise, trouble will erupt every time a contract-training program strikes a deal that bends or breaks the normal academic rules.

And innovative programs will bend the normal rules. Take, for example, Lane Community College's recent agreement to provide pre-employment training to prospective workers for Sony and Symantec in Oregon. For years a sacred tenet of community colleges has been that they were open to anyone. But for this partnership, Lane College and the participating companies will screen applicants to the program. And it will be the companies' hiring standards that determine who is admitted.

Lane's Warford admits that his approach may raise the hackles of some traditionalists, but he defends the arrangement. "Our college still has an open-door policy, but that no longer means you automatically have access to everything within the college. This is the new model for contract training," says Warford. "If we aren't working in concert with business and industry, we might miss the target."

You Don't Know Me

Some community colleges run first-rate contract-training programs but remain largely unknown to their potential customers. Illinois, for example, is a hotbed of contract-training activity. Last year 46 different community colleges in the state provided customized training to nearly 2,000 companies. And yet, random calls to half a dozen Illinois companies found training directors who were unaware that community colleges provide this sort of service. Kenneth Lund, director of corporate training at Sandoz Agro Inc. in Des Plaines, IL, says he can't recall seeing a marketing brochure from a community college, though he receives dozens from four-year schools all across the Midwest.

"Marketing is truly one of the missing pieces," says O'Banion. "I'd guess about half the companies in the United States don't know what community colleges are doing these days."

Business's Role

There is, of course, another piece in the community college-business partnership and that's the role business plays. By way of illustration, Joan Leonard, a former executive at California's EdNet tells this story:

For years Caterpillar Inc. dealerships in California had drawn their technical work force of diesel mechanics from community colleges and vocational schools. But in the early '90s they began to notice a drop-off in graduates' skills. Caterpillar asked EdNet to conduct a survey of diesel programs at community colleges to find out what had changed. "What we found," says Leonard, "was that the newest equipment at any school was at least 20 years old." At the same time, Nissan and Toyota were having no problem finding qualified automotive mechanics. But the carmakers had been donating the latest equipment to schools and had established programs to allow instructors and students to visit plants and regularly sponsored job fairs. "The lesson," says Leonard: "Business has to be in the equation."

One company that's taken note of that is Whirlpool Corp. in Benton Harbor, MI. The company last year organized a network of eight community colleges across the country and has been holding roundtable meetings with representatives of the schools. Next year it plans to familiarize the schools with its proprietary training and performance-measurement methodology.

According to Craig Hendricks, director of training and education at Whirlpool's North American Appliance Group, Whirlpool plants across the United States have used local community colleges for contract training in the past. While they've been generally pleased with the low cost of the training, the quality has varied dramatically. "We need consistent quality, whether it's in Marion, OH, or Oxford, MS," says Hendricks. It's to ensure that quality that Whirlpool has elected to establish a formal relationship with the schools.

Hendricks says the company could probably work with a network of private-training vendors and get volume-pricing discounts that would bring their fees within range of what community colleges charge. But cost isn't the only reason for the arrangement. "We like to work with institutions that are part of the community," he says. "They are in a position to understand our long-term needs and strategies as a major employer in the area. They also provide a fresh pool of new employees, which is something private contractors don't do."

From such beginnings, long-term training partnerships have been known to develop, though sometimes the first steps have been shaky. "When we approached GM in the early '80s, they looked at us and said 'By what stretch of whose imagination do you think you can help us?'" recalls Delta College's Jonker. "But we delivered, one step at a time — first with a good college-credit program, then by putting qualified people in their learning centers, later by providing ongoing training to Mr. Goodwrenches. Every time we did a good job," says Jonker, "we got another opportunity. It took a lot of small successes, a lot of networking with GM dealers, and an attitude of customer service."

Notes:

More See Community Colleges as an Attractive Outsourcing Option

BY CHRIS BUSSE

Outsourcing select types of training — especially basic skills or technical training — to local community colleges is certainly not a new idea in training circles. But with continued pressure to deliver more training with smaller staffs, partnering with community colleges has become an even more valued way to stretch a training budget without sacrificing program quality.

Several indicators point toward an increased use of community colleges as outsourcing tools and explain why more businesses are taking advantage of the partnerships.

• A 1992 poll of 608 community colleges by the Washington, DC-based Southport Institute for Policy Analysis found that 69 percent of those surveyed offer retraining for corporate workforces. More than half of those schools started programs in the five years from 1987 to 1991.

• According to *TRAINING Magazine's* 1993 Industry Report, 6 million more people were slated to receive some kind of training last year — an increase of 15 percent over 1992 — the largest ever measured by the study. But overall training budgets went up by an average of only 7 percent. Increased use of commuity colleges may partly explain the disparity, according to the survey analysis, as well as the fact that spending on off-the-shelf programs increased by 15 percent, far outdistancing spending on hardware such as computers, video cameras and slide projectors.

• Estimates vary, but one company that partners with community colleges, Wells Fargo Bank in San Francisco, says the institutions are 10 to 20 percent cheaper than other third-party trainers it has used for equivalent courses. Some community colleges now even "guarantee" graduates of their technical programs. Under the guarantee, if a company is unhappy with a graduate's new skills, the employee can take refresher courses at no cost until the employer is satisfied. So far, all Illinois community colleges, plus most schools in New Jersey and Texas, offer the guarantee, according to *BusinessWeek*.

Burlington Northern: On the Right Track

Increased use of community colleges results in some unique partnerships. Take, for example, the arrangement between the operations center of Burlington Northern and Johnson County Community College (JCCC), both in Overland Park, KS. In the late 1980s, when the railroad sought to expand its technical training center, JCCC approached the company, suggesting that Burlington Northern locate its training center on the campus and use the college as a resource for training, facilities and equipment.

The city of Overland Park got involved by establishing industrial revenue bonds for the construction of the facility, and the result is Burlington Northern's national training center which is part of JCCC's Industrial Training Center, a 100,000 square-foot, $20 million facility.

But the ties between the railroad and college go beyond sharing real estate. According to Ed Butt, Burlington Northern's Director of technical training, the arrangement saves the railroad tens of millions of dollars a year while boosting training quality, and grosses JCCC $6 million a year in salaries and fees associated with program management. And in 10 years, when the railroad has paid off the bonds, the college will take ownership of the training center.

Additionally, Burlington Northern looks to JCCC to develop curriculum, train thousands of employees, and prepare instructors from the company to teach classes at the college. Butt says a total of 32 instructors — made up of both railroad and college staff — teach 65 courses, ranging from techncial writing to welding. Currently, more than 8,000 people (most, but not all, are Burlington Norther employees) are enrolled in courses. The classes are made up of engineers, conductors, brake and switch operators, telecommunications workers, and train traffic controllers. Since the center opened in 1988, Butt says more than 20,000 people have gone through the various programs.

Trainees at JCCC earn college credit for their work. Electrical and electronics workers attend courses for two weeks every six months, earning an associate degree after about 2.5 years. "There's an enormous psychological benefit to being on campus," Butt says, "in that it's a true learning environment. The employees who go throught this training are hands-on people who may not have done well in school. This setting allows them to break down barriers that may otherwise come up in traditional classrooms." Indeed, trainees only spend about 20 percent of their campus time in the classroom; the rest is hands-on time spend learning the tools of the trade, including working on a full-scale locomotive simulator at the center or on the road in railroad facilities across North America.

Trainees also have access to the college's library, gymnasium, dining facilities, and other perks associated with quality community colleges. But that's just icing on the cake, says Butt. "The key ingredient is the courseware, how it is structured and presented. We look to the college for that kind of help, and they are very good at it." How good? Burlington Northern credits the JCCC training with influencing huge improvements in productivity, reliability and effieciency. Since 1986, according to Butt, the mean time between system failures has improved from 53 days to 84 days, accidents caused by poor management of the railroad's 1,000 trains a day have declined by nearly 15 percent, and improved operating procedures have increased fuel efficiency by 8 percent.

Long Distance Partnering

Another example of a unique partnership comes from a Hewlett-Packard plant in Boise, ID. Its self-paced, interactive learning center — designed to bolster production workers' skills — is managed entirely by the College of San Mateo (CSM), a California-based community college located 650 miles away.

"We wanted the provider to tailor the curriculum to meet specific business needs, to have expertise in the development and management of learning centers, and have a vision of where the program could go in the future," says Lauren Malmon, technician development program manager. "We eventually decided upon CSM based on its ability to meet those needs and their willingness to provide employees an associate degree."

The 45 Hewlett-Packard employees enrolled in the electronics program attend "classes" at a 24-hour, on-site learning center equipped with multimedia workstations. The program is based in interactive video instruction and a self-paced workbook, so trainees work through courses by completing computer tutorials, reading assignments and evaluating their skills via computerized tests.

CSM developed the curriculum specifically for Hewlett-Packard, following a series of interviews with company technicians and their supervisors. The interviews were an effort to design lab exercises and study guides that reflect Hewlett-Packard

job procedures and equipment capabilities. Currently, employees can receive an associate degree in two different courses of study, but Hewlett Packard plans to eventually offer curriculum in six areas.

Since the program is self-paced, there is no need for instructors, although the center is staffed during peak hours by part-time aides from CSM. They administrer midterms and finals, but work primarily as mentors to trainees. Those aides also handle all administrative duties of the center, such as billing individual departments for training received.

Malmon says the company is pleased with the results of the program, which is still in its pilot stages. "The program has resulted in better-equipped technicians for the company," she says. "And while there are obvious differences in training practices and philosophies between industry and educational institutions, we were able to communicate as partners and reflect on one another's needs. That's the reason for our success."

Solving Time and Money Problems

Because its stores are spread throughout Pennsylvania, Hoss's Steak and Sea House has found the community college to be extremely beneficial in time and cost savings. Currently, the Duncansville, PA-based company is partnering with two com-

munity colleges — each on opposite ends of the state — to train managers in Lotus 1-2-3. "It's difficult to bring everyone to a central site," says Walt Lang, vice president of training, "and the fact that the community college can train groups of 12 to 20 people allows us to pull managers from nearby geographical areas. That keeps drive time down and makes for a reasonable day for trainees."

Though quality of instruction was the main criterion Hoss's used in choosing community colleges over other third-party options, Lang says cost was also a key determinant. Hoss's pays the community college a flat rate per class, and employees attend computer courses separate from the college's general student population. "The price of the community colleges is the $50 per person per day range, versus upwards of $100 for other sources. But quality came first, and for the introductory and intermediate classes we were looking for, I was very impressed with what the colleges were delivering."

Lang says the partnership also allows his department to spend more time on other training issues. "The partnership frees up resources here to teach more general courses to everyone," he says. Lang has found time, for example, to develop and deliver a general communications class and a course on business writing as a result of the partnership.

GUIDELINES HELP IN CREATING PARTNERSHIPS WITH COMMUNITY COLLEGES

What does a training executive need to know about establishing or building a relationship with a community college? Here are some factors to weigh, based on the experiences of other training executives who have successfully created those kinds of partnerships.

• **Be flexible.** Among the most successful partnering models in the country are a relationship between a business and a community college separated by 650 miles, and a community college that helped push through funding for a $20 million training facility to be built for a partner company on its campus. So don't be limited by traditional ways of conceiving these partnerships. As one training executive says, inflexibility is one reason "you rarely see established universities involved in these programs."

• **Take advantage of networking resources.** One, for example, is the League for Innovation in the Community Colleges, a nonprofit consortium of community colleges and corporate CEOs. The consortium serves as an experimental laboratory for workforce training and hosts national conferences and regional forums on community

college and business partnering.

• **Try for accreditation.** The ability to offer associate degrees to employees who complete training at community colleges often provides them with a huge psychological and career boost. Having accredited courses also builds credibility for the training function.

• **Be prepared for the time commitment.** The most common mistake, says one training executive, is thinking that creating this sort of partnership is easy and self-sustaining. Not so. One estimate says a company can expect to dedicate one additional worker-year toward tasks directly related to the partnership. That doesn't necessarily mean you need to add staff, but you must be prepared for a substantial time commitment.

• **Be prepared for the money commitment.** Cost depends on what kind of partnership you establish, but the initial expenditures for space, materials, salaries and other intangibles often obscure the benefits that will be reaped down the road. Stay patient, say training executives, and be persistent in your defense of the relationship to upper management.

Can You Outsource Your Brain?

A major training outsourcing deal at DuPont
may hail a new age in company-supplier partnerships —
or merely another round of staffing cycles.

BY MARC HEQUET

Can you outsource your brain? If training departments constitute the gray matter of the corporate organism, that's the question some face as companies downsize and outsource more and more of the functions that once were regarded as in-house musts.

In 1988, Corning Inc. cut a deal with College Center of the Finger Lakes (CCFL) under which CCFL delivers and administers a large share of the company's training, freeing Corning's internal training staff to focus on areas of particular strategic importance.

And one year ago chemical giant E. I. du Pont de Nemours and Co. of Wilmington, DE, and The Forum Corp., the big Boston-based consulting firm, joined in a training partnership in which Forum acts as DuPont's corporate training function. Forum says it's talking to more prospective partners for similar pairings, hoping to sign up "one or two" in the coming 12 months and up to 20 in the coming five years.

Why outsource the training function? The argument goes like this: A training department is permanent, embedded overhead that costs a company every minute of every day. Ideally, an outsourced function costs only when you use it. Such an arrangement is supposed to leave a company with a lower unit cost on its product and with more cash available to deploy quickly elsewhere.

Companies have long turned to outside suppliers for selected training needs — bringing in an outsider to lead management-development workshops, for example. Observers suspect that this kind of thing is hap-pening more and more. But DuPont and Corning arguably have relationships with training suppliers that are different in kind, not just in degree.

In the DuPont-Forum deal, Forum will develop and deliver courses for its partner. Twenty former DuPont trainers who now work for Forum, teaming up with other Forum consultants, will scour DuPont for business needs; develop or buy curricula not

---

What if a big vendor made a pitch for the whole corporate training function? "We would listen to them," says US West. "It makes sense."

---

already in hand; schedule DuPont, Forum or outside instructors to teach courses; and measure the effectiveness of their training for DuPont. In short, says Forum Chairman John Humphrey, "We are their training department."

Forum won't disclose its fees or DuPont-related revenue, but says DuPont pays either on a per-day or more often on a per-project basis. In comparison, Corning pays CCFL on a per-enrollee basis, with about 7,000 employees per year attending courses that cost between $65 and $300 per person.

Forum says its DuPont deal helped boost its 1995 revenues to about $50 million. The consulting company, with 260 full-time employees and another 190 part-time, is growing at a rate of about 25 percent per year.

Corning's partnership allowed it to double its training volume and meet an ambitious corporate goal of 5 percent of employee time spent in training, without increasing staff. Outsourcing to CCFL, moreover, let it focus on courses it wanted to keep internal for their strategic leverage — including training in quality, diversity, union-management relations, partnership-building and new employee orientation. Corning Inc. turned over 60 courses it considered less strategic to CCFL, including effective presentations, accounting, selling skills, and statistical process control.

Fear and Outsourcing

Outsourcing most certainly focuses trainers' attention. Indeed, the very word has unnerving connotations. DuPont and Forum call their arrangement "insourcing." "When you use the word 'outsourcing,'" says a training director at another company who declined to be interviewed on the record, "it strikes fear in people."

Some observers say the DuPont-Forum deal does indeed hail a new age of utilitarian pairing between business and training firms. Others predict it will prove to be merely a new wrinkle in a familiar cycle: staff up, lay off, outsource, staff up.

Clearly, many training departments have become intermediaries for outside suppliers. "Today's training organization has turned more into a brokering function," says Bill Jackson, selection and assessment services vice president with Development Dimensions International Inc. of Pittsburgh. "Forum is taking that to its next logical step."

An Ill-Tended Garden

DuPont says its partnership with Forum is about core competencies — and DuPont has decided human resources development is not a DuPont core competency.

Three years ago DuPont, deep in a period of self-examination and restructuring, found that its training organization had gotten to be like an ill-tended garden. In the Wilmington area alone, DuPont uncovered about 500 employees spending more than half their time on training and development.

Many were specialists seeking a chance to teach their specialty. "They were running around like ministers in search of a congregation," says Ty

Alexander, DuPont human development, staffing and personnel relations director. Adds Steve Crawley, senior engineer and training manager for DuPont's Chambers Works Specialty Chemicals site in Deepwater, NJ: "It used to be, 'Here's what we offer. Take it or leave it.'"

Over a two-year period DuPont cut trainer numbers from 500 to 100 by centralizing the training function, reassigning some trainers, and giving severance packages to others. But one more step was in order. "We needed something dramatic," says Ed Trolley, DuPont's training and education manager. "It wasn't just about incremental change."

DuPont starting talking with Forum in 1992, while it was shopping other training firms as well. DuPont settled on the Boston-based firm in May 1993, and signed a contract in August 1993 that took effect Jan. 1, 1994. Recently, the partners were at work renegotiating it to a five-year deal.

'Window Shopping'

Under the contract, Forum delivers all DuPont's training and development services worldwide except training for chemical plant operator mechanics (which is provided by community colleges and technical schools), and safety and diversity training, both of which DuPont has kept in-house as a part of its corporate "heritage," says Gerald Jones, Forum's executive vice president and general manager of the DuPont/Forum partnership.

On the human resource development side, Forum takes over. It provides assessments for DuPont and schedules classroom instructors from Forum or from other suppliers. Buying from outside through "one window" — Forum — DuPont hopes for better-managed purchases and volume discounts. Forum promises cost savings from reduced travel and less worker downtime.

Forum has drastically cut back DuPont's curriculum, slashing its client's course catalog from 1,000 offerings to about 150. Little-attended courses went. So did courses that scored low on trainee evaluations, like one on coaching for new managers. Evaluations said the course raised awareness but provided no skills. DuPont once had 54 time-management courses. Now it has two. Once it had more than 20 writing courses. Forum

kept the best two and axed the rest.

Formerly, managers were each allocated a certain amount of training for their department, and used it as they saw fit, whether they needed it or not. Now managers pay for their department's training out of their business-unit budget as an inducement to target training more carefully. "They're making an investment decision about something that's connected to their business success," says DuPont's Trolley.

Forum runs 50 or more courses per month for its big client's 23 business

---

When you use the word "outsourcing," says one training manager, "it strikes fear in people."

---

units. What's to keep Forum from using materials it developed for DuPont elsewhere — or even leaking DuPont proprietaries? The partners' contract spells out restrictions on what Forum can and cannot do with its curricula developed for DuPont.

The partnership keeps office in a DuPont facility in Wilmington — eating lunch with DuPonters, running into them in the hall, learning their acronym-laced language and the subtleties of their culture.

How much internal resistance have DuPonters mustered? "A fair amount," admits DuPont's Trolley. "At every tactical level, there were objections from the original training organization. It meant that organization was no longer going to do that work."

Bold Alliances?

The new arrangement places a premium on the partnership's performance. For Forum, "it says you're not going to be able to differentiate yourself on the basis of your latest leadership research," says Humphrey. "We're going to have to differentiate ourselves on the basis of, 'Can you make a difference in the client?'"

It may be an auspicious moment for bold alliances. Big companies are looking at every aspect of their operations. Continued downsizing may mean more outsourcing of departments, training included. More com-

panies downsized in 1994 than the previous year, though the average reduction was smaller and came with job creation as well, according to the American Management Association's eighth annual survey of corporate downsizing. And one in four responding companies planned to downsize before the end of June 1995 — the most ever in the survey's eight-year history.

Is Internal Better?

US West, in the midst of a 9,000-job cut, says its training staff has been centralized and reduced by 40 percent. Nevertheless the conviction persists at US West that internal trainers are better for assessing, designing and delivering courses. "We believe that internal people who have been here and know the nuances of the organization are better and can get at it quicker," says Maryanne Johnson, who directs leadership and professional development centers for US West.

And yet US West has discussed major outsourcing of training. What if a supplier made a pitch for the whole corporate training function? "We would listen to them," says Johnson. "I believe vendors are undoubtedly at the beginning of a wave of strategic alliances and partnerships. It makes sense to me. I'm keeping my ear to the ground on this one."

At Northern Telecom Ltd. in Canada, an effort to make training offerings more uniform nationally began in 1989. The goal was to eliminate redundancies and ensure equity — for example, the company wanted workers in Calgary, Alberta, to get the same training opportunities as those in Ottawa. Uniformity achieved, it means that a supplier could step in and provide training nationwide without missing a stride.

Indeed, Northern Telecom says it has already heard such pitches — and declined because the supplier didn't quite measure up and didn't cover all the bases. Geographically, at least, some supplier somewhere no doubt qualifies. "It's only a matter of time before one big firm comes to us and says, 'We've got partners based wherever you do business,'" says Rod Brandvold, senior manager for executive development in Ottawa.

Too Close to Heart?

Some trainers welcome the prospect of a major partnering, seeing it as a chance to shed grunt work and focus on corporate priorities. "I have friends that have been in the field 20 or 25 years. Their heart and soul is in this profession," says Barry Arnett, education and training strategy director at IBM in Atlanta. "A lot of them see this as by and large good, because it lets them focus on higher-order skills, the more strategic part of the job."

But many trainers are of two minds. Arnett balks at the idea of outsourcing anything as close to a company's heart as the training function. "The training arm of a company is a major change agent and is one of the key ways you can get improved human performance," he says.

Whether companies are indeed outsourcing more is hard to document. *TRAINING Magazine's* annual *Industry Report* (see October 1994 issue) shows spending for outside products and services hewing stubbornly to about 20 percent of total training budgets. Spending for off-the-shelf training packages has risen slowly but steadily since 1990, however, and spending for custom packages and outside services has shown more recent upticks.

Nearly everybody outsources some training already. A 1994 Society for Human Resource Management survey of 913 companies found that 92 percent have used an outside training source sometime in the last five years, with suppliers including private firms, industry groups, colleges and universities, and vendors of off-the-shelf packages or books.

Typically, organizations rely on a combination of inside and outside suppliers. Outsiders are more likely to be exclusive providers of training for certain types of employees. According to 1994 *Industry Report* respondents, outside suppliers are the sole source for 31 percent of training for executives, 20 percent for senior managers, and 18 percent for professionals. Those numbers have remained stable for the past five years, which argues against any broad-based outsourcing trend.

Why Not Outsource?

First Interstate Bancorp, a Los Angeles-based 13-state bank holding company, is in the midst of a 3,000-worker downsizing. The training function, however, has been relatively untouched. Indeed, says Sara White, vice president and manager of corporate training, her own staff increased by two to 14 from internal transfers.

She's wary of outsourcing too much of the training function and relying on what could be ham-handed off-the-shelf efforts by suppliers trying to solve intricate internal problems. "I would question whether it would be more cost-effective in the long run," White says.

Outside suppliers don't know the corporate culture or language, don't understand the nuances, don't know the hot buttons. Then there are the inevitable pockets of resistance. Even if a training effort seems fully supported from the top of the organization, consultants often encounter guerrilla defiance. When your responsibility is the entirety of a giant corporation, as is Forum's at DuPont, the potential for such heel-dragging multiplies enormously.

Another concern: What if an outsourced training function gradually loses its freshness, its independent judgment? What if it takes on the bureaucratic cadence of its host? "I could see it — being treated like and acting like overhead," muses DDI's Jackson. "You would have to remain intensely customer-focused."

Any training department will find a multitude of reasons not to enter such an arrangement. Some organizations use trainers for more than just training — running focus groups, for example. If you let those people go or reassign them, some internal scrambling is inevitable.

Any supplier who could deliver consistently good courses across a broad geographic area would deserve a look, acknowledges Northern Telecom's Brandvold. But it would be a long, hard look. "Personally, I suppose my reservations are the same as anyone who doesn't want to be dependent upon one supplier," Brandvold says. "I also believe there are pockets of innovation happening in training firms all over, and fear that if we line up with just one vendor they might not be as innovative as we want them to be."

Brandvold has one more concern. "We find that when we've teamed up with external designers, we are dragging them to catch up to where we are," he gripes. "If the vendors would get ahead of us, we'd use them. But it's hard for vendors to understand what's going on in a corporation unless they're living there."

Trend or Cycle?

Nevertheless, some suspect a fundamental change is afoot. That conclusion depends on whether you believe downsizing is a trend or a cycle, says IBM's Arnett. "It looks like there's some permanent downsizing going on, and if that's true then the pressure will be everywhere on corporations to keep looking for opportunities to do more with less."

But outsourcing your training department? Heaven forbid! Isn't that like outsourcing your brain? Is that any way to be a learning organization? "Learning doesn't take place in the training and development department," retorts Forum's Humphrey. "The training and development department facilitates a learning organization."

So, does the DuPont story herald a relentless trend that will transform the business landscape? Or is it just another swing in a cycle of insource-outsource-insource?

Time will tell. Either way, every training manager faces a difficult decision about what learning should be kept close to the corporate heart, and how much can be turned over to a partner in a strange new mating dance.

Choosing the Right Training Solution

With all the training suppliers out there,
how do you select the one that best fits your needs?
Here are two quick decision aids.

BY THOMAS D. CONKRIGHT

I n case you haven't received a dozen telephone calls this week or 75 pieces of advertising or 16 letters "just for you," let me bring you up to date. There are a lot of companies and individuals offering training products and services. They offer a vast array of training solutions.

How do you decide whether they offer anything appropriate for your needs? The first and most obvious question is: How do these suppliers propose to handle the content of the training program — the information that will be taught? After all, you teach topics, don't you?

Two interrelated and overlapping continua show how training suppliers treat the content of training programs. One continuum measures how much the supplier already knows about the topic in question. The other measures the degree to which the supplier uses existing material to meet your specific needs. Many points along these continua could be described, but I have picked four key ones for each.

And by the way, I'm writing from the supplier's perspective, since I am one.

Continuum of Knowledge

A supplier's content knowledge falls somewhere among the following points:

1. We don't know nuttin'. We are design and production specialists. We are a clean slate and will glean the content from your subject-matter experts (SMEs). We may also be media producers, computer-based training programmers or whatever you need. How well and how quickly we learn your topic and deliver the finished product varies a lot. Some of us are really good at it. Some of us are slower. A few of us may struggle and, perhaps, cost you extra time and energy.

2. We know sumthin' about your subject area or industry. Since we have done a project or two for others in your industry, or a project similar to the one you're considering, we know the general content area — computer

---

Off-the-shelf materials have an important place in the market. Smaller companies simply cannot afford custom development.

---

applications, say, or selling skills or product knowledge. Again, we may have learned a lot and become quite good at applying what we know. Or maybe not.

3. We know the specific topic. We built a course on radiation-worker training, so we can build one like it for you. Our "expertise" may be greatly influenced by how much the SMEs on the previous project knew. You need to tell us how much the topic varies from one environment to another. Soft-drink bottling may be the same the world over, or Coca-Cola and Pepsi may use entirely different methods. And each thinks theirs is the right one. Uh-huh.

4. We are experts in the field. We know, for example, total quality management techniques as well as any other supplier, and we know how to teach them. We may have a tendency to push our preconceived solutions on you and fail to listen enough to your input. But you don't have the expense and bother of supplying your own experts.

The ideal solution is the person who knows both content and training methodology. But to the degree that the content is unique to your company — residing only in the heads of your SMEs or in your own policies and procedures — you will be pushed toward a supplier whose only relevant expertise lies in the design and delivery of effective training, regardless of content. Such expertise is nothing to sneeze at. Just as building a highway requires highly skilled engineers, building a good training course demands skilled instructional technologists.

Continuum of Existing Material Use

Whether I know a little or a lot, I can still offer you two options: I can build a unique solution for you, or I can bring you the already-completed solution to be implemented. The degree of customization varies according to a second continuum.

1. Everything's new. We won't taint your program with anything someone else has used. It will all be specific to your performers. It will be an original, like a painting by Van Gogh. We will jointly create a training solution that is creative, efficient and exciting.

2. Here's a need: What do we already have that we can use? We work with a client, based on our level of content understanding, to design a solution that is just right for her. Then we "borrow" whatever we can from existing programs to speed up the development and production process. This may include graphics, test questions or just a good, solid content outline. Especially in computer-delivered solutions, borrowing from graphics libraries and using subroutines and conventions from existing programs improves productivity considerably. We can use clip art, existing slides and stock video footage. The solution is still tailored to the need, but may be more cost-effective than a program that is 100-percent customized.

3. Here's a solution: How much of what we have fits? The other approach is to begin with an existing product and see how much of it can be used to meet a specific need. This is not your best instructional-design theory, but it may be quicker and cheaper. The danger lies in the temptation to use something that almost, but not quite, fits. We modify the product, and repackage it with your logo. Or we may keep key elements — such as the video, hardcopy textbooks or whatever — intact, and then build other pieces to fill in the cracks. The result may look a little piecemeal, but the learners are smart enough to figure out how to smooth out the rough spots.

4. We don't build anything. We just prepare a site or conduct a specific "packaged" program. This works sort of like your history class, in which the teacher told you to read chapters 1 through 4 in book one, chapters 3, 4 and 10 in book two, and half of *Mein Kampf*. (Oh, and by the way, it's due Tuesday. Hope you enjoy the homecoming weekend!) The instructor doesn't really develop anything except his personalized presentation of the material.

Most vendors begin from one end of the continuum or the other. Depending on their orientation, they either build products or they don't. Some product vendors are very protective of their intellectual property and are reluctant to make even minor modifications. Others use existing materials as if they were items in a grocery bag or kitchen cupboard, and pull out the ingredients for the meal you want. Add a little more spice? No problem.

Custom developers often use past experience and materials both directly and indirectly. Never mind plagiarism questions; the new materials look sufficiently unique that no lawyer could question them. Lawyers and courts know so little about training development that they will never touch it anyway.

Off-the-shelf materials have an important place in the market. Smaller companies simply cannot afford custom development. They benefit from the in-depth research, additional packaging, presentation support, and the quality control necessary to create a product for the open market. The advantage of custom materials, of course, is that they are explicitly designed to fill the need. They are generally more efficient and effective, and with larger audiences, are the least expensive over the life cycle of a course. But they can suffer from budget limitations that often result in cutting corners and leaving off the so-called frills.

If only one of these approaches worked, suppliers that follow the others would have gone out of business long ago. Obviously, this has not happened. As a training buyer, you need to choose the approach that's best for you. Then find the vendor who has the experience and reputation to do the best job of implementing your chosen approach.

Notes:

How to Choose a Feedback Instrument

To see ourselves as others see us...a great gift indeed. But before you bestow the blessing on managers, do some shopping for a good questionnaire.

BY ELLEN VAN VELSOR AND
STEPHEN J. WALL

Every organization would like to use training more effectively as a means to achieve strategic goals. With management development courses, in particular, the challenge is to ensure that training focuses on things that are truly relevant to managers' jobs. What behavior or attitudes should individuals try to change in order to manage more effectively and help drive the organization in the direction it wants to go?

That question is the force behind the increasing popularity of instruments that provide "back-home" feedback; that is, questionnaires that can be used to gather not just managers' self-perceptions but also the perceptions of bosses, subordinates and peers. The idea is to allow managers to see themselves as others see them.

In the past 10 years, the number of feedback instruments available on the market has increased dramatically. Nearly 100 different questionnaires are now being marketed, compared with maybe 25 only a decade ago. With so many available, making an informed choice is more important but more difficult than ever. Here are some guidelines for evaluating the quality of an instrument and its suitability for your purposes.

Objectives

The first consideration in narrowing the field of possibilities is how well an instrument addresses the needs of your target population. Before you look at the various instruments on the market, be sure you know what you are trying to accomplish. What do you want managers to understand or do differently as a result of the feedback they will receive?

Every instrument is derived from some model of management or leadership effectiveness. To begin evaluating an instrument, read about the model it represents. What does it include? Does it provide managers with feedback on their behavior? Their leadership style? Their knowledge and skills, such as financial ability? Does it focus on personal characteristics like charisma or likability? Is the model appropriate for the level of manager who will be using it? Does it deal with competencies that are important to your organization?

How Was the Instrument Developed?

A model is no more than a hypothesis until it has been tested. While there are more instruments on the market now than ever before, probably no more than one in four has been professionally developed and adequately tested. Spend some time finding out where the model came from and how sound it has proven to be.

The "items," or individual questions people respond to in the questionnaire, may be derived from one or more studies of leaders or one or more theories of leadership effectiveness. Or, the author may have started out with a list of items that he or she personally believed reflected leadership skills. When looking at individual items, consider these questions:

• Do the items have face validity? That is, do they seem to make sense? If you were a manager looking at them for the first time, would you believe they were important to your effectiveness?

• Is the wording of the items clear and unambiguous?

Pay attention to the scales, which are the categories into which the items are grouped. In some cases feedback is provided only on the scale level. It is important to find out how the scales were developed; in other words, how were items grouped to form a category? There are two aspects of scale development: the statistical and the rational. Both methods should be used.

Statistical methods (factor or cluster analyses, item/scale intercorrelations) are clustering procedures that group items into scales based on similarities in the responses of raters. For example, if subordinates rate a manager high in "having frequent meetings with direct reports," do they also tend to say that this manager frequently seeks feedback from them on her own performance? If so, are these two tendencies really grouped together more often than either one is with other items, such as monitoring progress toward group goals or delegating appropriately to subordinates?

While a statistical approach to scale development makes obvious sense (you would not want an item in a scale that was not really associated with other items in that scale) it can be taken to such extremes that it produces silliness. Therefore, the statistical approach is usually supplemented with a rational approach: The author's knowledge or experience about how skills and behaviors relate to one another is used to modify the scales. If, for example, statistical analysis shows that public-speaking skill is correlated with strategic planning ability, these items do not necessarily belong in the same scale, since it's hard to see how they overlap conceptually. Perhaps they are statistically related only because the sample on which the analysis was based contained a group of experienced executives who were skilled in both areas.

How Sound?

How important is it, really, for an instrument to have been tested for validity and reliability? After all, questionnaires with face validity are developed every year by smart and experienced people who ought to know what effective managers and leaders do.

Our view is that when you give managers feedback from others on a set of scales, you are implicitly asking them to trust that the instrument is relevant and well-constructed. In fact, you are asking managers to use this input to change their behavior in some way. Thus, it is crucial that instruments actually measure what they purport to measure — and that the behaviors, skills or attributes they do measure are actually related to effectiveness on the job. That's what validity means.

We recognize that poring over technical reports is time-consuming and daunting for many people. Yet there are several relatively simple things to look for to determine a questionnaire's soundness.

Reliability and validity are different things. We'll take them one at a time. There are three basic tests of an instrument's reliability: test/retest reliability; internal reliability; and inter-rater agreement. Let's look at each briefly.

Test/retest reliability is the instrument's stability over time. Would raters' scores remain relatively stable over short intervals if there were no change on the part of the manager being rated? If Jane answers an item about Bob in one way today, would she select the same response tomorrow?

Because of their wording, some items have higher stability over time than others. For example, an item such as "tends to be conservative" might have a low test/retest reliability. If the rater has just seen his boss allocate a huge sum of money for a risky project, he might say the boss is not conservative. But a week later, if the two of them have a conversation about politics, the rater might characterize the boss as conservative — with no real change on the boss's part.

Some questionnaire authors claim that test/retest studies are not applicable to their instruments because the instruments are designed to create change in the manager. This argument ducks the issue of measurement: You cannot use an instrument to measure change unless you know that the items or scales will remain constant under conditions of no change.

To find out about an instrument's stability over time, ask for a technical report that details the research and validation that have gone into its development. Look for a section titled Test/Retest Reliability. Numbers for each scale should be a minimum of .4; .6 is considered good for a feedback instrument.

Next, look for a study of the questionnaire's internal consistency. This type of reliability refers to the scales on which feedback will be given. Internal consistency tells you whether all the items that make up a scale are, in fact, measuring the same construct and whether there are enough items to measure it adequately. If all the items are measuring the same construct, then managers who exhibit one of the behaviors that define the scale should also tend to exhibit the behaviors described by other items on that scale.

Internal consistency should be in the .65 to .85 range. If the reliability coefficient is low, either the scale contains too few items or the items have little in common. If it is very high, the

---

Before you look at the various instruments on the market, be sure you know what it is you are trying to accomplish.

---

scale may contain more items than is necessary. For example, in a scale such as "team orientation," adequately high internal reliability would mean that all the behaviors represented by items within that scale are indeed measuring "team orientation" and that the number of items is sufficient to assess that competency.

Finally, look for a study of inter-rater agreement — how much agreement there is among people who should tend to see the manager similarly (among peers, for example). While raters with different perspectives (peers vs. subordinates) may disagree in their assessment of a manager, raters with the same perspective should show at least moderate agreement. Very low inter-rater agreement would signify that the scale(s) lacked stability or interpretability among people who have similar relationships to the manager.

That said, however, do not expect inter-rater reliability to be as high in statistical terms as the other measures of reliability. Regardless of how well-constructed the instrument, people rating a manager are untrained observers and will understand and interpret items differently. Statistically, .5 is considered a high degree of inter-rater agreement.

Validity

Next, look at the studies that gauge the instrument's validity, or its integrity. These tests are done to ensure that the instrument measures what it claims to measure and that scores on the questionnaire are in fact related to effectiveness on the job. Indeed, if we don't know whether the instrument we're using is valid, why in the world are we giving this feedback to managers and suggesting that they pay attention to it and use it to set some goals for change?

As consumers of these products, we need to see some basic evidence that there is indeed a relationship between scores on the instrument and some other measure of performance.

The most convincing evidence will be that scores on the instrument are related to data from an independent source: actual performance appraisals, perhaps, or effectiveness ratings on a different instrument completed by a different set of raters. This kind of data is not always available, so many studies use ratings from the same source. That is, the same people who rated managers on the instrument being tested are asked to rate them on some different scale of overall effectiveness or performance, as well.

In the technical report, headings may refer to different kinds of validity (construct, content, concurrent, and so on), but look for evidence of at least one study showing significant relationships between scores on the instrument and some measure of actual effectiveness on the job. The details of this study and its results should be described.

Finally, read the description of the norm base, as well as the sample used in the validity studies. Is the type and level of manager used in the research similar to the type and level of manager who will be using the instrument in your organization? If you plan to use the instrument internationally, has its validity and reliability been studied in populations outside the United States?

Feedback

You can narrow the field of possible instruments considerably just by examining them for evidence of reliability and validity. Next, ask to see a sample feedback report. This will show you how the instrument displays the feedback it gathers for the manager being rated. In other words, how much information does the manager actually get about how he is perceived, and in what form is this information presented?

There are hundreds of ways to present managers with data. Choosing among them involves some inherent trade-offs. The key is to match the strengths of an instrument's feedback display with organizational needs.

For example, consider the length of the feedback display. Very short instruments tend to have very short displays, which may allow for quicker interpretation. The trade-off is obvious: A short display may give managers less information, or only a superficial understanding of a specific area of feedback. How useful is it to learn, for instance, that you are rated "above average" in "team orientation," with that term defined only as "ability to work well with others on team projects"?

Next, examine how the raters' feedback is presented. Does the breakout of rater data meet your needs? Is feedback from groups of peers, direct reports and supervisors displayed separately? Each one of these groups observes a somewhat different slice of a manager's total set of skills and behaviors. In addition, some items and scales will apply more to working relationships with one group than they do with others. For example, scales having to do with supervision speak only to relationships with subordinates. Therefore, there can be great advantage to seeing data from various groups presented as distinct categories of feedback.

On the other hand, if you are using the instrument to give feedback on supervisory behavior only, or on cross-functional influence only, you may not need all of these groupings of data. Another consideration: Breakouts of rater data can violate rater confidentiality or compromise the honesty of rater responses.

Confidentiality is an issue in its own right. The question usually gets stickiest when feedback from the boss is presented separately. If only one superior completes an instrument on the manager, that person's ratings will be undisguised. While this kind of feedback is critical, both the manager and the boss should understand from the beginning that the boss's ratings will not be anonymous. Both parties should also agree that the impact of the boss's ratings will not minimize the impact of feedback from subordinates or peers.

Interpretation

Look at the feedback format and consider this question: Does the format help the participating manager interpret the data?

Changing your behavior is difficult, even when you've gotten comprehensive feedback on your performance. The difficulty occurs partly because feedback can be overwhelming. It can overwhelm not just because there's a lot of it, but also if it is mostly negative or if it comes from many different perspectives. Without some road map that highlights the most important findings, the recipient can get lost, ignore important data or give up on trying to process the information.

Built into the instrument's feedback display should be some kind of framework for interpreting the data. This might include:

• Denoting which areas were rated most important to the manager's job or to success in the organization.

• Highlighting large discrepancies between self-perception and the perceptions of others.

• Providing standardized or percentile scores for comparison of individual data to instrument norms.

• Including recommendations for what observers feel the manager should "do more" of or "do less" of.

• Listing rater responses to the individual items.

• Using text or narrative to help the manager interpret and remember the meaning of the data.

To illustrate the benefit of these interpretive frameworks, suppose we're using a hypothetical instrument with five feedback scales: "Planning," "Delegating," "Getting Information," "Influencing" and "Self-Management." A hypothetical manager has ratings (on a five-point scale) as follows:

	Average of Rater Responses	Self-Rating
Planning	4.5	4.0
Delegating	4.4	5.0
Getting Information	4.0	4.2
Influencing	3.8	3.9
Self-Management	2.1	3.1

Having nothing with which to compare her own scores, this manager might conclude that 3.8 is a satisfactory score for "Influencing." However, if she knew that subordinates saw "Influencing" as extremely important in her job or if she knew that the norm for all managers was

---

CHECKLIST FOR SELECTING A FEEDBACK INSTRUMENT

The Questionnaire
1. Does the kind of feedback provided meet the needs of the target population and help achieve your management development objectives?
2. Do the items have face validity?
3. Are the items clear and unambiguous?

The Technical Report
1. Were the scales developed using both rational and statistical methods?
2. Has test/retest reliability been studied, and are the results .4 or better?
3. Has internal consistency been studied, and are the results between .65 and .85?
4. Has inter-rater agreement been studied, and is it at least .4?
5. Has the instrument been tested for validity, and are the results significant?
6. Was the sample population used in validation research similar to your target population?

The Feedback Report
1. Is the length of the feedback report appropriate for your uses?
2. Does breakout of rater data meet your needs?
3. Is rater confidentiality adequately protected?
4. Does the feedback format include multiple methods of presenting the data?

The Support Materials
1. Are materials available to help managers summarize their feedback and plan next steps?
2. Does the guidance and support offered to trainers meet your needs?

4.5, she might decide she needed to improve that skill. Similarly, this manager might be delighted that raters awarded her a score of 4.5 for "Planning." However, if the raters also were asked what she should "do more" of and "do less" of, perhaps they'd say she should do less planning. Maybe they're feeling smothered by her cautious, deliberate style.

Not atypically, this manager overrates herself in four of five areas. Left to her own devices, she'll probably pay attention to self-rater differences greater than .4 (as with "Self-Management"). But how does she know whether the gap for "Getting Information" is large enough for concern? Feedback can be enriched when it shows which self-rater differences should be considered significant.

Finally, it is difficult to understand how to change or improve abstract competencies. "Self-Management" is an example. Does a score of 2.1 on "Self-Management" mean that the raters think the manager is unaware of her own strengths and weaknesses? That she doesn't manage her time well? That she's spreading herself too thin? Feedback on the "item" level rather than just the scale level would be very useful here. That is, how did raters respond to the specific, concrete behavioral items on the questionnaire that were combined to form the "Self-Management" scale?

Most instruments do not make use of all of these strategies simultaneously, and it is not critical that you look

---

How much information does the manager actually get about how he is perceived?

---

for one that does. Two or more strategies in a single instrument are preferable, however.

Support Materials

Suppose you've found an instrument with a clear feedback display and appropriate strategies for interpreting the information. Now the question becomes, how do you ensure that managers can make constructive use of the feedback they receive? What do they do with the stuff?

Managers will need a summarizing and goal-planning process specifically geared to the feedback. Some instruments include materials to facilitate such a process. Others provide more in-depth information about the model or quick reference guides that can be used as a manager works to improve.

Also, look for specific guidance or support for trainers. How will you learn to use and interpret the feedback? Is certification required to purchase or use the instrument? Are trainers' materials available? How is the instrument scored — by the vendor, by you or by the managers themselves (manually or using computer software)? Again, you'll have to make trade-offs based on your organizational needs, objectives and resources.

As must be all too obvious by now, the careful selection of a feedback instrument can be a time-consuming endeavor. Yet because of the enormous value of good feedback, it is effort well-spent. Seek out the instrument that best matches your needs and goals — the one that has been proven reliable and valid, the one designed for maximum clarity and impact. You'll have a powerful and intriguing tool for helping managers understand and improve their effectiveness on the job.

Notes:

How to Choose a Video Producer

Looking for a professional to make your training video? Here's a shopping guide.

BY ROY B. COHN

You've identified a training need and decided that video is the best medium for the job. Now you need to hire someone to make the video. But with literally thousands of production companies plying their trade in the corporate marketplace, how do you choose a producer who understands the special needs of training and development and can deliver a video that gets results? Before you pick a producer, it's important to understand the playing field.

Producers generally fall into one of six categories. Here are the usual suspects:

• **Full-service audiovisual production houses.** This type of vendor is a meeting-services company that offers video along with other services including slides, print production and staging. The specialty of a full-service house is filming large corporate meetings and trade shows. However, for the right price they'll do your training video and wash the windows, too. Full-service houses offer high-quality work and hand-holding provided by an account representative. Remember, though, that those marble lobbies don't come cheap. Often these vendors rely extensively on free-lancers and subcontractors. If they understand training issues and know your industry, you're in good hands; if not, be wary. You could be paying through the nose for a video that looks great but accomplishes little.

• **Production companies.** These are smaller shops, creative-services boutiques that function as general contractors. They generally don't own much equipment but work closely with facilities to assemble a production package. The principals of these small houses are usually experienced producers who maintain a low overhead by serving as both creative director and account representative. On the plus side, if this vendor has the training expertise for your project, the quality will be top-notch and the price should be less than a full-service house would charge. The downside is that smaller production companies won't have the organizational depth to juggle more than a handful of projects at one time.

• **Independent producers.** In this category we find the one-person shop whose quality depends almost entirely on the talents of a single individual. Often working from home, the independent producer may be a multitalented "hyphenate" — a writer/director/producer who can flawlessly execute a broad range of projects. If this person happens to specialize in training videos, you may have found a great source for a professionally produced video at a reasonable price.

• **Videographers.** These vendors own their own equipment and earn a good portion of their income from event photography such as weddings and bar mitzvahs. While they may be a great choice for inexpensively taping a meeting for archival purposes, do not expect them to add much value to a training video by selecting or shaping the material.

• **In-house departments.** Many large companies maintain fully equipped, state-of-the-art production facilities staffed by in-house personnel. If your company has such a facility and you're not looking for an outside perspective, one big advantage of working in-house is that the staffers will already understand your corporate culture and will know what has worked reasonably well in the past. Also, depending on the nature of your charge-back system, the cost of these services may be available to you at below market rates. The drawback is that internal departments, with some notable exceptions, do not offer the same level of service or creativity as their more profit-oriented counterparts.

• **Facilities.** Apart from videographers and some production companies, producers typically don't own much equipment. Instead, they buy time and space from facilities. A facility is an impressive-looking place containing rooms of equipment that resemble the bridge on the starship Enterprise. Facilities are either studios (where your video may be shot), "post houses" (where your program will be edited), or a combination of the two. In addition to your corporate video project, the facility may be working simultaneously on more glitzy programs for cable, network television and ad agencies. For the most part, facilities do not act as producers. In some smaller markets, however, facilities may have a separate producing arm. Be cautious if you choose this type of vendor; it's easy to be seduced by showbiz glamour and high-tech equipment, and lose sight of the fact that what you really need is an effective training video.

"My Brother-in-Law Knows a Guy..."

You'll probably begin your search for a producer with at least one or two names in hand. These may be gleaned through personal contacts, advertisements, or referrals from colleagues. If you don't already know someone, ask a training professional who works regularly with video to refer vendors in your area. Be advised that with video, as with life, you generally get what you pay for. If someone tells you they know a guy who knows a guy who can do the job cheap, chances are a cheap-looking video is exactly what you're going to get.

As you begin to contact producers, don't be intimidated by your lack of technical knowledge. Although video technology is indeed complex, a good producer will shield you from most of the jargon. The only major technical decision you should have to make relates to the desired level of "production values," or overall program quality. If your program is going to be beamed via satellite to an audience of millions, you should select a producer capable of delivering a "broadcast-quality" production. This generally means shooting Betacam (a broadcast-quality format not to be confused with Betamax) and editing your final product to one-inch tape, D2, or another high-end format. On the other hand, if you're just taping a meeting as an archival record, a low-cost format like VHS or Hi-8 may be perfectly adequate.

As a rule of thumb, the quality of your program should be high enough so that the viewer doesn't notice it. The production values should be invisible. If poor audio or lighting make it difficult to understand your message, you've got a problem. On the other hand, a slew of expensive digital effects that overwhelms your content can be equally distracting.

"Don't Worry, We'll Fix It in Post..."

If you had to choose a trainer to lead a diversity workshop, you probably wouldn't begin your search by interviewing consultants specializing in sales training. Similarly, video producers have different areas of strength and weakness. The producer who shows you an award-winning video about a Mt. Everest expedition is not thereby demonstrating that he can produce an effective video that illustrates how to conduct a performance appraisal.

The producer you want will have previous experience with training subjects and will grasp the basics of instructional design. Above all, she will understand your underlying business issues and will be able to deliver a script that addresses them.

Ninety percent of what ails most training videos can be traced back to the script (see box). Your producer should have strong scriptwriting credentials or work regularly with a writer who does. A writer/producer with a background in training can be a tremendous asset. Not only will he have a feel for dialogue and narrative structure, but he will collaborate with you to clarify objectives and suggest creative ways to achieve them. A good writer/producer will also use the potential of the video medium to take the training to a new level — whether through comedy, drama, or simply editing together taped interviews in a narrative structure.

Beware of training consultants moonlighting as scriptwriters. Although they may have excellent com-

---

IT'S (ALMOST) ALL IN THE SCRIPT

It has been said that a film is actually made three times: once in the scriptwriting, once in the production, and once again in the editing.

Nowadays it's increasingly rare to find a professionally made video that fails because of shortcomings in either production or editing. Our society has produced enough competent video pros — directors, editors, camerapeople, sound engineers — to ensure that most productions are competently executed. Of course there will always be instances where misguided direction, poor casting, or some sort of technical glitch will mar a production, but these cases are rare.

It is far more common to find a handsomely made production that flops because it either lacks the necessary content or does a mediocre job of communicating that content. This type of problem almost always can be traced back to the script. By "script," I mean not only the document containing the dialogue and camera direction but also the overall creative approach.

Some common video-script problems:

• The writer has failed to clarify the program's objectives, so the script meanders without a strong focus.

• The writer has failed to limit the number of learning points, so the script becomes an endless laundry list of information.

• The writer has a poor sense of dramatic structure, so the script lacks a beginning, middle or end, as well as a sense of pace.

• The writer has a poor sense of dialogue, which detracts from the clarity of the message as well as the credibility of on-camera performers. How many training videos have you seen in which the people modeling the desired interpersonal skills come across as repugnant androids whose speech and behavior no sane person would wish to emulate?

• The writer tries to spice up the script with humor or drama, but chooses a concept that is either tedious or hokey.

• The writer succeeds in spicing up the script with humor or drama, but does such a good job that the entertainment value buries the learning points.

• The writer fails to spice up the script, and the audience tunes out the message because the delivery vehicle is so boring.

— R.C.

---

mand of the subject matter, this does not necessarily translate into an engaging, tightly crafted script. Novice scriptwriters usually lack a feel for dialogue, as well as the ability to tell a story visually. On the other hand, it's often helpful for the writer/producer to meet with your consultants during the project's instructional-design phase to develop a sound creative approach. Remember, no amount of special effects or high-level production values will overcome a poorly crafted script.

Taking a Meeting

When you first meet with prospective producers, you should ask to see their demo reels. These reels contain samples of producers' better work and will cue you in right away to their overall professionalism, as well as their core competency. If the demo reel features lots of dramatic vignettes, chances are the producer considers this type of program an area of

strength. But reels can be misleading. While they're often provocative and fun to watch, they contain just enough of a program to entice you, but not enough for you to evaluate its effectiveness.

If you see something that looks impressive, ask if you can view the program in its entirety. Also ask the producer about her role in the project. Who's idea was it? Who actually wrote the script? How did she work with the client? What did the project cost? Of course, it's also helpful to talk directly with the producer's client to determine the effectiveness of the video and to gain additional insights about the producer.

If you don't see exactly the type of program you're looking for on a producer's demo reel, don't necessarily write him off. Just because a producer normally works, for example, in the financial-services industry, doesn't mean he won't have the capacity to deliver an effective video for a consumer-products company. A true professional is a quick study, and will hone in on your business issues by asking good questions and bringing his problem-solving ability to bear.

A Few Good Proposals

After meeting with several producers, you may find that one stands head and shoulders above the rest. If the fees are within your budget and the producer comes highly referred, there's nothing wrong with engaging that person immediately for your project. If you have several good candidates in mind, it's customary to ask them to submit competitive bids. The proposal process need not require a formal RFP document, but it's often helpful to write down your objectives, timetable, and other pertinent information.

Most producers view the preparation of proposals as a necessary cost of doing business. If your program requires a creative solution, good producers will recognize this and submit "treatments" that will sketch out how they propose to address the challenge. If your project or account is large, a producer will expend considerable time and effort to develop a creative approach that will win your business. Be clear with a producer if you're still awaiting budget approval or if the budget may be limited; it's unfair to make a vendor jump through hoops for a job that isn't real.

Another question of proposal etiquette may arise if you find yourself preferring one producer's creative approach, but feel that another producer may offer superior pricing or quality. You're under no obligation to pay for proposals written "on spec." However, if you'd like to incorporate the first producer's ideas without actually engaging him for the project, it makes good business sense to compensate him for the treatment. That way, you won't be burning any bridges.

The Price Is Right

Buying a creative service like video production is different from purchasing a commodity or even from purchasing other services. Yet many clients approach video pricing as if they are trading in pork bellies; then they're surprised by the wide range of bids they sometimes receive. Although some version of standard pricing may apply to camera rentals or on-line editing, there is no easy rule of thumb for the more intangible creative services. Is an excellent director who commands $2,000 a day really worth four times more than a competent journeyman who charges $500? If the success or failure of a $100,000 project hangs on the director's unique talents, the $2,000 may ultimately prove to be a bargain.

In the absence of dramatic quality differences between producers, variances in pricing are sometimes due to the size of the producer's markup. Most producers charge a markup on their services, which can range from 10 percent to more than 100 percent for some full-service houses. This amount is what they have determined they must charge to earn a profit and cover such overhead expenses as office support, marketing, and their own professional development. In general, producers with lower overhead will charge less of a markup. A high markup is not necessarily a sign of bloat or excess, but neither does it automatically translate into higher quality.

Another source of differences in pricing is the assumptions producers build into their job estimates. Producer No. 1 may assume that taping a teleconference with the company's CEO will require a minimum of five cameras; Producer No. 2 may assume that three cameras will be adequate. Unless you dig into their underlying assumptions, you may be comparing apples and oranges — and jump to the conclusion that Producer No. 1 is wildly overpriced.

In the event that an otherwise solid proposal is beyond your budget, ask if the producer will work with you on price. Producers are loath to cut their markup, but they can often lower their price by fine-tuning the assumptions used to arrive at the budget totals. For example, a producer's budget may provide for four days of location shooting. By working with the producer to tighten the schedule, it may be possible to compress the shoot into three days. Such creative problem-solving is often the first indication that you will be able to work with the producer as a true partner.

The Satisfied Client

I have often heard producers grouse about the unreasonable demands or expectations of their clients. For many producers, the expression "satisfied client" has become an oxymoron. When the common goal of both producer and client is to produce an outstanding training video, how is it that relations often break down?

By selecting a well-qualified producer, you will certainly minimize problems. But now the work is only beginning. You must manage the client-producer relationship by infusing it with the same ingredients necessary for any successful partnership: honesty, respect and enthusiasm. Step to the other side of the table, and you will discover that what really motivates producers is the desire to make you happy by creating good work. Give them the freedom and support to do their jobs, and they will produce videos of which you will both be proud.

Notes:

Out of the Can:
How to Customize
Off-the-Shelf Training

Prepackaged training programs are fine, but sometimes you want to add a little spice of your own. Where do you start?

BY BOB FILIPCZAK

Who's got time to cook anymore? OK, so maybe on weekends you put together a dinner of fresh tomato-basil spaghettine followed by tiramisu and a latté. But when you've done a full eight hours or more at work you're more likely to reach for that can of Campbell's soup. Sure, you might add some oregano or garlic salt or pepper to whatever slops out of the can, but the real mission here is to get food into your family's stomachs before you collapse for the evening.

Time and energy are even more precious commodities at work these days. We've been hearing about the reasons for years: downsizing, doing more with less, being lean and mean. While *TRAINING Magazine's* research (see *Industry Report*, October 1992) shows that training departments haven't borne more than their share of the cuts, they've certainly felt the ax in terms of reduced staffing and budgets. Consequently, when a manager approaches the training department with a request for training on, appropriately enough, time management, the harried director of training often looks for an off-the-shelf course.

Saving time is not the only reason trainers are drawn to packaged training. Using off-the-shelf courseware staves off a deep-seated fear of redesigning the wheel, of building a course from scratch only to discover some professional training company has a better program that has been proven successful time and time again. An outside supplier probably would have saved money and, ultimately, time.

Expertise is also a key consideration for many who buy off-the-shelf training. Susan Keen, a management and professional development specialist for Sunquest Information Systems, a software company in Tucson, AZ, says she investigates packaged training courses when she doesn't have the internal expertise to design the program. Most training suppliers do extensive research into a subject before designing off-the-shelf courseware, something Keen says she has neither the staff nor the time to do. Pure expedience — she needs a course right away — is usually only the secondary reason she considers packaged training. Her first concern is getting a course that has been well-researched and proven to work in pilot tests and with other clients.

Adjusting the Spokes

Off-the-shelf courseware saves you time and money, is the product of extensive research and testing, and has a proven track record. So why customize it? Good question.

Anecdotal evidence might persuade you that customized training is more effective than packaged programs, but harder evidence is sparse. A typical example: Ed Mohebi, chief operating officer of Cogent Technology Training, a Seattle software training company, says one of his clients estimated a 20 percent increase in skill transference after Cogent customized a packaged course. But that's only a guess.

Rachael Tayar at the department of health services for the state of California in Sacramento, taught an off-the-shelf business writing course to employees both before and after she customized it. Her gut feeling is that the customized version was more effective and that the trainees got more out of the program because she used examples of poor writing taken directly from the employees' departments. But she didn't conduct any statistical research to validate what she intuited.

A lot of the reasons people customize training fall into the gut-level commonsense category. It just stands to reason that if you use engineering examples when teaching engineers the principles of good business writing, the training will stick better than if you use office automation examples. And if the training is more relevant in the classroom, common sense also dictates that the training will transfer back to the job better. Which is, after all, the objective of the entire exercise, isn't it?

And, to be honest, who can really resist the temptation, without reinventing the wheel, to adjust the spokes a little?

Jim Kouzes is chairman and CEO of Tom Peters Group Learning Systems, a Palo Alto, CA, consulting firm that sells off-the-shelf training programs. Kouzes adds one more factor to the customization equation: the customer. As our economy evolves beyond customer service to customer intimacy, he says, companies will deal with customers as individuals instead of demographic groups. As he points out, Julie Nixon and Grace Slick are part of the same demographic niche, but you probably won't sell them the same set of goods.

Part of customer intimacy is tailoring products for individuals, says Kouzes. Levi Strauss, for example, is now testing the market for custom-tailored jeans. You go to a Levi's store, get your measurement taken and, presto, within weeks you receive made-to-fit-you Levi's jeans. Likewise, says Kouzes, training must be increasingly customized to meet the needs of the ultimate customer: the trainees. So the more relevant you make your training, the better you serve your constituency — the employees being trained.

Joe Lipsey, manager of corporate training and development for Mutual of Omaha in Omaha, NE, says that training departments in general don't do a very good job of reaching their customers by addressing the specific issues important to trainees. He suggests that adjusting training to fit the customer is a matter of accountability, that trainers who don't deal with the precise problems of the trainees are shirking their responsibilities.

Teaming Up with a Supplier

Once you've decided to customize a training course, where should you begin? Most experts and practitioners agree that the process begins with a traditional needs assessment — essentially trying to figure out what the audience already knows, what it needs to know, and what kind of training will bridge the gap. Some even take a further step back and start with the perennial question: What's the problem and what can training to do to solve it?

Another camp in the customization debate suggests that the first step is finding the right supplier and establishing a long-term relationship. You save time if the company selling you the training also does some of the customization work for you. The training company comes in, asks some questions, does some interviews and modifies a course it already sells for you, rather than just dropping workbooks and videos on your desk and letting you figure it out.

In fact, many suppliers of off-the-shelf training discourage practitioners from customizing a course without input from the company that designed the training. Sometimes the issue is copyright infringement and the desire to protect intellectual property, which we'll address later. But suppliers' careful research and testing can be undone by well-meaning trainers who don't understand the methodology behind the packaged training. Cutting a lot out of a course or patching together a bunch of courses are two ways to compromise the objectives of packaged training.

Even so, there are trainers like Mike Perry, a site training administrator for Texas Instruments in Dallas, who prefers to get his hands on packaged courseware and customize it himself. He's impressed with training companies that will send him material on a CD-ROM so he can pick and choose what to include in the course. "I find that it's faster — as long as it's an easily customizable thing — than me trying to teach them exactly what I want," says Perry.

Rich Wellins, senior vice president of programs and marketing for Development Dimensions International (DDI), a training supplier with headquarters in Pittsburgh, also encourages companies to let DDI customize off-the-shelf products to keep the integrity of the training intact. DDI does some needs-assessment work and alterations, when requested, as part of the relationship between customer and supplier.

DDI has "almost developed a packaged approach to customizing," says Wellins, with its "tailored to fit" program. The program allows for changes that range from putting the client company's logo on the materials to adjusting the skill practices to better fit the company's environment — in other words, hospital examples for health care companies or factory scenarios for manufacturing facilities. Wellins considers a fully customized course one that involves a radical overhaul of the program or combining pieces of two or more DDI programs.

Exercising Your Options

There is no universal agreement what customizing an off-the-shelf training program means. Customizing is often a matter of degrees, ranging from changing the logo on the cover of the workbook to reshooting video footage that reflects a particular company's problems.

Wellins contends that making purely cosmetic changes to packaged programs can be effective. Often, the off-the-shelf program fits quite well with the needs of the customer and just a little tweaking is needed.

Kerri Reid, a training specialist for the Federal Judicial Center in Washington, DC, has spent up to a year completely reshooting videos in an effort to customize a canned program for her audience. Her main problem with packaged training is that most of it is designed for private industry and doesn't translate to the public sector very well. For example, profit is the bottom line emphasized in many training programs, a concept unfamiliar to her audience.

If you've decided to customize a packaged program on your own — and you've done your needs assessment — your next step may be to look at the student exercises, case studies and role plays. Practitioners use participant-focused events, in which trainees actually do something besides

just listen to a lecture, as likely targets for customization. And that makes sense: This is where the rubber of a training course meets the road of actual skills practice. So altering the student exercises in workbooks, handouts, overheads or computer-based training is an effective way to customize a training program.

Mary Walter, principal of NewLeaf Consulting in Atlanta, often customizes canned training programs for clients and goes for the exercises first.

She customizes with an eye toward "option-optimization," adding three or four exercises that will deliver the same point for every exercise the canned program suggests. That way, she says, trainers can customize on the fly, adjusting to different audiences with participation appropriate for each circumstance. In case audience members show significant reluctance to talk to each other, for example, Walter offers optional exercises that will reinforce the learning points, but allow participants to work on their own. Her definition of customization is fairly simple: "giving myself more options than they give me," says Walter.

Reid likes going after the student exercises first, because it gives her the chance to get more of her peers involved in the customizing process. She picks an exercise out of a training program, faxes it to 10 other trainers who work for the federal courts, and asks them how they would change it to make it more specific to the organization.

Sunquest's Keen agrees with this strategy. She often contacts people in the target audience and "vacuums their brains" for ideas on how to make the student material more relevant. If you can limit the customization of a program to just the exercises and leave the rest of the course alone, she says, you'll be in good shape.

Customizing for the Individual

In addition to altering student exercises, other strategies can also make packaged training programs more relevant to your audience. Scott Parry, chairman of Training House, a Princeton, NJ, supplier of off-the-shelf training courseware, encourages his customers to "take it out of the can" and customize the training for each participant.

On the flip side, he also encourages participants to customize their own training. "The ultimate customization

— the last analysis customization — is on an individual basis, and each participant is ultimately the best person to decide what is relevant in his or her work area," says Parry.

Trainers can encourage this individual buy-in by asking each trainee to come up with an action plan, an outline or document that states as precisely as possible how the training will be applied back on the job. Parry says he tells participants to consider the training course a kind of cafeteria plan, a collection of skills and knowledge from which they should pick and choose to assemble the action plan that they will take back to their supervisor. But not everything in the collection will be completely relevant, he warns, so trainees shouldn't just take one of everything from the cafeteria line.

Parry also uses a method he calls "critical incidents." He encourages trainees to come up with real situations from their own work that demonstrate the training concepts and to discuss these incidents with the other participants. The instructor then collects these examples and points out the similarities to the group. Moreover, says Parry, trainees themselves can become important sources of case studies and role plays for future training sessions. He's even seen ambitious trainees go off and develop case studies on their own time. These, too, can be included in future training sessions, creating an environment in which customization of an off-the-shelf program becomes an ongoing process.

Finally, Parry encourages clients to use both internal trainers and key managers to co-facilitate his packaged training. This partnership makes training more effective in two ways. First, the internal trainer can translate generic language into company-specific terms that make more sense to the trainees. Second, by including a key manager as co-trainer, trainees see that the managers — sometimes an obstacle to implementing training back on the job — are supporting the training. "It lends a lot more credence," says Parry, because trainees think, "It's no longer a canned program, because it's being delivered by our key managers."

Action Learning

Another way to customize a packaged training program is to incorporate action learning principles, says Mutual of Omaha's Lipsey. Action learning is a training method that brings real problems into the classroom; participants learn to apply new principles or techniques by solving these real problems. If, for example, you were using action learning to train managers in strategic planning, the group would assemble a real strategic plan during the program. This plan wouldn't be hypothetical; it would be the plan the group would implement in the future.

In this way, Lipsey customizes each packaged program by having participants bring real problems to the class and solve them while they learn. "You find out where they are having problems, what they are trying to accomplish, what their success factors are," says Lipsey, and then you incorporate those into the course.

Action learning, which his company now uses to customize all off-the-shelf courseware, also addresses issues like transfer of training and

MASSAGING THE MEDIA

BY BOB FILIPCZAK

If you're planning to customize a course, you probably want to figure out how easy it will be to customize it before you buy. There seems to be a consensus that text-based materials like workbooks, overheads and handouts are the easiest to alter to fit your company's mission, vision or industry. And if the text is sent from the supplier on disk, it's even easier to change.

"Getting something on a disk that is compatible with your current operating system is like dying and going to heaven," says Susan Keen, a management and professional development specialist for Sunquest Information Systems, a software company in Tucson, AZ.

Customizing computer-based training can be tricky, especially if you want to do it yourself. Most CBT is developed using authoring software, so if you don't know how to operate an authoring system, and particularly the authoring system that was used to assemble the packaged training program, customizing a course that runs on computer may be difficult. In the hands of someone who knows the appropriate authoring system, making changes can be pretty straightforward, but it still takes more specialized knowledge than operating a copy machine.

A lot of attention is currently centered around multimedia training in general and courseware stored on CD-ROM in particular. That second part of the acronym — rom — stands for "read only memory" and that means whatever is on that disk is unalterable. So if you want to customize the training on a CD-ROM, you're either going to have to do it with software on the hard disk of the computer or remaster the CD-ROM disk itself.

In the past, altering a CD-ROM seemed unthinkable, but with CD-ROM recorders plummeting in cost and rewritable optical disks becoming more prevalent, this may not be such an insurmountable obstacle in the future. As it is, though, the CD-ROM you buy is pretty much what you get.

The most expensive media to change is video. It's not hard to record or duplicate a tape, but reshooting footage can quickly turn into a nightmare if you're not familiar with the intricacies of video production. Just the shoot — setting up a site, hiring actors and a crew, adjusting lighting, and doing a number of takes — is a complicated and costly affair. Tape editing, where you put your customized scenes back into the original video footage, is also an expensive and labor-intensive process.

The advice from those who have been there boils down to this: If you want to customize a video to fit your corporate culture, be sure you know in advance what you're in for. Kerri Reid, training specialist at the Federal Judicial Center in Washington, DC, actually reshoots whole videos — not just segments of them — for her audience. But she also has a staff of video technicians to handle this kind of major customization. Reid rewrites the scripts, based on the principles of the original video material, and hands them over to the technicians to reshoot.

validity. Lipsey says he doesn't worry about training transfer because participants actually do the work; the training becomes what he calls a byproduct of the process. As far as validity is concerned, Lipsey says "if our customer says this works for them, that's enough validity for me." A work group that goes through a class using action-learning principles also signs a contract that makes members accountable for using what they've learned back on the job.

One quirky way to customize an off-the-shelf training program comes from Ann Petit, author of *Secrets to Enliven Learning: How to Develop Self-Directed Training Materials.* She puts a little life into a packaged course by changing the name and trying to make it fun. She took what she described as a deadly program on how to do a needs assessment and renamed it "A Ferndale Tale." She rewrote the needs assessment exercise as a story about a French restaurant in Ferndale, CA, and set up the room to look like a bistro, including croissants and French music. If you don't put a little life into a course, says Petit, "people come into the room and they sit down and they want to die" of boredom.

It's All Mine Now...Not

Just as there are many useful ways to customize a packaged training program, there are several ways it can be done badly, and a couple of ways you can get in trouble. The most contentious arguments about customization are over copyright and intellectual property rights.

Suppliers accuse some trainers of buying a training program, altering it to fit their needs, and then reproducing the materials ad infinitum because the trainers think the program now belongs to them. Suppliers contend, however, that the training principles and ideas remain their own intellectual property, protected by copyright laws. Some training departments, they insist, try to get around paying for a course by altering the product a little and claiming that the program is now their original work.

When Parry's company surveyed customers about copyright infringement, 35 percent admitted to wrongful copying of training materials. A 1987 study sponsored by the Training Media Association and conducted by Lakewood Research, a subsidiary of *TRAINING's* publisher, Lakewood Publications, found that more than 30 percent of training videos are illegally copied. Kouzes suspects the numbers are similar for training software and packaged programs. He says that the training industry is rife with people who would never even contemplate stealing a car but who readily steal training programs.

To be on the safe side, Audrey Choden, president of Training by Design, a Kansas City, KS, firm that customizes other suppliers' canned training for corporations, always checks with the supplier of the training to find out what kind of rights the customer has to alter the material. She also advises trainers who customize to check with their legal departments and with their suppliers when they make changes — just to be sure they stay out of legal hot water.

One of the prevailing reasons for customizing training is, for want of a better term, a pick-and-patch approach. Let's say you find two packaged programs you like, and you take what you think is the best stuff from both and patch them together to make one course. Choden says a significant number of the requests she gets for customization are from companies that want her to make a hybrid course from two or more packaged programs.

Other practitioners admit that combining the best parts of multiple programs or approaches is a common way to create a new training course. Aside from the aforementioned copyright violations this approach invites, Kouzes of the Peters Group contends that this creates less effective training. "The worst customization I have seen is when something isn't designed as an integrated whole. There's no system to it, there's no sense of integrity or wholeness to it. It's stuff that's stuck together," says Kouzes.

For the sake of argument, he suggests applying the pick-and-patch approach to car assembly. Imagine what you'd end up with if you took the best transmission from one company, the best engine from another, the best chassis from another, and tried to assemble a car from these high-quality but incompatible parts. Likewise, making a milk shake training course of principles from Margaret Wheatley, Peter Block, Warren Bennis, and his own theories is probably not a very effective approach, says Kouzes.

Another even more prevalent reason to customize training, especially lately, is to trim hours or days from courses to save time. Many experts and practitioners agreed that "customizing" a two-day course down to a two-hour course is becoming commonplace. The danger, of course, is that you end up just dumping information on hapless trainees and essentially wasting those two hours.

Choden has noticed a tendency to chop all the exercises out of programs to save time. "The question is, what do you want to achieve with this training? Because if you've taken out all the skill building — which takes time — and you've taken out some specific things to help them transfer the learning, the program just isn't effective at all," says Choden.

If you cut a program to fit a time slot, consultant Walter advises, also cut out some of the objectives. In other words, if you start cutting the time, you have to cut some of the meat of the course if you want the remainder to be effective. And being both effective and cost-effective is what customized packaged training is all about.

It's not that the training sold by many training companies isn't good enough; there's just this tendency to tweak and edit it so it's even better. The suit analogy comes up quite often; a suit off the rack may look pretty good, but when it's altered to really fit you, it looks that much better. Laura Lind-Blum, a training coordinator, added this to a computer on-line discussion of customizing packaged programs: "Sometimes (I'll admit it), I customize an off-the-shelf training program to 'make it my own'... I think there is something about human nature that causes us to believe on some level that we can do it a little bit better."

As the movement toward one-to-one customer intimacy increases demand for customization, technological improvements will make it easier and quicker to accomplish. What happens when everything — text, visuals, video — is on disk and it can be mixed together by someone who isn't even one of the computer cognoscenti?

DDI's Wellins postulates a future that looks like this: "Nothing will be shelf product. When customers order, their workbooks and materials will be produced within 24 hours and shipped to them with their logos, their exercises, everything that would make it relevant to their organization."

RECOMMENDED RESOURCES FOR MANAGERS

MAIL ORDERS TO:
LAKEWOOD BOOKS
50 S. Ninth Street, Minneapolis, MN 55402
800-707-7769 or 612-333-0471
Or fax your order to 612-340-4819.

Please send me the following publications:

Qty.	Title	$ Amount
_____	Creative Training Techniques Handbook, Vol. 2. By Bob Pike. $49.95	_____
_____	Creative Training Tools. By Bob Pike. $14.95.	_____
_____	Making Training Work. By Berton H. Gunter. $27.00.	_____
_____	67 Presentation Secrets to Wow Any Audience. By Dianna Booher. $22.95.	_____
_____	Dynamic Openers & Energizers. By Bob Pike. $14.95.	_____
_____	Managing the Front-End of Training. By Bob Pike. $14.95.	_____
_____	Motivating Your Trainees. By Bob Pike. $14.95.	_____
_____	Optimizing Training Transfer. By Bob Pike. $14.95.	_____
_____	Powerful Audiovisual Techniques. By Bob Pike. $14.95.	_____
_____	The HR Handbook, Edited by Elaine Biech and John E. Jones, $59.95	_____
_____	101 Games for Trainers. By Bob Pike. $21.95.	_____
_____	101 More Games for Trainers. By Bob Pike. $21.95.	_____
_____	TRAINING Magazine. 12 issues/yr. $78 U.S., $88 Canada, $99 Other Int'l.	_____
_____	Creative Training Techniques Newsletter. 12 issues/yr. $99 U.S., $109 Canada, $119 Other Int'l.	_____
_____	Training Directors' Forum Newsletter. 12 issues/yr. $118 U.S., $128 Canada, $138 Other Int'l.	_____
_____	The Lakewood Report on Technology for Learning Newsletter. 12 issues/yr. $195 U.S., $205 Canada, $215 Other Int'l.	_____

SUBTOTAL   **Subtotal:** _____

In Canada add 7% GST #123705485 (applies to all products)   **Add GST:** _____

In MN add 7% sales tax; in WI add 5% sales tax
(does not apply to newsletters)   **Add Tax:** _____

Add $4 for first book; $3 each additional book
for shipping & handling   **Add S&H:** _____

TOTAL   **Total Amount Enclosed:** _____

❏ Check or money order is enclosed. Check payable to Lakewood Publications. (U.S. Funds on a U.S. Bank)
❏ Please charge: ❏ VISA   ❏ MasterCard   ❏ American Express   ❏ Discover

Card # _____ Exp. ___/___ Signature _____
(Required for Credit Card Use)

NAME _____
TITLE _____
COMPANY _____
ADDRESS (No P.O. Boxes) _____
CITY/STATE/ZIP _____
PHONE (_____) _____ FAX (_____) _____

H607